Strangers in Their Own Land

Part-Time Faculty in American Community Colleges

John E. Roueche • Suanne D. Roueche • Mark D. Milliron

Copyright 1995 the American Association of Community Colleges

Printed in the U.S.A.

Published by the Community College Press, a division of the American Association of Community Colleges
One Dupont Circle, N.W.
Suite 410
Washington, D.C. 20036
(202) 728-0200

Coordinator of Publications: Ron Stanley
Manuscript Editor: Vicki Whitaker
Design: The Magazine Group, Inc.
Printing: Jarboe Printing

ISBN 0-87117-283-6

This volume is dedicated to

our friend and mentor

TERREL H. BELL

U.S. Secretary of Education,

1981–1985

whose courageous leadership

began, and continues to

inspire, a renewed national

commitment to improved

educational quality in

American schools and colleges.

TABLE OF CONTENTS

P r e f a c e

The employment of part-time faculty in American community colleges is not a new phenomenon. However, over the last decade, we have been observing what has been—for the majority of colleges—a silent explosion. Part-time faculty are increasing in number, they represent an upward spiraling percentage of total community college faculty, and they are responsible for ever-larger percentages of colleges' instructional contact hours. Yet, they have been so long in the shadows of higher education that most colleges know little about them—they are indeed strangers in a land that they have chosen and that we have invited them to inhabit for a portion of their professional lives. The majority of part-timers move in and out of our teaching institutions silently and remain, for various reasons, for brief periods; others remain in our company for a much longer time—many part-timers have served for five, ten, fifteen, or twenty years. They teach for myriad reasons—some intrinsic, some extrinsic: they teach to perform, to contribute, and to support themselves and their families. Their heterogeneity makes the label of "part-time faculty" far too simplistic; the term itself does not provide a realistic and accurate picture of who they are. We wanted to know more about them and about how colleges respond to them—not only because part-time faculty are an important component of American community colleges, but because even the most conservative observers of this expanding phenomenon note that they are playing and will continue to play a critical role in our collective futures.

Struggling to meet the challenges of escalating demands for their services and declining revenue streams, American community colleges are finding it more and more difficult to meet these demands with their current cadre of full-time faculty. The traditional strategy of hiring more full-time faculty cannot solve the demand problem; new full-time faculty will represent substantially increased costs for far fewer courses than will part-timers who can be employed for less cost but who could add significantly to the number and array of courses. Moreover, new course or program requirements, particularly in the technical areas, require skills and expertise that are not as developed among faculty whose teaching responsibilities have limited their opportunities to participate in out-of-the-classroom, state-of-the-art training. These realities are but two of the many reasons that colleges are turning to increased employment of part-time faculty.

Many college administrators and full-time faculty told us that they were surprised, if not shocked, when they documented the actual number of part-time faculty employed on their campuses, and that their surprise turned to concern—not only were the numbers frequently larger than they had believed, but they were on the rise. Many recalled that their next concerns (not necessarily in this order) were about how part-timers represented their colleges; how they affected the teaching and learning environment—for example, cost, scheduling, and quality of service; and how they fit into the college—for example, what roles they actually played. The challenges that part-timers represent are not isolated in particular components of a college; rather, they impact the entire institution and must be addressed by everyone.

In this book, we seek to document trends in the employment and integration of part-time faculty in American community colleges. We recognize that the issues surrounding part-time faculty have become lightning rods for arguments and counterarguments over the last decade. Regrettably, as K. Patricia Cross observed in *Accent on Learning,* "The problems are clearer than the solutions" (1976, p. xi), and we too frequently dwell on the problems and drain the critical energy we need to create and develop viable solutions. As we read the responses to our survey questions, and as we conducted follow-up interviews, we learned that many colleges were developing such solutions; many had established policies and procedures that would be useful to others who were looking for ideas with which to shape unique and successful strategies of their own. We choose to feature some of them here.

The topics of the following chapters reflect the major components of our survey, as well as the essential elements of the information we gleaned from our interviews about college policies and procedures affecting part-time faculty use and integration.

Chapter One, "Focusing on the Problems: Part-Time Faculty in American Community Colleges," describes the economic, technological, and demographic imperatives that are generating American community colleges' increased employment of part-time faculty; the array of beliefs and realities accompanying their integration; and current pictures of the relatively silent cadre simplistically labeled "part-time faculty."

Chapter Two, "Taking a Wide-Angle Picture: Surveying How American Community Colleges Use Part-Time Faculty," describes the methodology and major findings of the survey.

Chapter Three, "Taking the Critical First Steps: Recruitment, Selection, and Hiring," reviews some of what we know about identifying and employing part-time faculty, drawn from the literature and general responses to our survey. With this chapter, we begin to focus on and describe the array of procedures and policies implemented by the colleges we selected.

Chapter Four, "Orientation: Welcome to the Community," reviews some of what we know about making part-time faculty familiar with the college and its students, and describes strategies by which colleges articulate their expectations and introduce new part-timers to the college's unique teaching and learning environments.

Chapter Five, "Faculty Development and Integration: Doing the Right Things for the Right Reasons," reviews some of what we know about the goals and objectives of successful faculty development activities, describes various activities that address the needs of part-time faculty and promote their integration—i.e., the removal of actual and mythical barriers between full-time and part-time faculty.

Chapter Six, "Inspecting the Expectations: Conducting Faculty Evaluation," reviews the essential objectives, components, and measures of effectiveness of successful faculty evaluation plans. It describes strategies for implementing collegewide faculty evaluation plans that promote growth and development for all faculty.

Chapter Seven, "Creating the Mosaic for a Common Cause: Putting the Pieces Together," briefly reviews the issues developed throughout the book, surrounding the employment and integration of part-time faculty in American community colleges. It concludes with recommendations, drawn from our study of successful responses to this developing phenomenon, for making friends of strangers and thereby better meeting the needs of American community college students—our common cause.

This study would not have been possible without the colleges and the people who responded to our requests for information by survey and interview. We are especially indebted to those who participated in our interviews; they not only responded to our questions, but they provided additional observations and numerous college documents that brought their descriptions to life. In addition, they accepted responsibility for proofing the final drafts of their particular descriptions that we had prepared for publication. (The colleges that are featured throughout this book, their presidents, and the individuals participating in our interviews are listed in Appendix C.) Their enthusiasm and candor provided the energy and support that we enjoyed through the research and writing process. Our experiences with them will remain as special recollections of this effort.

Arriving at the project mid-way through the survey phase and early in the interview phase, Steve Johnson, a graduate student in the Community College Leadership Program, contributed an extraordinary expertise that made us all more computer-friendly. He brought the same high level of commitment to this project that he brought to all of his graduate work. And, equally important, his good humor was a welcome relief during some tedious processes.

Finally, we pay special tribute to those here at home who read and considered every word of this manuscript and who, thereby, made it more than we could have alone. Special thanks to Sheryl Fielder, NISOD administrative assistant; Julie Leidig, currently completing her work as a graduate student in the Community College Leadership Program; and Teri Rucker, graphics editor for NISOD's *Linkages* newsletter. And, we owe a collective thank-you to those friends, family, and colleagues who endured months of blow-by-blow descriptions of writing travails. When they receive some of the first copies of *Strangers,* we hope that the books are more than graphic reminders of their ordeals; we hope that they are proof that their patience with us was for a good cause.

Austin, Texas   John E. Roueche
January, 1995   Suanne D. Roueche
                                                      Mark D. Milliron

CHAPTER 1

There is no longer any point to arguing over the place of part-time faculty in American colleges and universities... While one might wish that the situation were different, and while in a perfect world it might be so, it is not so now.

—Gappa and Leslie, *The Invisible Faculty*, 1993

FOCUSING ON THE PROBLEMS

Part-Time Faculty in American Community Colleges

ommunity colleges have long pointed with pride to what, for the majority, is their middle name: *community*. They boast of being *in, of, about,* and *responsive to* community and all that this notion implies. Their pride is obvious as they describe themselves as *communities*—especially their concern for their students, their faculties and staffs, their larger communities and townships. Yet, many who have studied their public pronouncements and their actual behaviors posit that they should take a more critical look at some of the incongruities.

Ernest Boyer, president of the Carnegie Foundation for the Advancement of Teaching, has observed that perhaps the most fundamental pathology among young people in our culture is the "sense of disconnectedness—their feeling that they do not belong, they do not fit" (Boyer, 1992, p. 4). Vince Tinto, a noted researcher of student attrition, has further warned that "individuals in college are rarely provided with formal rituals and ceremonies whereby...connectedness is ensured," that they "are left to make their own way through the maze of institutional life," and that "many will leave" (1987, pp. 98–99). While these researchers of college and university life address the unsettling nature of the student experience, their observations and warnings are strikingly poignant reminders of the experiences of others in that educational milieu who through resiliency and tenacity may not disappear, but who nevertheless are significantly affected by the conditions in which they find themselves.

In all institutions of American higher education, but especially in community colleges, there is a large and growing cadre of faculty who move silently in, around, and out of our college communities relatively unnoticed. Institutions have assigned them various names—"associate faculty, temporary faculty, community faculty, reserve faculty, supplemental faculty, and percentage instructors" (Biles and Tuckman, 1986, pp. 25–26), even *temporary part-time faculty*. The literature has described them in terms such as "the invisible faculty" (Gappa and Leslie, 1993), "gypsy faculty" (Tuckman, 1981), a "corps of unregulated personnel" (so named by the National Education Association and cited in Leslie et al., 1982), "expendable, interchangeable components of a 'Tinker Toy' system of staffing" (Richardson, 1992), and "a new academic underclass" (Smith, 1990, p. 7). Other labels, rare or nonexistent in the literature, surface with some regularity in oral histories about the part-time faculty phenomenon—perhaps the most jaded and ubiquitous of all labels is "freeway fliers," describing part-timers as dashing along expressways and freeways from one teaching site to another.

Today, American community colleges struggle to meet the serious challenges of staying up-to-date in disciplines and programs, offering more courses and programs to larger numbers of students, and battling shrinking budgets. It is the part-time faculty, this group that heretofore has remained remarkably nondescript, that colleges are relying upon in greater numbers to carry the day. However, serious questions about part-timers are being raised—how part-timers are employed and integrated into the "communities of learners" about which colleges boast, and how their employment affects the quality of teaching in these colleges that publicly regard themselves as "premier teaching institutions" (O'Banion and Associates, 1994). These questions reflect real concerns about actual, potential, and mythical problems that demand thoughtful answers and successful interventions. Initially, the answers will be found in the cool-headed assessment of our educational, social, and economic reality; and, finally, they will result in the design of strategies that truly reflect the community college's belief in the importance of community—a community whose members are not strangers in their own land.

NOT A NEW PHENOMENON

Employing part-time faculty to teach community college students is not a new idea; part-timers have been employed as faculty since community colleges were first established. In fact, Eells (1931) reported that in the late 1920s more than half of the instructors in Texas community colleges were part-timers and that in 1921 more than 90 percent of the staff in eight California junior colleges were part-timers. When community colleges were young and still relatively small, Eells argued that employing secondary school instructors to teach such subjects as physics, chemistry, and biology would provide "more expert knowledge" for students than would a full-timer who more likely would be a generalist. Moreover, he noted that hiring these instructors could make "for closer coordination of the curriculum in high schools and colleges" (p. 396). Furthermore, he recommended hiring university professors who would better coordinate university and junior college curricula, and bring some of the prestige accorded to universities to the junior college. He also argued that as these colleges grew larger, part-timers could further expand and diversify the colleges' offerings and increase enrollment by teaching specialized courses, such as foreign languages not typically offered in more traditional language programs, specialized topics important to new career programs, art, or religion.

Since those early days, the number of part-time faculty in American community colleges has steadily increased, especially over the last twenty-five to thirty years. In 1966, approximately 38 percent of the faculty in community colleges were teaching part-time—that is, one or two courses (Heinberg, 1966). In 1980, between 50 and 60 percent of all faculty in community colleges were part-time employees (Scheibmeir, 1980; Cohen and Brawer, 1982; Palmer, 1987). While these percentages represent an increase in the use of part-timers, full-time staff percentages, by contrast, have been relatively stable. For example, between 1973 and 1991, full-time faculty increased by only 15 percent, while part-time faculty tripled (American Association of Community Colleges, 1991). And, in 1992, the American Association of Community Colleges reported that in all fifty states and U.S. territories combined, full-time faculty totaled 74,373 and part-time totaled 145,155—*part-time faculty in community colleges outnumbering full-time almost two to one, and representing 55 to 65 percent of all community college faculty* (American Association of Community Colleges, 1992). Nine states report percentages greater than 65. Furthermore, if the estimate provided by the National Center for Education Statistics (1993) that a part-time instructor represents about one-third of a full-time equivalent instructor is correct, then part-timers currently teach about 30 to 40 percent of the full-time equivalent contact hours in American community colleges. Employment trends record that between 1987 and 1989, 41 percent of community colleges increased their hiring of part-time faculty; between 1990 and 1992, that number jumped to 60 percent (Hawkins, 1993).

This part-time staffing trend represents the most widespread use of part-time instructors in all of higher education. The U.S. Department of Education's *Digest of Education Statistics* (1993) last reported that part-time faculty represent only about 36 percent of the faculty across *all* colleges and universities. While the overall percentage of part-timers may be lower in four-year colleges and universities than in community colleges, the trend toward the increasing use of part-timers is not. All levels of postsecondary education appear to be experiencing an increase (Gappa and Leslie, 1993; Kelly, 1991; Spinetta, 1990).

No general trends or other indications forecast a reduction in the use of part-timers. Rather, there is ample evidence—fiscal constraints, faculty labor market factors, shifting demands for academic programs, and the like—that the numbers of part-timers will increase (Bowen and Schuster, 1986; Bowen and Sosa, 1989). Economic considerations, in particular, will drive the number and responsibilities of part-timers upwards. College budgets will continue to suffer from reductions, and part-timers, regarded as a less expensive alternative to additional full-timers, will increase. Enrollments will increase as waves of older returning and first-time-in-college adults swell the college rolls (Graves, 1994). If for no other reason, these two trends alone would support hiring part-time faculty to maintain existing college services and expand the college's offerings. As Gappa and Leslie observed in *The Invisible Faculty*, "this alternative, which started out to be a 'temporary solution,' has become a 'permanent fix'" (1993, p. 3).

EMBRACING THE PERMANENT FIX

How has this "permanent fix" been embraced? Today, the general mood is cautious, concerned, and somber. Generally, it appears that part-time faculty are "considered a necessary evil, rationalized as an important strategy for saving money and maintaining flexibility...a cheap fix" (McGuire, 1993, p. 1). The Commission on the Future of Community Colleges reported, "The increasing numbers of part-time faculty at many colleges are a disturbing trend. We urge that the unrestrained expansion of part-time faculty be avoided." The commission recommended that "a majority of credits awarded by a community college should be earned in classes taught by full-time faculty" (1988, pp. 12, 14). The authors of *Involvement in Learning* proposed that because part-time faculty cannot make a primary commitment to the institution, they cannot bring the level of responsibility to their teaching that is required for effective learning. They concluded that "one full-time faculty member is a better investment than three part-timers" (Study Group on the Conditions of Excellence in American Higher Education, 1984, p. 36). The Education Commission of the States warned that the use of part-time faculty can "inhibit faculty collegiality, instructional continuity, and curricular coherence" (Working Party on Effective State Action, 1986, p. 19). In 1991, the Texas Higher Education Coordinating Board issued a set of guidelines on the use of part-time faculty; the guidelines, while not binding on any institution, were described as representing "good practice." They warned: "Institutions should examine their present practices in light of appropriate use of part-time faculty and set goals to eliminate excessive use" (pp. 3–4). The trend is viewed as deprofessionalizing to full-time faculty (Cohen and Brawer, 1982) and as an ebbing away of valuable time available for students outside of class, for developing curricula and relationships with other faculty, and for opportunities for professional development (Richardson, 1992; Cross, 1990; Friedlander, 1980). Boyer (1987) questioned the part-timers' impact on the "spirit of community on campus." Gappa and Leslie (1993) observed a general assumption among college and university faculty and staff that part-time faculty have a negative impact on the quality of instruction—a concern clearly articulated by Patrick McCallum, former executive director of the Faculty Association of California Community Colleges, when he recently warned: "We in California use too many of them and that impacts quality" (Hawkins, 1993, p. 6).

Part-timers are concerned and dissatisfied, as well—albeit in radically different ways than are those outside the part-timers' camp. In interviews with 240 part-time faculty at eighteen college and university sites, five of which were community colleges, Gappa and Leslie (1993) documented reports of general dissatisfaction with status and working conditions.

> If you fall in love, you want a commitment. The institution won't make a commitment [to me]. Thus, as a part-timer I am vulnerable.

> We are basically in the same position as migrant workers. There is a lot of wasted energy and unnecessary expense in trying to stay alive with part-time teaching.

> There is confusion—power, guilt relationships, and powerful feelings. The tenured faculty [have power] over the part-time. They are expendable. The part-time [have power] over the tenured. We have the numbers and we control the enrollment. The tenured faculty have their schedules and [other perks] at our expense, and they feel guilty. They know there are inequities (1993, pp. 42–43).

Observations by some part-timers are less strident. One part-timer, who in a recent semester taught courses simultaneously in two states, Virginia and Maryland, made two memorable observations about her juggling act: "I have enough work. The key is getting enough contracts [including private sector consulting] to make a full-time salary....This is like taking a tour of Europe. If it's Tuesday, I must be in Maryland" (Dervarics, 1993). Others described a rather common transformation experience:

> Moving from the ranks of a fifth-year adjunct instructor to a full-time position for me was the equivalent to stepping from the shadows to center stage, from invisible understudy to recognized performer. In reality, my role didn't change; it merely expanded. But perceptions changed. From my students' angle as audience, I had always been a key performer. But from the vantage point of the full-time cast, I was usually invisible, swallowed by darkness. Suddenly with a full-time position, the shadows vanished. Even though I hadn't done anything differently, special effects lighting illuminated my place on the stage (Roslyn Bethke, Johnson County Community College, KS).

The alienation that part-timers feel from their teaching communities is recounted in their stories, cited in recent research, and reflected in current college responses to how they are managed and integrated into community college faculties. However, there are no indications that their numbers will diminish; indeed, there is every indication that they will grow stronger and have an ever-larger impact on students and curricula. Many observers of these trends caution that alienating such a critical mass operating within any segment of higher education is risky business. Especially among faculty, administrators, and staff who take pride in being a community, it is unconscionable behavior and poor policy.

WHO ARE THE PART-TIMERS?

As Gappa and Leslie observed, part-timers are not, as many stereotypical descriptions would suggest, "an anonymous mass of laboring drones" (1993, p. 17). The diversity of their demographic characteristics, their academic backgrounds, their experiences, and their motivations to teach part-time makes it impossible to assign them simple or inclusive labels. These two researchers, drawing from interviews and a specially commissioned analysis of data on part-time faculty from the 1988 National Center for Education Statistics' National Survey of Postsecondary Faculty (cited as NSOPF '88), described part-timers as:

- younger than full-timers as a group, completing academic and professional training, beginning their families, and deciding upon mobility

- representing racial and ethnic minorities in a slightly lower percentage than full-timers (9.2 percent)

- 58 percent men and 42 percent women (NSOPF '88); about equal representation in interviews; evidence of gender-related issues

- married men and women in fairly equal numbers; family commitments leading to geographical immobility

- one-half of a dual-career academic couple in which one partner assumes part-time status to accompany a full-time spouse

- in community colleges, specifically, a large majority with at least one master's degree, many with extensive work experience, in mid-career, choosing teaching over pursuit of higher degrees

- serving at the college over widely varying lengths of time

- choosing to teach for a variety of intrinsic and extrinsic reasons

- somewhat (46 percent) or very (41 percent) satisfied with their jobs (NSOPF '88); interviewees citing the excitement and challenge of teaching but dissatisfaction with many aspects of employment (Gappa and Leslie, 1993, pp. 17–44)

There have been attempts to develop typologies of part-time faculty. The first was developed from interviews with more than 3,500 part-time instructors (Tuckman, 1978). A modified and expanded version of this original description of the seven categories of part-timers (from Tucker's *Chairing the Academic Department,* 1993) is included here:

1. *Full-mooners* are persons who, in addition to their part-time jobs, hold full-time positions elsewhere of at least thirty-five hours per week for eighteen weeks of the year. This group, comprising 27.6 percent of the sample, includes many full-time faculty members at nearby universities and community colleges, as well as local business and professional persons. A good example of a full-mooner is a certified public accountant who is recruited to teach introductory accounting courses.

2. *Students* are persons employed in departments other than those in which they are seeking degrees. These part-timers, 21.1 percent of the sample, are often graduate students from nearby or distant colleges or universities. Some are still doing coursework while others are writing their dissertations. It should be noted that graduate teaching assistants within their own departments are usually not reported as part-time instructors by the universities for whom they work. If they were counted, the numbers reported would be quite different.

3. *Hopeful full-timers* are persons holding part-time positions because they are unable to find full-time employment, and they comprise 16.6 percent of the sample. These fully qualified persons are becoming a national concern because they represent a generation of scholars who are unemployed due to the lack of academic jobs. They hope that their part-time positions will develop into full-time employment.

4. *Part-mooners* are persons who simultaneously hold two or more part-time jobs of less than thirty-five hours per week for more than one week. They comprise 13.6 percent of the sample and, like the hopeful full-timers, often seek full-time employment. Members of groups 3 and 4 are the so-called itinerant or gypsy scholars of the 1980s.

5. *Homeworkers* are persons who do not want full-time employment because they are taking care of a relative or child at home, and they comprise 6.4 percent of the sample. These individuals are often unemployed spouses who possess a variety of graduate credentials and experiences. Along with the full-mooners, they provide a stable cadre of part-time instructors.

6. *Semiretireds* are persons who seek activities to fill time made available by retirement, and they make up only 2.8 percent of the sample. These individuals, who often possess considerable talent and ability, may also contribute to the stable core of part-timers. They may need the extra income to compensate for inflation and rising taxes, which have reduced their fixed retirement income. In rural areas, homeworkers and the semiretireds can be the main sources of part-timers.

7. *Part-unknowners* comprise the remaining 11.8 percent of the sample. They give a variety of reasons for becoming part-time that do not fall into any of the other categories (pp. 120–121).

It is instructive to note that the majority of the part-time faculty interviewed in the Gappa and Leslie study fit the various descriptions of this typology in roughly the same percentages as they appeared in Tuckman's typology, drawn more than fifteen years ago.

Another taxonomy classifies part-timers more particularly on the basis of their employment situation. This approach to classifying part-timers was applied in a doctoral research study that sought to define specific rights for part-timers based on their degree of attachment to their employing institutions and to research policy considerations for employing part-time faculty in public community colleges:

1. *Moonlighters:* Persons who are employed in another job but who teach one course. They have no fringe benefits, no tenure or sabbatical accrual, no advisees or committee work, and no departmental vote.

2. *Twilighters:* Persons who are not otherwise employed, but to whom the institution chooses not to give a regular part-time faculty position. They have no departmental vote but receive prorated fringe benefits and have longer contracts.

3. *Sunlighters:* Regular faculty appointments who are like regular full-time faculty in every way except the amount of time they work. They receive prorated fringe benefits, committee assignments, and advisees and are eligible for tenure and sabbatical accrual. Their probation period is no longer than seventeen semesters, and they have an opportunity to negotiate for full-time faculty status at a later time.

4. *Persons on occasional part-time leave:* Those whose regular full-time faculty appointment is retained and whose probationary period is extended proportionately. They may extend their part-time leave or return to full-time status at any time. This category of part-time faculty is not restricted to women who have small children, although the expectation is that such people will use it most (Biles and Tuckman, 1986, pp. 12–13).

Clearly, part-time faculty are a diverse group, and the various attempts to assign defining labels have failed to provide a workable vocabulary to explain who they are or their role in the institution. What we have learned from these attempts is that we still know relatively little about them and what they can bring to a teaching and learning community. Moreover, the diversity of their backgrounds and the needs of the part-timers make it difficult to design solutions that will address their disparate needs.

Why have part-time faculty become such a controversial, contentious, and compelling topic for discussion in higher education over the last decade? They have been in our colleges for decades—long before the mid-1980s, when the infrequent ripples of literature about their employment first began to swell into ever-larger waves. What issues have converged to focus our attention on this heretofore little-understood, little-acknowledged group? There are many, and they share a common characteristic: each is a curious mix of advantages and disadvantages for both colleges and part-timers. Thus, the problems that each can pose are as multifaceted and complex as the larger part-time controversy itself.

INSTRUCTIONAL QUALITY

For many part-time and evening students, part-time faculty *are* the community college. "Each day and night of instruction, millions of students judge community colleges on the basis of the performance of adjunct instructors" (Richardson, 1992, p. 29). Yet, there is the generalized concern that part-time faculty, no matter how qualified, competent, or conscientious in performing their duties, lack the permanent commitment required for sustained teaching effectiveness. The concerns over instructional quality generate the most intense discussions among full-time faculty and college administrators regarding the use of part-time faculty. The question is whether community college students are being short-changed in the classroom with the expanded use of part-timers. Are there relevant differences in instructional quality between full- and part-time faculty?

Major reviews and research on full- and part-time faculty argue that part-time faculty differ from full-time in almost every measure of instructional practice:

> Part-time instructors were found to have less teaching experience, to have taught fewer years at their current institution, and to hold lower academic credentials. The adjunct instructor also differed from the full-timer in that he had less choice in the selection of materials to be used in his course, assigned fewer pages to read, used less instructional media, recommended or required students to attend fewer out-of-class activities, and placed less emphasis on written assignments in determining student grades (Friedlander, 1980, p. 34).

Researchers posit that full-time faculty are more experienced with the community college, have longer tenure and a clearer understanding of college systems, and are in a better position to counsel students and provide important degree-planning information. Furthermore, they observe that part-time faculty are more likely to be transitory and as such are not so "secure" in the eyes of students. Finally, full-time faculty are more involved in instructional improvement and professional development activities than are part-timers (Cohen and Brawer, 1982; Leslie et al., 1982).

Yet, while these researchers' perspectives on the differences between part-timers and full-timers appear to suggest that hiring part-time faculty is a highly questionable activity, the perspectives of colleges and part-timers themselves bring some different realities to the table.

From the perspective of the college. Gappa and Leslie (1993) observed two themes when they queried department chairs, deans, and vice presidents or provosts about the quality of instruction by part-time faculty: they either are not as effective, or are at least as effective as full-time faculty. Almost all of the respondents qualified their statements, admitting that their responses were not based upon hard evidence. In regard to the first theme, they worried about their own inadequacies with selection and hiring practices that can bring unqualified instructors into the institution, about part-time faculty teaching course content that may be out of sync with others in the same program, about evaluation of part-timers' teaching effectiveness, and about whether the part-timers were up-to-date in their fields. In regard to the second, they believed that part-timers brought an enthusiasm to their teaching that many full-timers had lost, that perhaps their youthfulness and newness to the teaching field generated a high level of energy and creativity, that their more recent experience with graduate education might have put them on the cutting edge in their fields, and that the instruction they provide is enriched with practical examples and diverse perspectives. Overall, the respondents observed that while the range of part-time instructors' teaching effectiveness might well be broader than that of full-time instructors—that is, while there are more obvious examples of poor performance and exceptional performance among part-timers, differences in classroom performance, on average, of part- and full-timers were unobservable. Yet, most researchers admit that supervision and evaluation of large numbers of part-time faculty is difficult. The lack of supervision and evaluation means that institutions know less about part-timers' teaching effectiveness than full-timers'.

From the perspective of the part-time faculty. The criticisms of part-time faculty are somewhat ameliorated by a closer examination of their characteristics and the unevenness in the level of responsibility that institutions take for professional development of all faculty. For example, part-timers are not as transitory as one might think from a cursory reading of part-time status reports. Many part-timers have taught at their institutions for a number of years. Research data indicate that in 1988, while 52.5 percent of the part-time faculty in public two-year institutions had fewer than four years teaching in their current institution, more than 35 percent had more than four, and some had more than twenty years (Gappa and Leslie, 1993, p. 35). And, while there are concerns about their relatively few years of teaching experience in comparison to full-time faculty, these concerns may be unwarranted. The majority of the nation's community college full-time faculty have been teaching for the greater part of their lifetimes; they are aging—over half will retire in the next five years (O'Banion, 1994, p. 313), and many may decide not to retire when traditional retirement ages occur, perhaps to pursue their careers "beyond reasonable limits and literally die on the job" (Lorenzo and Banach, 1994, p. 7). Most part-time faculty are much newer to the community college scene. While there is little argument that many part-time faculty are likely to have less experience than full-time instructors, the link to instructional quality is tenuous. Indeed, a counter-argument can be made that part-time faculty are more likely to have more recent graduate training and as a result more current education and training than full-timers. Simple degree attainment comparisons are problematic as well; many part-time faculty are hired not because of extensive academic preparation, but because of "real world" experience, an especially important feature in highly technical fields.

Another counterargument to the claim of lessened instructional quality is suggested by the body of research that supports part-time faculty instructional quality. Empirical studies to date have found no significant difference in student ratings, class retention, or student achievement in subsequent classes between students taught by part-time faculty and those taught by full-time faculty (Cohen and Brawer, 1982; Leslie et al., 1982; McGuire, 1993). In one study of freshmen composition students tested over a four-year period, students taught by part-timers did not perform in any significantly different fashion on exit exams than those taught by full-timers (Boggs, 1984). Moreover, in a recent national study of community college faculty, part-time faculty were observed to use the lecture plus discussion method of instruction—a method that has been severely criticized for its negative effects on instructional quality—less often than full-time faculty (Keim, 1989; Roueche and Roueche, 1993a). Part-time faculty, albeit by a slim margin, are also more likely than full-timers to have attended a community college (Keim, 1989); it could be argued that these faculty might be better suited to relate the choices the college provides, and that they may be particularly empathetic to the part-time student, as both are managing multiple identities and responsibilities. In fact, in the study of freshmen composition students, students performed better in subsequent English composition courses when their developmental composition course was taught by a part-time instructor than when taught by a full-timer (Boggs, 1984). This finding is particularly interesting since a majority of developmental teachers in many regions of this country are part-timers (Abraham, 1992).

Despite the heated debate over instructional quality and part-time faculty, more than twenty years of research points to little or no difference in the instructional ability of part-time faculty. In fact, there is little evidence that in any way implicates part-time teaching as the culprit in any instructional quality "crime" (Gappa and Leslie, 1993). In fact, much of it points to the notion that "in a sense...part-timers may be held to a higher standard of teaching performance on the average" than full-timers (p. 125).

UP-TO-DATE EXPERTISE, PROFESSIONAL AND COMMUNITY LINKAGES, AND "REAL WORLD" EXPERIENCE

A counterbalance to the research on teaching effectiveness is the knowledge that many part-time faculty enhance the quality of their instruction by bringing current, up-to-date expertise to the classroom (Bender and Hammons, 1972; Guthrie-Morse, 1979; Hammons, 1981; Roueche and Comstock, 1981). And, although one long-time researcher of part-time faculty questions the equivalence of such expertise to scholarship (Tuckman, 1981), the specialization that part-time faculty bring to the classroom continues to be an important motive cited for their employment.

From the perspective of the college. Part-timers offer insights from the "real world" and emerging disciplines (Albert and Watson, 1980). They are in a unique position to give students a sense of current professional trends and a connection with the working world (Albert and Watson, 1980; Eliason, 1980; Gappa and Leslie, 1993). Using part-timers creates a connection between the college and the community when community professionals teach for the college (Eliason, 1980; Gappa and Leslie, 1993).

Part-timers can help answer the question: Can today's educational institutions meet the new demands of an elite business community? The sad truth is that our bureaucratic organizations have accepted the status quo for so long that students are quickly learning that they can attend proprietary schools that, although costly, have instructors with the up-to-date technical skills required to teach relevant courses to help students get high-wage, high-skills jobs. In contrast to this scenario, many full-time college faculty are people who graduated in the '50s and '60s, and whose skills in some technical areas are far surpassed by the high school graduates enrolling in their classes. Lifelong learning is not a new concept, particularly in community colleges; but it has been largely ignored by hundreds of faculty members simply because the need to maintain up-to-date technical skills has not been required or because a means to update their skills has not been available to them (Gianini and Sarantos, 1995).

In contrast, many part-time faculty members are currently working in the field they teach. In academic courses, a student may learn about business ethics from a part-time faculty member who is a lawyer confronting ethical dilemmas daily. A freshman English student may learn paragraph construction from a local journalist who can show how the rules followed in class are followed daily in the local newspaper. In vocational courses, a student may learn welding from the owner or the operator of a welding shop.

Research on instruction has long shown the importance of demonstrating the application and relevance of knowledge for quality instruction (Roueche and Pitman, 1973; Cross, 1976; Roueche and Roueche, 1993a). Part-time faculty can provide community college students with "real world" linkages that bring learning to life. This is not to say that full-time faculty cannot or do not do the same, only that many part-time faculty members have a natural venue for creating such learning opportunities. With part-time faculty, students experience an important professional and community resource that can enhance learning, inspire career choices, and connect students with professions and the community through outside affiliations. Students receive the special opportunity to learn from someone who is actively using the skills being taught outside of the college setting.

SALARY AND BENEFITS

In the 1960s and '70s when community colleges first began to hire part-timers in especially large numbers, they emphasized the advantages of bringing special insights and an expanded contact with the "real world" into the classroom—insights and contact that are not always available among full-timers who have been teaching for many years. Actually, in some disciplines, such as nursing, it is impossible to attract full-time employees at prevailing faculty wages; hiring specialists for part-time service has been an acceptable alternative (Bender and Hammons, 1972; Leslie et al., 1982). As hiring continued and expanded, colleges reluctantly admitted that economic realities were responsible for the continued hiring of an ever-larger number of part-timers (Texas Higher Education Coordinating Board, 1990; Pedersen, 1993). In many colleges, part-timers have become an essential component of the instructional core as entire budgets are set up to employ a less-expensive teaching cadre to meet instructional demands (Gappa and Leslie, 1993; Hauff and Berdie, 1989; Parsons, 1980c). Simply put, part-time faculty can be employed for far less compensation than can full-time. In fact, their compensation per class has remained between one-third and two-thirds as much as the salary of a full-time faculty member, and they rarely are provided or allowed access to such benefits as health insurance or retirement (Cohen and Brawer, 1982; Spinetta, 1990; McGuire, 1993).

This wide variance between salaries of part-timers and full-timers has given birth to yet another issue: How can a college justify the disparity between these salaries? Are part-timers not worth more than they are paid? Are full-timers worth what they are paid, are they productive enough, and could they accept additional responsibilities and eliminate some of the reasons that part-timers are hired? Should full-timers be teaching more courses and assuming more responsibilities for other student services (Cage, 1991)?

From the perspective of the college. College administrators currently admit that "there is too much teaching to be done with too little money," and hiring part-time faculty is a solution that can be implemented handily (Gappa and Leslie, 1993, p. 108). Yet, while there have been no long-term studies to determine the actual costs associated with hiring so many part-timers, there are clear warnings that over-reliance on part-timers may not be a good idea. Over the long term, the "magnitude, if any, of real savings becomes highly questionable" (Gappa and Leslie, 1993, p. 108), and colleges too easily succumb to the "false economies" of part-timers (p. 102). Part-timers may increase productivity, and enrollment increases may occur, but little consideration is given to the additional responsibility that full-time faculty must assume as a result—for example, additional advising and counseling responsibilities that must be assumed because part-time instructors are not always available (Tucker, 1993), or the expanded work of committees and departments (Gappa and Leslie, 1993).

Moreover, although some colleges report that part-time faculty provide them with solid pools for selecting future full-timers, there is concern that by hiring part-timers who are hopeful full-timers, community college administrators may be setting them up for dissatisfaction. Much of the literature on part-time work and satisfaction supports this assumption. While reports vary as to the actual number who prefer full-time employment to part-time, most researchers observe that those who teach part-time because they cannot find full-time employment want and expect full-time employment when positions become available. These employees report greater dissatisfaction with their work (Feldman, 1990; Smith, 1990) and are more inclined to file suit when full-time employment is not forthcoming (Biles and Tuckman, 1986).

From the perspective of part-time faculty. The response to the use of part-timers for purely economic reasons has been fierce. Part-time faculty generally feel exploited when comparing their compensation with that of full-timers employed at the same college or district (Gappa and Leslie, 1993; Tucker, 1993). In California, part-time faculty unions have become powerful players in the community college ranks, mandating legislative responses to part-time faculty concerns (Spinetta, 1990). Even in non-union states, some part-time faculty associations have developed a powerful collective strength; for example, in Texas, one association provided major support for candidates sympathetic to their requests for increased salaries and benefits and delivered the votes that earned them places on the college board of trustees (Smith, 1994).

FLEXIBILITY

Hiring part-time faculty gives a college more flexibility to respond to rapid enrollment changes and special program and scheduling demands, thereby offering opportunities to cut costs and protect full-time positions.

From the perspective of the college. As demands on the community college to expand programs increase, as populations of life-long learners (Gleazer, 1980), part-time students, returning adults, and underprepared students swell the student rolls, colleges face uneven and unexpected enrollment fluctuations. Part-time faculty provide the flexibility that these fluctuations require (Friedlander, 1980; Erwin and Andrews, 1993). Moreover, enrollment demands of part-time and older returning students include more evening, weekend, and off-campus programs. Late afternoon and evening classes have become more common as part-time and returning working adult students have increased. The younger, more traditional college student who enrolls primarily in daytime courses and takes all courses on one central campus is becoming more and more an atypical college figure (Graves, 1994; Tucker, 1993).

Colleges are being challenged by cost-saving demands, and many would argue that they are losing the ability to staff their programs with the very best faculty, faculty who understand the college and the students, faculty who have commitment and ties to the college—in other words, full-timers. They argue that fiscal pressures brought on by state appropriation cycles and the impending shortages of faculty limit their freedom to select and keep the best faculty for their institutions (Mortimer, Bagshaw, and Masland, 1985). Moreover, because enrollment fluctuates from term to term, colleges can find themselves searching for part-time faculty on a last-minute call basis. Unless there is a solid pool of part-timers with experience at the institution, their calls may bring people who have limited knowledge about the college and its students. Finally, there is little opportunity to conduct critical hiring procedures when screening opportunities are diminished and hiring is not done in a timely fashion (Texas Higher Education Coordinating Board, 1990).

Finally, not only do part-time faculty allow colleges to meet their needs for flexibility in course scheduling, some researchers note that they provide the flexibility that colleges need to meet affirmative action guidelines for the employment of women and minorities (Eliason, 1980); others document that there is little evidence of affirmative action in the recruitment and hiring of part-time faculty from minority groups (Gappa and Leslie, 1993). The early arguments surrounding affirmative action and part-time faculty centered around the opportunity part-time faculty positions provided administrators in fulfilling affirmative action guidelines (Eliason, 1980). With part-time faculty staffing, there is an increased opportunity to hire strong minority role models. Additionally, the college might attract these minority part-time faculty members into full-time positions as they become available.

While these are noble aims, the data do not indicate that they have been achieved (Gappa and Leslie, 1993). Part-time faculty pools, in general, tend to be less diverse and represent more of a problem than an opportunity for affirmative action. The controversy increases when part-time faculty are given priority in the hiring of full-time positions, as the applicant pool tends to be skewed away from minority applicants.

From the perspective of part-time faculty. Many part-timers appreciate the opportunity to teach at times that will not interfere with full-time jobs, young children's school schedules, graduate school responsibilities, and a host of other restrictions on their time that make full employment difficult. For example, part-time faculty who are employed full-time elsewhere and work a traditional eight-hour day more likely would have only late afternoons, nights, and weekends available for teaching. Parents who want to accommodate their children's school schedules might prefer to teach at off-campus sites, particularly if they are located near their homes.

Yet, for part-time faculty whose personal and professional schedules permit a wider range of course times, having only the opportunity to teach late evening and weekend classes that most full-time faculty would prefer not to teach increases the part-timers' sense that they are second-class citizens in a bifurcated system.

PROFESSIONAL DEVELOPMENT

Institutional practices critically affect the quality of instruction. The support functions that are available to full-time faculty within their departments and within the larger college family are not as accessible to part-time faculty, and there are fewer opportunities to enjoy the collegiality and professional development that are available to full-timers.

Faculty are critical to student success (O'Banion, 1994; Roueche and Roueche, 1993a; Tinto, 1987); yet, ironically, this expanding faculty cohort is the least likely to receive organizational support to improve their teaching (Erwin and Andrews, 1993; Gappa and Leslie, 1993). The critical relationship between part-time faculty and the institution now depends largely on the department chair (Gappa and Leslie, 1993; Tucker, 1993). Department chairs and division heads often have sole responsibility for recruiting, selecting, and orienting part-time faculty in their areas. Yet, most department chairs are "underprepared and administratively overwhelmed in trying to deal responsibly with part-time faculty issues" (Gappa and Leslie, 1993, p. 12). Chairs receive little training in hiring processes, affirmative action concerns, orientation processes, or staff integration; yet they are the key administrators in supervising the largest faculty cohort in today's community colleges.

From the perspective of the college. The incidence of comprehensive professional development programs for part-time faculty is uneven among community colleges. Colleges report that their efforts to provide staff development are limited by the time constraints that part-timers have, by the college's own inability or unwillingness to provide compensation for participating in such programs, and by a reluctance to commit additional funds for employees who have loose ties to the college and may well be gone within a matter of months.

From the perspective of the part-time faculty. Part-timers typically feel as though they are left on the fringes of the college, and they report strong feelings of alienation and concern over the severely limited opportunities and incentives for professional growth and development (Parsons, 1980b; Spinetta, 1990; Richardson, 1992). Their contention is that the college does not do enough to weave part-time faculty into the communicative fabric of the institution. Few have offices at the college or access to an office, although most have a mailbox at the college (Keim, 1989).

> The most common problem for the adjunct is the relative difficulty of communication. Unlike regular faculty, he does not have lunch, coffee breaks, and casual conversation with colleagues or administrators. Being set apart from this community, he can expect to receive requests for information several days after the deadline for furnishing it. To illustrate, I was once given a mailbox two hours drive away, which I was presumably expected to check several times a week! (Beman, 1980, p. 83)

They enter college classrooms to teach, but they are encumbered by inadequate support systems and limited knowledge of the community college philosophy and its students (Smith, 1980, pp. 17–18). In a social vacuum, without social status in the academic community, the part-time teacher sees himself denied the opportunity to become a part of the intellectual mainstream of the college (Greenwood, 1980, p. 56). This state of affairs for part-time faculty seems alive and well in most community colleges (Richardson, 1992; Erwin and Andrews, 1993; Gappa and Leslie, 1993). Helping "what's his face" feel at home is a challenge for the institutions that employ part-timers (Beman, 1980; Greenwood, 1980). Yet, from those colleges that implement staff development programs for part-timers come remarkable discoveries that encourage others to "become stronger and more effective because they integrate part-time faculty in the core activities of teaching and learning" (Gappa and Leslie, 1993, p. 213).

THE STUDENTS THEY TEACH

Part-time faculty and part-time students are both increasing in number. As enrollments increased in the 1970s with the influx of part-time students, part-time faculty staffing became more common (Leslie, 1978). Today, it is a common characteristic of institutions with higher percentages of part-time students (for example, urban institutions) to staff greater numbers of part-time faculty. Moreover, the times most often available to part-time students for academic work make them more likely to be students of part-time teachers—that is, late afternoons, evenings, and weekends.

The part-time faculty member is also most likely to wrestle with the instruction of the growing numbers of underprepared students—one of the most important and expanding missions of the community college. *Between A Rock and a Hard Place: The At-Risk Student in the Open-Door College* (Roueche and Roueche, 1993a) details the challenges that increasing numbers of underprepared, at-risk students pose to community colleges. Underprepared, at-risk students combine work and school; they are single parents, minorities, first-generation college students, students with economic and child care needs, students with a history of academic difficulties, or some combination of these categories. These students are often referred to as "at-risk" because they are those most likely to drop out of higher education. Quality faculty are essential to serving their needs.

> Faculty...are representatives of the institution; what they say...and what they do...significantly affects what students believe about a college or about the quality of the college experience (Roueche and Roueche, 1993a, p. 103).

> The heart, the key to student success resides in the faculty selected to implement programs and teach students (p. 257).

A 1993 report to the Florida State Board of Community Colleges documented that from 1987 to 1991 there had been a 63 percent increase in the use of part-time faculty to teach general education courses; the same report cited another from the Illinois Community College Board that documented heavy staffing of general education and remedial courses by part-timers (Armstrong, 1993). Finally, Gappa and Leslie's (1993) recent study found that part-timers are frequently used by colleges to teach the lower-level courses that full-time faculty find undesirable, and that often developmental and general education courses are the only courses part-timers are allowed to teach.

Teaching poorly prepared students is "considered a low-level enterprise, often left to part-time faculty members hired specifically for this purpose" (Astin, 1985, p. 104). The Southern Regional Education Board, in a late 1980s survey of program characteristics of its colleges' remedial and developmental programs, discovered: "Institutions rely heavily on part-time faculty to teach remedial students—typically, about half the faculty [of institutions responding to this survey] providing such instruction are part-time" (Abraham, 1992, p. 4).

Given research findings that most part-timers are haphazardly selected, poorly oriented, and weakly supported (Erwin and Andrews, 1993; Parsons, 1980b; Richardson, 1992), the use of part-timers in general education and remedial instruction poses a unique challenge. It appears that the underprepared student in the community college is very likely to be taught by an "underprepared" instructor—at least in terms of organizational support.

THE WARNINGS ABOUT USING PART-TIME FACULTY

Warnings about the overuse of part-time faculty in community colleges are common and widespread, and while they have changed little over the past fifteen years or more, they appear to resurface with different faces as the debate continues. In 1988, California legislated staffing ratios of 70 percent full-time faculty to 30 percent part-time (Armstrong, 1993). Boyer, reporting on a study of the college experience for undergraduates in American colleges and universities, recommended: "It is our position that a balance must be struck between full- and part-time faculty. Specifically, we propose that no more than 20 percent of the undergraduate faculty be part-time and that when part-time faculty are used, it is essential that their employment be educationally justified" (1987, p. 137).

However, there is a curious absence of any evidence to support any policy for appropriate ratios of part-time to full-time faculty. Lack of research and absence of hard data about part-timers and their teaching performance make even more curious the hand-wringing and nay-saying positions taken by legislative bodies, by college administrations, and by full-timers. Most of the "evidence" is based on perceptions and is tied to two dimensions: student evaluations of part-time faculty; and vague concerns about the limited time that part-time faculty have to serve on curriculum committees, tend to instructional details, and keep office hours. In reality, there are limited hard data to support whether part-time faculty are any better or any worse than full-time faculty.

The current thinking appears to be a wait-and-see attitude, a bowing to the complexity of part-time faculty issues, a notion that there may well be no appropriate ratio. Howard Simmons, executive director of the Commission on Higher Education of the Middle States Association of Colleges and Schools, has observed that the focus used to be on numbers but is now on results—"we have found that setting numbers doesn't work or make for quality. There are too many different kinds of schools and disciplines to have a blanket requirement" (Morgan, 1993, p. 6). Sandra Elman, associate director of the Commission on Institutions of Higher Education of the New England Association of Schools and Colleges, reported, "It is the thinking of the commission that it is not prudent to set ratio standards" (Morgan, 1993, p. 6). John Petersen, executive director of the Accrediting Commissions for Community and Junior Colleges of the Western Association of Schools and Colleges, noted, "We can tell an institution that they need to hire thirty full-time faculty members, but if they don't have the money to do it, that doesn't help anybody" (Morgan, 1993, p. 6). In the final analysis, agreement runs strong that the bottom line is quality and effectiveness, that achieving both requires colleges to monitor themselves and determine if their mission and purposes are being achieved with their current faculty.

LOOKING INTO THE EYE OF THE STORM

The increasing use of part-time faculty in the community college may well be inextricably linked to two significant economic trends that do not yet have a mature definition, but that, with some focused attention, can be identified by tracking the changing demands of the workplace. Over the last twenty years our shifting economy has created a new trend—part-time work is on the increase (Jackofsky and Peters, 1987). IBM, once the Goliath of the corporate world, has noted that by the year 2000 more than 80 percent of its workforce will be contract part-time. And, Dow Chemical is now only hiring individuals with specialized skills—for example, chemists and mathematicians—to accomplish specific and specialized tasks for specified time periods (Gianini and Sarantos, 1995). In a similar fashion, colleges are using increasing numbers of part-time faculty to staff experimental programs to test the student market before making firm commitments to pay expensive start-up costs. Part-timers are proving to be so useful that some institutions are converting some of their full-time positions into a greater number of part-time positions (Tucker, 1993). Attention to the bottom line will require organizations to consider increasing their use of part-time, temporary employees.

But perhaps even more unsettling than having to rethink our traditional patterns of staffing is the prospect that we must also rethink our notion of the larger concept of "jobs" as a way of organizing work. Even as escalating costs increase the use of part-time employees, there is evidence that jobs as we know them are changing, that they are social artifacts, going the way of the dinosaur.

> To an extent that few people have recognized, our organizational world is no longer a pattern of jobs, the way a honeycomb is a pattern of those little hexagonal pockets of honey. In place of jobs, there are part-time and temporary work situations. That change is symptomatic of a deeper change that is subtler but more profound. The deeper change is this: Today's organization is rapidly being transformed from a structure built out of jobs into a field of work needing to be done.

> Tomorrow's organization certainly must turn a significant part of its work over to a contingent work force that can grow and shrink and reshape itself as its situation demands. But note that even the most creative work design begs the question of how unready most organizations are to manage this work force of temps, part-timers, consultants, and contract workers effectively (Bridges, 1994, p. 64).

While the majority of American community colleges have a long history of using part-time faculty, many have not yet recognized the widespread effects of employing increasingly large numbers of part-timers, nor have they recognized fully the need to integrate, train, and provide part-timers with acceptable levels of institutional support services.

CONCLUSIONS

Over the last twenty to thirty years, even as the number of part-timers have been escalating, there has been an underlying assumption among full-time faculty, administrators, and professional and legislative entities that once the extraordinarily heavy demands on our colleges dissipated, when budgets began increasing again, the need for significant numbers of part-time faculty would be reduced. There would be a return to "normal behavior," to a more traditional mode of delivery. More full-time faculty would be hired, and they would provide the bulk, if not all, of colleges' educational services.

There are indications that suggest those days will never come. Recently, Clark Kerr, speaking to the Southern Regional Education Board, observed "that all sectors of higher education should turn over their lower division courses to part-time instructors." And, one commentator proposed that perhaps colleges, in their efforts to best use the skills and talents of all faculty, should consider organizing departments by clusters of ten or more part-timers, with each cluster supervised by one full-time faculty member who would participate in the part-timers' classes and serve as a "conduit of information between…part-timers and the college, and between the students…and college support services" (Pedersen, 1993, p. 4). Lorenzo and Banach, writing as members of the Institute for Future Studies, posited that if Bowen and Schuster (1986) are correct—that higher education faculty will experience a faculty shortage of 500,000 during the twenty-five-year period from 1985 to 2010—then a shortage of well-qualified professional staff could drive community college planners to consider solutions "ranging from lowering credentials to using more paraprofessionals" (1994, p. 7). Moreover, they asked: "Is there an optimal mix of…full-time and part-time employees?… Is there need for a new class of employee, somewhere between full-time and part-time?" (p. 8). And, could that "new class" be a combination of technology and human— telecourse-based associate degree programs (Cross, 1994, p. 22)? Can a variety of nontenurable, limited-contract "full-time temporary" positions, with appointments limited to three to five years, provide more instructional continuity and allow the college to cut back on the numbers of part-time faculty (Gappa and Leslie, 1993, p. 119, p. 156)? The number of considerations are expanding as colleges search for staffing solutions.

In every decade of American history, some issues have so captured our imaginations or so threatened our traditional values that they have become synonymous with the times. By studying the ways in which we as a nation have responded to these extraordinary issues, we can chart how they have affected the quality of our collective lives. Sometimes that study strengthens our faith in our ingenuity and spunk—our history is resplendent with examples of seemingly impossible tasks that, once they were identified as critical to our society's well-being, were accomplished. Yet, sometimes history has recorded that we have fallen short; we have failed to anticipate the complexities of the mission, or have been too divided in our battle plans, or too meek in our actions to mount a substantial attack—American ingenuity and spunk have been momentarily derailed by faulty thinking.

Undeniably, present-day uncertainties are testing the American approach to solving problems. Perhaps at no time in our history have we been compelled by necessity to tackle so many seemingly disparate problems at once—problems that appear unrelated but that collectively are affecting mightily the social, economic, and educational foundations of our society. Crime, drugs, troubled education and health care systems, to name but a few of the current devastating realities, threaten to dull our competitive edge in the global economy and weaken the very fabric of our society. These problems are joining forces to write a terrible history. To this mix, one must add the reality that we have no reliable responses with which to address these changes in our society, no foolproof templates for designing strategies; tried and true answers to these tough questions just do not exist.

Everything somehow seems fundamentally different…it's readily apparent that both alignments and priorities are in flux…the hows, whens and whys of almost everything we do have changed…it's crystal clear that perpetuating the status quo will have ominous consequences in this period of fundamental uncertainty (Lorenzo and Banach, 1994, p. 1).

Historically, community colleges have boasted of their ability to respond quickly and effectively to change. They have likened themselves to speedboats— quick, unencumbered, and responsive—and they have likened their more tradition-bound four-year college and university sisters to considerably less responsive battleships. However, with age and development, most community colleges would now agree that while they have not earned full battleship status, they have not maintained their status as speedboats either. In fact, they may have become much more comfortable with the notion of being pleasure boats. Inflexible systems, typically associated with more established institutions, are now more common at community colleges. Growing comfortable with the status quo, some leaders have decided to perpetuate it. To continue in nautical terms, they are creating major wind drags on progress.

However, historical precedents document that perpetuating the status quo has never been a path to success. Pundits warn that "if we are not getting better, we are getting worse; if we are not going forward, we are going backward." Internal demands, such as the increasing number and diversity of students, and external demands, such as burgeoning technological advancements and competitive global markets, warn us that maintaining the status quo is an irrational, foolhardy, if not suicidal, response to the need for inevitable change.

CHAPTER 2

It is not enough to understand what we ought to be,
unless we know what we are.

—T. S. Eliot

TAKING A WIDE-ANGLE PICTURE

Surveying How American Community Colleges
Utilize Part-Time Faculty

his study began with three major goals:

- to review important issues in the part-time faculty debate
- to describe the current extent of community colleges' reliance on part-time faculty
- to identify and showcase selected successful part-time faculty utilization and integration programs.

The broad-brush views of the most common and controversial issues in the part-time faculty debate, touched upon in the opening chapter, will be explored further as we showcase institutional responses to part-time faculty concerns and issues in the remaining chapters. The current extent of American community colleges' use of part-time faculty will be described here as we share institutional responses to our national survey questions (see Appendix A for the full text of the survey). And, finally, we will end this discussion of survey responses by turning to the information we gathered through a final request of survey respondents— the information that became the primary focus of this investigation.

We paid extraordinary attention to this final request for information from survey respondents, but it is important first to describe the survey responses that make up our wide-angle perspective on the part-time faculty picture. These survey responses provide a current benchmark of college employment of part-timers; more importantly, they paint the current landscape upon which we have drawn institutional program particulars from selected community colleges.

PART-TIME FACULTY DEFINED

The first step in developing and administering our utilization survey was to clearly define what we meant by part-time faculty. We began with a simple definition of the group we were studying: part-time or adjunct faculty are those individuals an employing institution recognizes, legally and contractually, as less than full-time. However, a few months into our investigation, we discovered that the terms *part-time* and *adjunct* could not be used interchangeably at many institutions, that the term *adjunct* sometimes identified a tenure-track or a "full-time part-time" employee. Therefore, we decided to abandon the term *adjunct* altogether for the purposes of this study.

As we studied individual colleges and their definitions of part-time faculty, we realized that if we embraced all of the various nuances of their descriptions, our own would grow too complex, and, in fact, take us away from our primary goal of showcasing successful programs for integrating part-time faculty into colleges. The definitions of part-time faculty were often as varied as the institutions employing them. Colleges defined them in remarkably dissimilar ways: they described legal relationships between employees and the college; they characterized employees by credit hours, type of courses, and day or evening responsibilities; they had established such distinctions as "full-time adjunct" and "degrees of part-timeness." Some institutions placed their faculty into categories of full-time, fractional full-time, and part-time—fractional full-timers carried a load more than half-time but less than full-time (Tuckman and Vogler, 1978). However, among the more common definitions were: in California community colleges, part-time faculty are those who teach not more than 60 percent of a full-time load; in Texas community colleges, most part-time faculty teach no more than 50 percent of a full-time workload; and the American Association of Community Colleges' survey data identify part-time faculty as teaching nine or fewer credit hours (full-time faculty were represented as those teaching nine or more credit hours). The definitions of part-time were not as simple, precise, or concise, as the definitions of full-time, and the varied definitions complicated the research issues considerably as we began to feel more and more obliged to attend to every nuance of each college's situation and perspective.

And so we settled upon the definition that, for purposes of this study, most effectively described the faculty that we chose to study: Part-time faculty are those whose employing institutions recognize them legally as less than full-time—that is, part-time faculty are those so recognized by their employing institutions. Moreover, we observed that the term had served other researchers of part-time faculty quite well—Biles and Tuckman defined them as "those who work less than a full-time load as...defined by their employing institution" (1986, p. 1); and, Gappa and Leslie defined them as "individuals who are temporary, nontenure-track faculty employed less than full-time" (1993, p. 3).

POPULATION AND PROCEDURE

We chose to survey the member colleges of the American Association of Community Colleges (AACC). Initially, we planned to conduct a simple random survey of all AACC member colleges, but a cursory study of AACC's membership showed that such a sample would likely increase the sampling error. Because a majority of AACC's members are small colleges and technical schools, they would be overrepresented in the survey population, when the large districts and colleges in AACC enroll the great majority of students attending American community colleges.

We chose, instead, a stratified random sampling procedure that would provide the benefits of randomness and allow for stratification along important population parameters (Kerlinger, 1986; Singleton, Straits, Straits, and McAllister, 1988). Member colleges of AACC were divided into categories prior to our random selection of colleges within these categories. Because these categories were more homogeneous, they would reduce the sampling error that simple random sampling would create (Rubin and Babbie, 1993). Additionally, this stratification would facilitate more complete analyses of specific categories and comparisons between categories. The categories for this sample were:

Category One. Community College Districts or Systems. American Association of Community Colleges member districts/systems. Population: 41. (A notable exclusion from this stratum was the Community College of the Air Force. The data from this institution, which represents some ninety-nine colleges and campuses, could have skewed the results for non-comparable institutions.)

Category Two. Large, Non-District-Affiliated Colleges. AACC's individual institutional members with 8,000 credit students or more, not associated with a district or system. Population: 153.

Category Three. Average, Non-District-Affiliated Colleges. AACC's community college members not affiliated with a district or system, with less than 8,000 credit students. Population: 644.

A census of Category One included almost 200 colleges and allowed for the comparison of district and non-district-related schools. This expanded reach also provided a larger source for our referential sample, by which we would identify community colleges with reputedly outstanding programs for part-time faculty integration. A random sample of fifty colleges was drawn from each of the remaining categories. While this was a small number of colleges in terms of the population/sample ratio for Category Three, we accepted the limitations of the smaller sample in order to keep it manageable. This was an important decision given the type of survey to be conducted. Our study sought data that would not be readily available (e.g., reports of credit hours taught by part-time versus full-time), and so conducting a phone survey would be impractical. A mailed survey of selected colleges was the best available option. To avoid the problems typically associated with national-scale mail surveys (e.g., low response rate, ranging from 30 to 40 percent), direct contact follow-up procedures were developed. These procedures, used in conjunction with a sample of manageable size, helped ensure a more representative sample.

There were further considerations. Because we sampled at the district level with Category One, as opposed to the college level with the others, we needed to ensure that district colleges were equally represented in the sample. To equally represent the influence of district colleges in our data, the scores for the district respondents were multiplied by the average number of colleges in the district sample and then added into the analysis of the data,[1] a common statistical weighting procedure. Statistical weighting was also used as a control for the disproportionate stratified random sample. Our survey sampled categories in different proportions than the proportions of the categories in the actual population. For example, average colleges represent more than 60 percent of the total population of American community colleges, but represent slightly more than 30 percent in our sample. Statistical weighting adjusts for these differences.[2] With these controls, our sample statistics better match the characteristics of the member colleges of AACC.[3]

We designed a survey instrument that would be appropriate for either a community college district (Category One) or a single community college (Categories Two and Three). Survey instruments were mailed to the CEO of each institution,

1. This statistical weighting procedure was conducted to ensure equal units of analysis. If the survey had sampled both districts and colleges, and then attempted to generalize from combined data, the findings would not apply; the effects of college-level units of analysis would be underrepresented in the district scores. The districts reported a census of all data from their member colleges; thus, by multiplying each district by the average number of colleges represented by districts, the college-level unit of analysis was retained.

2. This statistical weighting procedure was conducted to equalize the disproportionate samples drawn from the strata (categories). Strata of interest in any population occur in different percentages. If the samples drawn from within the stratum are not equal in proportion to the percentages of the population stratum, the findings would, in effect, misrepresent the true population parameters of interest by inflating or deflating different stratum contributions. This effect was controlled by statistically weighting the disproportionate stratum samples to adjust their contribution to equal the proportion of those of the population stratum.

3. Comparisons between and within the categories do not necessarily have to be statistically weighted. The effect of statistical weighting in this case would be to restrict unnecessarily the variance of a given sample. However, by not statistically weighting these samples, the unit of analysis is no longer AACC colleges, but AACC organizations (i.e., colleges and districts). Therefore, when interpreting data from within a stratum, findings can be generalized only to the organizational-level unit of analysis.

or in the case of a district, to the district CEO only; a cover letter described the study and requested participation. Our letter requested data from fall 1993 and assured anonymity of individual responses, if requested. Non-respondents were contacted by phone and asked again to complete the survey.

Our sampling plan facilitated comparisons between community college districts, large community colleges, and average community colleges. Our final sample included colleges and districts from forty-nine states, and the collected data represented the state-of-the-art of part-time faculty use in almost one-fourth of all American community colleges. [See Appendix B for a list of responding colleges and districts.]

RESPONSE RATES

Our overall response rate was 62.4 percent. The response rate within Category One was 59 percent (n=24). The statistical weighting of the other categories was based on this proportion. Careful analysis of this category sample revealed no systematic differences between the responding colleges and non-responding colleges in terms of geographic region or district size. The response rate for Category Two was 62 percent (n=33); an analysis of responding and non-responding colleges showed no significant differences in terms of institutional size or region. The response rate for Category Three was 66 percent (n=33), and the colleges were evenly distributed in size and geographic region.

The overall response rate in this investigation is higher than that of typical national mail surveys. The sample represents approximately one-fifth of the member colleges in AACC. Additionally, many of the results reported here are very similar to recent surveys reporting on part-time faculty (e.g., Keim, 1989; Erwin and Andrews, 1993). Thus, even with the inevitable limitations, the data reported here can be regarded as effectively representing trends in the employment of part-time faculty in AACC member colleges and, more specifically, within the stratified districts and colleges.

PERCENTAGE OF PART-TIME INSTRUCTORS VS. FULL-TIME INSTRUCTORS

Our first general questions asked participating colleges and districts to report the number of part-time faculty and the number of full-time faculty employed in fall 1993. These data were then converted into percentages for trend comparison and analysis. The percentages represented the trends in the employment of 68,699 faculty nationwide and indirectly represented all faculty teaching in AACC member institutions.

Our study revealed that part-time faculty represent 58.28 percent of all faculty teaching in AACC-member institutions. The percentage of part-time faculty ranged from 3.7 percent and 8.8 percent in two of the small colleges responding to the survey, to 89 percent in one large, non-district college. These data were compared with full-time faculty, who represented some 41.72 percent of the faculty

Figure 2.1
Differences in Faculty Utilization Percentages

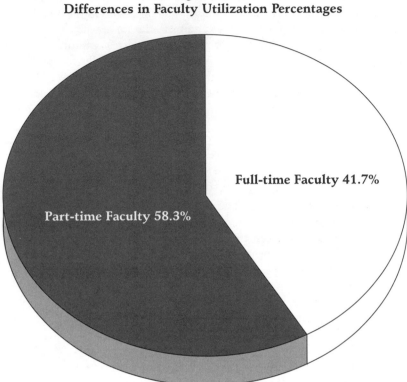

across all institutions.[4] These data were similar to those reported in the 1991 AACC annual survey and by Keim (1989).

An analysis of variance tested for significant differences between categories. The results revealed a significant difference between districts, large colleges, and average colleges in the percentages of part-time faculty employed (n=88, df=2, F=7.412, p<.001).[5] Community college districts employed an average of 62.51 percent part-time faculty, compared with 68.25 percent for large colleges, and 54.85 percent for average colleges, indicating that large colleges and districts are more likely than small or average colleges to employ higher percentages of part-time faculty.

4. There was a large standard deviation (sd=16.56) due to two extreme outliers, but otherwise the data were normally distributed. For example, when the median was used as the measure of central tendency, the percentages only changed one percentage point either way.

5. ANOVA with unequal group n's is largely unaffected if the ratio of the largest n to the smallest n is smaller than 1.5/1; the ratio in this case was 1.36/1.

Figure 2.2
Differences in Faculty Employment by Category

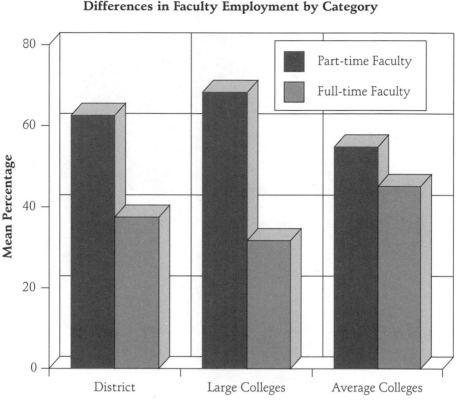

Sample Categories

Clearly, part-timers represent the largest cohort of instructors in the total number of community colleges, particularly in community college districts and in large community colleges. These part-time faculty percentages do not clearly represent relative teaching impact on community college students, given that part-time instructors typically teach only one or two courses per term, compared to the five taught by full-time faculty. Yet, a major issue with regard to the employment of part-time faculty is the percentage of part-time faculty instructional delivery, or the percentage of credit hours taught by part-time faculty.

PERCENTAGE DIFFERENCES IN CREDIT HOURS OF INSTRUCTION

Survey respondents were asked to report the total number of credit hours taught by part-time faculty and by full-time faculty. These data were again

Figure 2.3
Community College Faculty Credit Hour Teaching Percentages

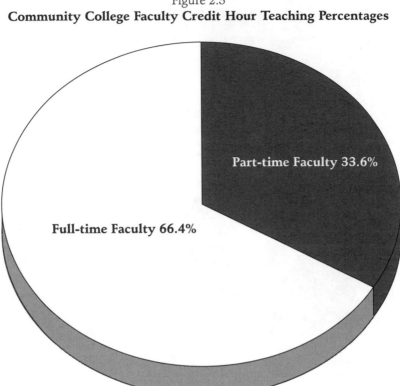

converted into percentages to facilitate comparison and analysis. We discovered that of all the instructional credit hours delivered by AACC member institutions in fall 1993, 33.63 percent were taught by part-time faculty and 66.37 percent by full-time faculty.[6]

Survey results revealed that approximately one-third of all credit hours delivered by these responding institutions were taught by part-time faculty, although the credit hour percentages were not the same across all categories. An analysis of variance tested for significant differences between the three categories. The results revealed a significant difference between districts, large colleges, and average colleges in the percentages of credit hours delivered by part-time faculty (n=88, df=2, F=4.726, p<.01). Part-time faculty delivered a mean of 38.73 percent of

6. The variability of these data was similar to the total percentage data (n=88, sd=17.33). Again, the standard deviation was inflated by two outliers. The distribution was otherwise normal and the median only one percentage point off either way.

Figure 2.4
Differences in Faculty Credit Hour Teaching Percentages by Category

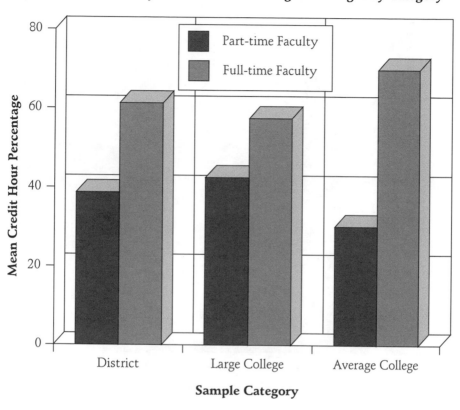

credit-hour instruction in district colleges; in large community colleges, part-time instruction represented 42.54 percent of credit hours delivered; in average community colleges, part-time faculty delivered a mean of 30.17 percent of the credit-hour instruction.

From these data we can infer that students are more likely to have a course taught by a part-time instructor if they attend a large community college or a community college in a district than if they are enrolled in an average non-district-related community college. Additionally, while full-time faculty still deliver the majority of credit-hour instruction in all colleges, somewhere between 30 percent and 42 percent of the instruction of community college students nationwide is being delivered by part-time faculty. In average community colleges, almost one out of three courses is taught by a part-time faculty member; in large community colleges and community college districts, approximately two out of five courses are taught by part-time faculty.

Figure 2.5

Distribution of Per Course Salary Means for Surveyed Colleges

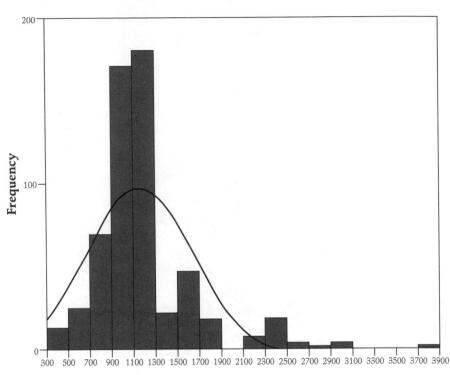

Per course salary for part-time faculty

Most colleges did not respond to survey questions about non-credit hour instruction. Of the twenty-seven colleges that did respond, the median percentage was 79 percent delivered by part-time faculty.[7]

AVERAGE PER-COURSE SALARY AND BENEFITS

We asked for salary information regarding part-time faculty (per-course estimates for a typical three-hour course without benefits). The salaries ranged from $424 per course paid by one small eastern college to $3,852 per course paid by one large western district. The mean or average per course salary was $1,196.70.[8]

7. The *mean* of 97 percent was inflated by three significant outliers. Again, these data were of little use, given the limited response and the wide variability.

8. There was a large standard deviation with these data (sd=481.50) because of outliers, which could make the median a better measure of central tendency in this case. The median part-time faculty salary was $1,100 per course, and the mode was $1,200.

Figure 2.6
Category Differences in Part-Time Faculty Mean Per Course Salary

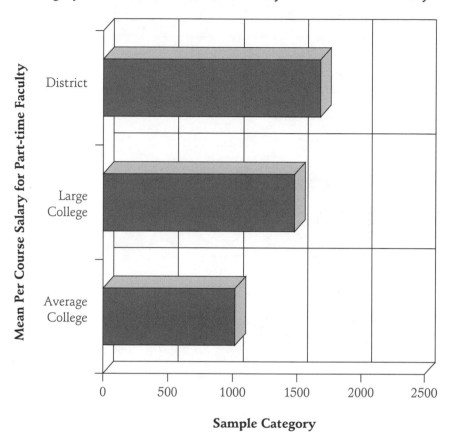

Sample Category

The cluster of scores to the right of the bell curve reflects salaries in districts and large colleges—albeit not *all* of the districts and colleges; but this outlying cluster of large colleges and districts increases the mean average salaries for these categories. Districts had a per-course mean salary of $1,678.45; the large community college per-course mean salary was $1,479.19; and the average community college per-course mean salary was $1,017. Analysis of variance revealed a significant difference between the category means (n=88, df=2, F=12.29, p<.000).

These data reveal a wide variability in the per-course salaries of part-time faculty nationwide. For example, type of institution appeared to account for some of the differences in per-course salary; in the case of a district, higher pay per course could be attributed to the reality that districts in large metropolitan areas must operate where costs of living are much higher than would colleges in areas with a

Figure 2.7

Faculty Salary Expense Differences for 30 Credit Hours of Instruction

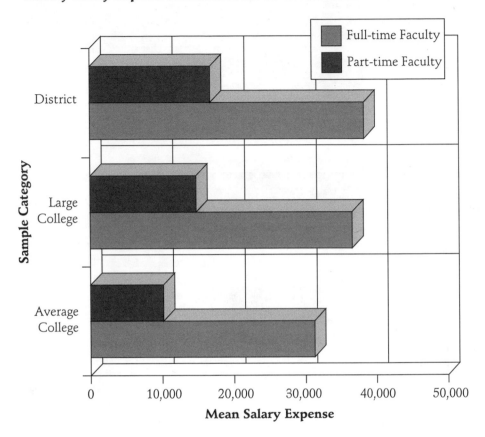

lower population density. Moreover, when the average per-course salary was cor-related with the same institutions' average pay for a beginning level full-time fac-ulty member, it was discovered that the institutions that are paying part-time fac-ulty more money per course tend to be the same institutions that are paying full-time faculty more [the Pearsons product moment coefficient was r=.50 (p<.000)]. While no "standard" salary emerged from this national-level analysis, salary did appear to vary by type of institution.

Less than 24 percent of the colleges and districts surveyed offered benefits to part-time faculty. At those that did, most faculty did not meet the minimum cri-teria for receiving benefits (typically, a load of three or more courses per academic term). Of the 24 percent of the institutions where part-time faculty were eligible, only 77 percent actually provided benefits (usually to less than five part-time fac-ulty per institution) as most part-time faculty failed to meet the eligibility requirements. Clearly, most of the colleges responding to the survey do not provide benefits for part-time faculty.

Survey results also indicated that the per-course salary for part-time faculty was a fraction of the per-course salary for full-time faculty. For example, when we asked community college districts to provide us with the average salary and dollar value of the benefit package for a new, entry-level, full-time faculty member, they reported a mean salary of $31,214, plus a benefits package valued at $7,011. The responses also indicated that these faculty were typically expected to teach ten classes during an academic year. The average expense to a college district for ten three-hour courses with new, entry-level full-time faculty is $38,225; a district could deliver the same ten courses with part-time faculty and save $21,440—the mean per-course salary for part-time faculty in community college districts was $1,678.45.

PART-TIME STUDENTS AND PART-TIME FACULTY

Part-time faculty are being asked more often than are full-time faculty to meet one of the greatest community college challenges—instructing the at-risk student. One characteristic of at-risk students is that they are likely to be part-time students. Often, part-time students can only attend at night because of outside employment, or they are merely testing the college waters (Roueche and Roueche, 1993a). Data from this study support the widespread notion that part-time students are more likely than full-time students to be instructed by part-time faculty.

Districts and large colleges, which have demonstrated higher percentages of part-time instructors than average colleges, tend to have higher percentages of part-time students, as well. [An ANOVA model comparing the different categories part-time student percentages reached significance (n=88, df=2, F=3.973, p<.023).] An examination of the category's part-time student percentage means revealed that districts and large colleges have approximately 8 percent more part-time students than the smaller average colleges. However, while we cannot assume a direct relationship between part-time faculty percentages and part-time student percentages based on these data, the data can make important contributions to the discussion of part-time faculty/part-time student relationships.[9]

There was a strong correlation between an institution's percentage of part-time instructors and the same institution's percentage of part-time students. [To test more directly for this relationship, a correlation (Pearsons r) was computed between the college's or district's percentage of part-time faculty and percentage of part-time students; results revealed a statistically significant correlation of r=.53 (p<.000).] Again, based on these data, we cannot assume that part-time instructors are instructing part-time students, but other studies have demonstrated that part-time faculty are most likely to teach at the times (night classes), at the level (developmental), and within the type of courses (general education) in which part-time students typically enroll (Abraham, 1992; Gappa and Leslie, 1993).

9. Research texts refer to this phenomenon as an "ecological fallacy"—assuming that because a population has coexisting characteristics that the characteristics are related.

Table 2.1
Part-Time Faculty Utilization Process Ranking Table

Rank	Utilization Process	Mean	Std Dev
1.	Selection/hiring of part-time faculty	2.33	1.62
2.	Orientation of part-time faculty	3.14	1.36
3.	Evaluation of part-time faculty	3.63	1.50
4.	Recruitment of part-time faculty	3.70	2.16
5.	Staff development of part-time faculty	4.22	1.86
6.	Involvement of part-time faculty in college life	4.97	1.90
7.	Retention of part-time faculty	5.66	1.65

ISSUES OF IMPORTANCE

We asked for the college or district CEO's opinion about the importance of particular issues regarding utilization of part-time faculty. When asked if the use of part-time faculty in American community colleges was an important issue, 98.9 percent of those surveyed agreed or strongly agreed that it was.[10] Almost two-thirds (65.9 percent) strongly agreed. When asked if they saw their use of part-time faculty increasing in the future, 54 percent agreed that part-time faculty use will increase, and 26 percent said it would remain the same. Only 19.3 percent believed their institutions would be using fewer part-time faculty in the future.

Finally, respondents were asked to rank, in order of importance, the processes involved in the use of part-time faculty. Literature addressing problematic issues around the use of part-time faculty typically addressed one or more of the following processes, but Parsons' model (1980b), which organizes the utilization processes of part-time faculty from recruiting through evaluation, appeared to offer the most complete and straightforward listing for our purposes. Based on his model, the following processes were identified as critical to effective utilization and so were included in our survey:

- recruitment of part-time faculty

- selection/hiring of part-time faculty

- orientation of part-time faculty

- involvement of part-time faculty in college life

- staff development of part-time faculty

10. Because the unit of analysis for these questions was the organizational CEO, the statistical weighting procedure was not used in these analyses.

- evaluation of part-time faculty
- retention of part-time faculty

Data revealed that respondents believed that selection, orientation, and evaluation of part-time faculty are the most important processes in the utilization of part-time faculty. Selecting/hiring part-time faculty was determined to be the most critical of all. (Because there was little difference within categories, further analysis related to differences within categories will not be included here.)

SUMMARY OF SURVEY FINDINGS

The findings of this survey can be summarized as follows:

- Part-time faculty represent approximately 58 percent of the faculty teaching in AACC-member colleges, and significantly greater percentages in district-related colleges (63 percent) and non-district-related colleges (68 percent) with more than 8,000 students.

- Part-time faculty are responsible for delivering more than one-third of the credit-hour instruction in AACC member colleges; in districts and large colleges, they deliver as much as 43 percent.

- Part-time faculty are clearly an essential component of AACC member colleges' total service to students.

- The national average salary for part-time faculty falls between $1,000 and $1,200 per course.[11] Salaries vary by type and geographic location of institution. District-related colleges typically pay higher per-course salaries than do large colleges, that, in turn, pay more than average colleges.

- Part-time faculty have a large role to play in meeting the challenges of the part-time student. Data demonstrate that institutions utilizing higher numbers of part-time faculty are the same institutions with higher numbers of part-time students. While a direct correlation cannot be demonstrated between the actual instruction of these part-time students and faculty, these data do support the notion that adjunct faculty are likely involved in some significant way with instruction of part-time students.

- Community college administrators agree that the use of part-time faculty in the community college is an important issue. Additionally, most agree that their use of part-time faculty is going to increase in the future, and that selection and hiring of part-time faculty are the most important processes to be considered in the use of part-time faculty (with orientation, evaluation, recruitment, staff development, involvement, and retention appearing in descending importance).

11. The median and the mode were used as measures of central tendency.

THE RESULTS OF REFERENTIAL SAMPLING

Of the three goals we identified early on, we believed that showcasing successful part-time faculty utilization and integration programs was the most critical. We had determined that, by far, it was the most useful of all the information we were gathering. In truth, we did not expect much to have changed during the last decade with the topics we surveyed. While evidence of the increasing interest in part-time faculty abounds in the literature, the wide variety of commentaries, descriptions, and studies have resulted in little more than a continuing affirmation of the notion that part-time faculty are a common "response to uncertainty" (Parsons, 1985). The general literature has not produced any evidence of national trends; no trends have emerged from these studies that indicate how best to effect part-timers' successful integration into college communities. It was apparent that the next step in the national study of part-time faculty integration must be to identify and study a significant number of community college programs and systems that appear to be working, identify the most common characteristics of their successes, and use them to craft broad-brush recommendations for institutional policy design and implementation.

Therefore, as the final request of our respondents, we asked for help in locating districts and colleges that have exceptional programs and policies for effectively utilizing part-time faculty. They were encouraged to identify themselves if they believed their own programs and policies were effective. We asked for the names of institutions and appropriate contacts at each. As we contacted the individuals and institutions identified in our survey, we asked for further information about other exceptional programs. This referential sampling procedure provided us with the names of the following institutions (and one organization). [The colleges that are featured throughout this book, their presidents, and the individuals participating in our interviews are listed in Appendix C.]

We requested all printed information available about institutional programs and policies for utilizing part-time faculty and integrating them into the college—e.g., part-time faculty handbooks, orientation profiles, and evaluation portfolios. Furthermore, we conducted telephone interviews with each contact. The interviews were conducted using a set of thematic questions centering on the recruitment, selection, orientation, integration, evaluation, and retention processes of each district, college, or department. These themes were developed from reviewing the broader literature on part-time faculty utilization. Transcribed and segmented by process into an ACCESS database, the data could then be compared across colleges. The policies and programs at each of the following thirty institutions are woven into the fabric of the following chapters as we describe effective strategies for employing and integrating part-time faculty into American community colleges.

- Central Piedmont Community College, North Carolina

- Centralia College, Washington

- College of the Canyons, California
- Community College of Allegheny County, Pennsylvania
- Community College of Aurora, Colorado
- County College of Morris, New Jersey
- Cowley County Community College, Kansas
- Cuesta College, California
- Cuyahoga Community College, Ohio
- De Anza College, California
- Greenville Technical College, South Carolina
- Hagerstown Junior College, Maryland
- Kirkwood Community College, Iowa
- Lakeland Community College, Ohio
- Metropolitan Community College, Nebraska
- Modesto Junior College, California
- Nassau Community College, New York
- Ocean County College, New Jersey
- Richland College, Texas
- Rio Salado Community College, Arizona
- St. Petersburg Junior College, Florida
- Santa Barbara City College, California
- Santa Fe Community College, Florida
- Schoolcraft College, Michigan
- Tarrant County Junior College, Texas
- Triton College, Illinois
- Truckee Meadows Community College, Nevada
- Valencia Community College, Florida
- Vista Community College, California
- Westchester Community College, New York

CONCLUSION

The findings from this national survey in large part replicate and extend prior research in the area of part-time faculty utilization. Judging from these data, it is apparent that part-time faculty represent a significant cohort in the total number of community college faculty, and their numbers will be increasing. They provide sizable credit-hour instruction for all students, and they receive significantly less compensation than do full-time faculty. In sum, part-time faculty are a critical mass in American community colleges.

Our attention must turn now to determining how best to utilize and integrate this critical mass. Solving the current part-time faculty problems cannot be accomplished by eliminating these faculty from college campuses; that simply will not occur in the foreseeable future, if ever. We must turn to exploring current strategies that have produced documentable success and offer recommendations for the adoption and adaptation of the most practical features of these strategies.

CHAPTER 3

The faculty make the college. They are the conjunction that connects the teaching and learning processes.

—Terry O'Banion, 1994

TAKING THE CRITICAL FIRST STEPS

Recruitment, Selection, and Hiring

I f community colleges intend to make good on their boast that they are indeed premier teaching institutions, then the critical first steps they must take and to which they must pay special attention are the recruitment, selection, and hiring of their faculty—the heart and soul of the college and the keys to the outcome of the teaching and learning experience. Two current forecasts bring an even more critical edge to these three processes: the number of part-time faculty in the majority of American community colleges will be increasing over the next decade, and more than one-half of all current full-time teachers in American community colleges likely will retire in the next five years. How and if these two forecasts will merge—for example, how many full-timers colleges will replace with part-timers—cannot be predicted in any reliable fashion. But whether or not they do will only partially affect the already increased likelihood that both full- and part-time students will be taught by some part-time faculty members in the course of their college experience. What we can predict is that these forecasts will all be realized in some measure and that they require clear-headed thinking now to make conscionable decisions about selecting *all* faculty—those individuals who, in fact, "will determine the real nature of community colleges for decades to come" (O'Banion, 1994, p. 313).

SPECIAL CHALLENGES FOR PART-TIME FACULTY

The Underprepared Student. One of the realities of the community college for the next few decades, if not beyond, is the continuing growth of the academically underprepared student population—those students whose academic backgrounds put them at risk of failure or, at the very least, of poor performance in regular college courses. Over the years, the faculty who teach the courses designed to prepare these students for the academic challenges of college-level instruction have been recruited and selected in strikingly different ways. In one of the first national studies of developmental education (Roueche, 1968), it was reported that remedial courses were typically taught by those instructors who had low status and low seniority, were less experienced than the average instructor, and were inexperienced with and knew very little about nontraditional students. Most of these teachers, in fact, did not have high expectations of the students and had little personal and professional commitment to teaching, primarily because they knew their colleagues had little regard for developmental courses and for the students enrolled in them. The author warned that the selection of instructors played a major role in ensuring a good fit between the remedial or developmental instructor and the demands of that role.

In 1972, researchers continued to find an almost total lack of institutional commitment to the programs or the students:

> Most community and junior college faculty are ill-prepared to handle the underachieving or low-aptitude student. Those selected for the job frequently enjoy low seniority and no tenure. Such assignments reflect the fact that teaching a remedial course is [still] a low-prestige assignment. The inexperienced faculty member, often fresh out of graduate school, has had little in the way of orientation or training in coping with the special needs of this group of students. Too few resources and inappropriate instructional materials conspire to defeat even the most conscientious instructor (Bushnell and Zagaris, 1972, p. 68).

Yet between 1968 and 1973, faculty selection did experience some notable changes. Colleges were moving away from assigning the least experienced faculty to teach developmental work, and moving toward assigning faculty who expressed a commitment to developmental education, who volunteered to teach the courses, and who were committed to helping students for whom other faculty had little regard or low expectations. Moreover, researchers who interviewed and observed these more committed faculty recommended unequivocally that developmental programs and courses be staffed only by teachers who volunteered to be there (Roueche and Kirk, 1973). Surveys of institutional changes in remedial and developmental courses and programs documented that by 1974, more than 56 percent of the faculty expressed an interest in teaching these courses and that 61 percent of these faculty had special training for working with underprepared students (Cross, 1976, p. 238). By 1977, researchers had determined that drafting instructors for developmental courses resulted in negative attitudes, and that faculty who expressed an interest in these courses were more likely to provide relevant instruction, use motivational strategies, discuss specific skill deficiencies and barriers to academic success with students, and help them overcome these barriers (Cross, 1976; Roueche and Roueche, 1977; Roueche and Snow, 1977).

However, while it was clear that revised selection and hiring practices had improved the conditions for developmental students, the programs did not yet fit easily into most community colleges where the majority of regular faculty, who had been in their institutions for many years, held on to views of their past.

> Traditional faculty members remember their college in the 1950s and 1960s, when they had well-prepared students. They may feel nostalgic, perhaps even betrayed because the conditions under which they entered the colleges have changed so. At the same time, they may be pleased that the segregated compensatory education programs remove the poorer students from their own classes....Nonetheless, the teachers in the compensatory education programs run the risk of becoming pariahs, similar in that regard to occupational education instructors in the pre-1960s era (Cohen and Brawer, 1982, p. 90).

By 1983, other researchers were warning colleges that a large supply of faculty eager to teach these courses was not available, no matter what the advocacy literature about developmental education said. They concluded: "Sadly, such is not the case" (Barshis and Guskey, 1983, p. 90).

What we knew about the "case," several years later, was that in two-year institutions, where the average number of remedial instructors was 20 per institution, approximately one-half had been hired specifically for the purpose of teaching remedial courses, approximately one-fourth had degree credentials specific to remedial education, and approximately one-fourth to one-third had been given specific training by the institution for their assignment (National Center for Education Statistics, 1991). Moreover, a 1991 study by the National Center for Developmental Education at Appalachian State University surveying all postsecondary educational institutions reported that in over one-half of these institutions, 100 percent of the developmental education faculty were teaching part-time, with 7.1 percent of the institutions reporting faculty teaching full-time in developmental education (Bonham and Claxton, 1992, p. 2). And, as was mentioned earlier, the Southern Regional Education Board reported that the colleges and universities in its region relied heavily on part-time faculty to teach remedial students (Abraham, 1992).

Keeping Up-to-Date in Technical-Vocational Programs. One of the reasons offered by community colleges for hiring and maintaining significant numbers of part-time faculty was the advantage of keeping close ties with developing business and industry, staying on the cutting edge with working professionals who were "on the job," individuals who had access to information about current trends in technology and business. They argued that full-time faculty, with their time and attention more focused on instruction and with less available time for staying up-to-date in their field, could not provide their students with all of their training needs, that part-timers could strengthen their technical-vocational programs with an infusion of "real world" perspectives.

While the local market appears to be a convenient recruiting pool, the competition with other employers; a lack of teachers with specialized, state-of-the-art skills; and complications created by teaching and work schedules diminish its value as a resource for teaching personnel. Yet, one recruitment strategy that colleges cite as especially compelling is the notion of personnel exchanges between colleges and businesses. Conflicts with teaching and working schedules are reduced dramatically when industry personnel are given time "on the job" to teach courses as a part-time instructor at the college, and college faculty are provided with opportunities to serve as consultants, trainers, teachers, and "learners" in the private sector's research and development activities. It is this "boundary spanning"—using part-time professional practitioners as primary sources to directly insert "appropriate norms, values, and information . . . directly into the curriculum"—that helps ease students from the classroom into the world of practice (Phelan, 1986, p. 8).

Early on, most researchers who studied the part-time teaching phenomenon in vocational and technical areas observed that part-timers were in abundant supply and that colleges would have no difficulty hiring them with little or no advance planning or notice (Hoffman, 1980; Vogler, 1980). However, over the last decade, colleges have discovered that these conditions have changed; student populations have become more diverse, technology and training needs have changed radically, and the competition from proprietary teaching institutions for students and from industry for employees has escalated (Biles and Tuckman, 1986). Not only must the majority of colleges put more effort into finding qualified individuals who wish to teach part-time, they must pay special attention to hiring individuals who have the credibility and experience that industry and business respect and expect, who can demonstrate a keen ability to maintain instructional standards upon which the college stakes its reputation in the community, and who can provide students with high quality instruction that meets accepted industry needs.

Nontraditional students and schedules. Colleges currently are offering increasing numbers of late afternoon, evening, and weekend classes, and often offer them at sites away from the main campus. More and more students have work and family responsibilities that limit their opportunities to take classes offered within what is still regarded as the more traditional class schedule. But these classes, according to many full-timers, are less desirable teaching assignments than those scheduled during more traditional daytime hours and those meeting on-campus. And, because more often than not it is the part-time faculty who teach in these time slots and at these sites, increasing numbers of students will come to know part-time faculty as representatives of the institution. While many colleges report that full-timers also teach within the more nontraditional schedule, they admit that, for a variety of reasons, they staff this schedule heavily with part-time faculty. Full-timers prefer daytime hours, part-timers find late afternoon and evening hours more convenient, part-timers who want to teach will take whatever they are offered, and so on.

What We Know About Recruitment and Selection of Part-Time Faculty

The practices and policies regarding the recruitment and selection of part-time faculty vary widely among community colleges. Because most part-timers form their first impression of the college and how the college regards them at this stage, these processes are critical. Some observations and issues, drawn from previous studies, provide a broad-brush view of what we know.

Most community colleges have standardized qualifications or criteria for appointment that are published in recruitment materials (Gappa and Leslie, 1993). Typically, these statements reflect academic qualifications part-timers must meet—e.g., a master's degree and a specified number of graduate credit hours or experience in the discipline. Minimum acceptable standards, whether written formally or understood tacitly and informally, can usually be met if the part-timer can provide evidence of experience that can be substituted for the standard. Some accrediting agencies that set and enforce hiring qualifications must be informed of any personnel hired with less than minimum qualifications and the college's justification for doing so. Accrediting agencies for more specialized licensing may require additional qualifications. Information about these qualifications and criteria is commonly shared either in the advertisements for available positions or when the appropriate personnel meet with the applicant. However, many colleges do not have clearly written terms of hire that will help them avoid problems that can arise when institutional policies, practices, and obligations are not spelled out prior to and during the actual appointment process.

Most recruiting is informal and conducted by word-of-mouth. Many part-timers recommend acquaintances who may be qualified and interested. Department chairs may telephone or write their counterparts at nearby institutions; may contact outstanding teachers at well-regarded local high schools; may seek out affirmative action officers and professional networks to help them address affirmative action issues (Fox, 1984; Gappa, 1984; Leslie et al., 1982); and may place ads in nearby cities and in local college newspapers, or air spots on local and countywide public television stations (Tucker, 1993).

The size and location of community colleges determine, in large part, the difficulty or the ease with which they can recruit part-time faculty. Colleges in or near large metropolitan areas have less difficulty recruiting and hiring part-time faculty than do colleges in more rural settings. When the majority of part-timers are drawn from local pools, as is the case for most colleges, there are extraordinary differences among colleges. Large pools of available talent—for example, in and near large cities—will directly affect the dynamics of the pool; rural colleges may find recruiting and hiring much more difficult as the size and specialized skills of the pool are dramatically reduced.

Affirmative action guidelines are infrequent considerations when recruiting and select-ing part-time faculty, even at institutions where faculty do not reflect the ethnic diversity of the larger community or the college's student population. An examination of employ-ment practices at most institutions reveals that the hiring of part-time faculty is usually based on "a combination of availability, teaching competency, willingness to accept relatively low compensation for services rendered, institutional needs at the moment, and academic credentials" (Biles and Tuckman, 1986, p. 16). Colleges that do not rigorously follow affirmative action guidelines argue that it is difficult enough to find and hire qualified part-timers without making affirmative action a primary concern; moreover, they argue that rigorous attention to affirmative action guidelines, in the face of the brief duration of a part-timer's time with the college, appears to be unwarranted. One study, however, reported: "Community colleges in urban areas tended to have the best representation of racial and ethnic minorities" and if fortunate enough to be in areas with corporations that empha-size affirmation action hiring policies, these colleges can benefit by "recruiting… part-timers from among [the corporations'] employees" (Gappa and Leslie, 1993, p. 149).

Hiring of part-timers is either centralized or decentralized—it either occurs in the col-lege's personnel office or at the departmental level. One study reported that when part-timers are hired at the centralized level, the following steps usually occur:

- the adoption, in principle, of federal affirmative action regulations through the hiring process

- a requirement for specific documents, such as an application, recommenda-tions, and transcripts, to be included in part-time faculty candidates' files

- a requirement for interviews with at least two administrators, usually a dean and a department chairperson

- a review of recommendations by the chief academic officer who finalizes appointments by letter or contract (Ross, 1982, p. 87)

The study summary suggested that when hiring is decentralized at the depart-ment level and becomes the responsibility of the department chair, the institution loses such valuable information as advertising sources, applicant files, selection criteria, measures of teaching success, and the relationship of these data to the selection of part-timers. Department chairs are more likely to be concerned with filling teaching spots and not so concerned with recordkeeping efforts.

Of the two levels, most studies report that department chairs are the principal contacts with part-time faculty, in most cases totally responsible for all communication the part-

timer has with the institution; to the part-timer, the department chair is the institution. Chairs provide appropriate personnel with information about departmental faculty staffing needs; they recruit and select, then hire—frequently making the hiring decision alone. Yet, department chairs are infrequently trained in interviewing techniques and have, more often than not, simply learned by trial and error.

Hiring of part-time faculty is not always planned. While colleges do not consider last-minute hiring to be in their best interests, there is widespread recognition that emergency situations can leave them with few other hiring alternatives. Some count on an established pool of part-timers who are well-known to the college for meeting such emergencies. Others plan to improve their methods for forecasting hiring needs, including better long-term planning for the hiring of part-time faculty as part of their institution's strategic plans for program development.

In our interviews, we asked the following questions about recruiting, selecting, and hiring part-time faculty:

- How does the college/district recruit part-time faculty (e.g., newspapers, television)?

- What sources does the college/district use for identifying potential part-time faculty (e.g., personal references, university contacts, graduate students)?

- What processes does the college use to select part-time faculty?

- Does the college/district have policies regarding selection procedures?

- Does the selection process differ for part-time and full-time faculty; if so, how does it differ?

- What are the minimum qualifications for part-time employment? What are the differences between minimum qualifications for part-time and full-time employment?

- Who has primary responsibility for hiring part-time faculty? Do department chairs (and/or others with such responsibility) receive training in selecting part-timers?

What Colleges Say About Recruiting Strategies

Following is what we learned from the respondents concerning recruiting strategies.

Location is a critical factor. Early in our investigation, we discovered that recruiting strategies varied among colleges, primarily because of their location; colleges operating in large, urban areas had fewer reasons to be concerned with adequate numbers or specialized training and experiences in part-time faculty pools. Our interviews confirmed this discovery. For example, **Community College of Allegheny County, Central Piedmont Community College, County College of Morris, Westchester Community College, Cuyahoga Community College, De Anza College,** and **Santa Barbara City College**—all located in or near major cities—said that formal recruitment efforts were unnecessary. County College of Morris reported that large numbers of active prospects—retired business and computer specialists and people working or studying in nearby universities—make frequent advertising of available positions unnecessary. And, De Anza College felt "blessed" with its part-time pool; located in the Silicon Valley near the San Francisco Bay Area, many applicants are professionals who want to teach to stretch themselves, improve their skills, or be part of an academic environment. Most part-timers initiate contact with these colleges. However, even those colleges—e.g., County College of Morris and Cuyahoga Community College—that reported little or no difficulty in establishing a sizable, high-quality part-time pool have discovered that some pools are drying up, including daytime part-time faculty in various disciplines, especially math and English; women who used to teach while their children were in school and are no longer available; and people qualified to teach specialized courses. Others, such as Westchester Community College, find that in many fields where average salaries are high and there are considerable numbers of available positions, many qualified people will not consider teaching at the college for such low salaries.

At colleges in more rural areas, such as **Centralia College**, respondents admitted that recruiting is more difficult—noting that "it is not as easy for us as it is for our urban cousins." Centralia College officials point to unattractive salary levels as well as a rural location as negative factors in their recruiting efforts. In fact, they note that sometimes they must be satisfied with candidates who hold less than a master's degree, even in transfer education. Centralia advertises through its personnel department for general areas. And, at **Cuesta College**, located in a rural area between San Francisco and Los Angeles, respondents observed that the high cost of living is a critical negative factor in the college's efforts to attract part-time faculty. While most recruitment occurs locally for many colleges, California's state chancellor has held job fairs in San Francisco to promote affirmative action hiring. Cuesta College's experiences with these fairs are mixed; while they have attended the last four annual fairs, the sizable fee for attending and the discovery that the fairs appear to have provided more help in identifying potential full-timers than in recruiting part-timers have raised some doubts about their value to the college. The college will frequently share part-timers with a nearby college and with the University of California–Poly Tech. Other than employing these two strategies, the college is limited to fairly typical advertising procedures; however, it notes that, particularly in areas such as nursing, the recruiting results often do not produce satisfactory numbers. And, **Modesto Junior College,** located far away from any metropolitan area, recruits primarily by advertising in newspapers. There are no formal job announcements made, and most recruiting occurs by word of mouth. College officials and representatives frequently make presentations to community groups and find that this interaction with the community is more likely to attract applicants than are more focused recruiting strategies.

Ties within the community, especially with business, industry, and civic organizations, are important recruitment tools. Colleges cite their ties, both existing and developing, with local and regional business and industry as valuable recruiting sources. At

Cowley County Community College, college personnel assume individual responsibility for making personal contact with businesses and industries in the area and for encouraging their professionals to provide important part-time instruction. Approximately 50 percent of CCCC's faculty in the vocational area come directly from local business and industry—"it has really benefited students to get a real application of their subject matter" from professionals who are on the job every day in those environments, according to Cowley officials.

Greenville Technical College's extensive advisory committee program plays a major recruiting role, as many part-time instructors are identified through committee contacts. In highly technical areas, college personnel find that contacting advisory committee members for referrals provides the college with well-qualified part-timers. In less specialized areas, such as math and English, more extensive recruitment is required because there are few specific organizations available for referrals.

Hagerstown Junior College works closely with two organizations—a military base and the Service Corps of Retired Executives. Retirements and down-sizing in the military have created some valuable pools of part-timers; retired executives, contacted through the chamber of commerce, are proving to be more educated and more vital than at any time in the county's history.

Expanding faculty diversity is a recruitment goal. **Cuyahoga Community College** reports that diversifying its faculty is a major goal for the college. Current efforts to identify minority applicants include networking with professional minority associations in the area. The college president has formulated strategies and procedures for identifying and reaching potential minority applicants. Presently, the office of affirmative action and diversity is preparing a brochure directed at enhancing faculty diversity at the college.

De Anza College is also addressing the part-time faculty diversity issue. The college reports that diversity within its pool of part-timers is not representative of its student body. The problem with this lack of representation loomed especially large when the college could document that the majority of its full-timers were hired from this pool. A strategy now in place for addressing this issue is the college's hiring of minority interns—who are enrolled at a nearby university but have not completed their master's degrees—to teach part-time.

And, while recruiting at **Santa Barbara City College** is very decentralized, with the various departments using their own idiosyncratic strategies to recruit their own faculty, the college responds to the affirmative action concerns at the state level by monitoring the various departments' hiring patterns to ensure diversity and by making diversity within the part-time pool an institutional priority. If the college believes that affirmative action guidelines are not being addressed, it initiates a districtwide advertising process that targets potential minority part-timers. College officials believe that this priority has helped various departments generate a number of qualified minority candidates. **Vista Community College** responds to statewide interest in expanding faculty diversity by recruiting minority faculty interns from graduate programs in the nearby university. Under a state-approved program for recruiting larger numbers of minority faculty, colleges are given special waivers to allow them to assign a full-time faculty member at the college as mentor to any minority graduate student who has completed at least 50 percent of the units toward a master's degree and chooses to teach at the college; the intern teaches under the guidance of the mentor. Many minority part-timers have an improved chance at available full-time faculty positions because of the keen interest in improving diversity among college faculty in the state.

The affirmative action office at **Truckee Meadows Community College** periodically reviews applicant pools and, if appropriate, encourages division chairs and directors to consider specific applicants. If an applicant pool contains a sufficient number of qualified applicants from underrepresented groups, the division chair or director screens applicants and makes selections from this pool. If an applicant pool is insufficient to meet affirmative action goals and objectives, the division chair or director may review applications from related pools. The affirmative action officer must sign off on all final hiring decisions.

Maintaining current databases helps organize the recruiting process. **Cowley County Community College** and **Rio Salado Community College** use database software to categorize part-time candidates by teaching area and discipline; at CCCC, each entry includes a brief biographical sketch of the applicant.

Most recruiting occurs via word of mouth and media advertising, but some colleges implement additional strategies to spread their recruiting nets more broadly. While **Santa Fe Community College** receives an ample number of applications, most unsolicited, for part-time positions, some departments in the college advertise for candidates each July. They encourage people who are new to the area, have recently completed degrees at the university, and are looking for employment to apply. A two-page description of "what part-time teaching is about at the college" is sent to all who express an interest in the positions featured in the July campaign.

At **Tarrant County Junior College**, all employment opportunities are published in a weekly newsletter circulated on campus, spreading the recruiting net among current faculty and their contacts. In addition, the college's telephone hotline provides callers with a list of available positions. Those who have previously submitted applications may also arrange for the college to add their application to the current pool for any particular position during their call. The college's cable television station includes advertisements for positions as well.

Triton College is developing relationships with high school faculty who are qualified to teach at the community college level, resulting in some important partnerships between area high schools and the college. These programs acquaint high school instructors with the policies and strengths of the community college, make them more willing to talk to their students about the community college as a postsecondary choice, and provide the college with important information about potential students.

Job fairs offer alternative recruitment opportunities. **Valencia Community College** recently instituted a job fair to recruit and inform prospective part-time faculty about opportunities at the college. The first job fair, held in the college gymnasium on a Saturday, attracted 200 prospective part-time faculty. Participants at the fair first enter an area where they are greeted and registered. They move to a nearby personnel department station where they receive an application form that may be completed and immediately submitted. This area includes a credential check station that identifies the courses for which prospective part-timers are qualified to teach. A general information video about the college plays continuously in the background.

Prospects who request an interview are given appointment cards that include the following information: an interview appointment time, the name of the department chair who will conduct the interview, and the courses the candidate is qualified to teach. At the appointed time, the prospect moves into an area of the job fair where tables and booths house the various instructional departments. Here the prospects meet with department representatives, are given specific information about teaching in the department, and receive a fifteen-minute interview.

The job fair is publicized in flyers distributed to area high schools and local agencies; in press releases sent to six radio stations, five television stations, and all area newspapers; and in paid announcements in the newspapers.

What Colleges Say About Selection and Hiring

As a general rule, academic qualifications for full- and part-time faculty are the same, except in some technical areas where exceptions for experience and special training are made. Department chairs are the primary college officials making part-time hiring decisions; they usually make decisions alone or are assisted at some stage in the process by a review committee of as few as one or as many as four members. There is usually no formal training for this responsibility. Colleges frequently do not scrutinize part-timers as carefully as full-timers in the selection and hiring process.

Centralia College's division chairs typically contact people from the applicant pool for interviews, screen the applicants, and make recommendations to the dean of instruction. There is no formal training for interviewing and hiring part-time faculty. College officials remarked that the interview process conducted for part-timers is far less rigorous than for full-timers and that "sometimes we have to hire adjuncts on the spot—offer them a job over the phone."

At **College of the Canyons**, two or three full-time faculty members screen and interview every qualified part-time candidate using approved questions provided by the personnel department. The majority of faculty, especially "lead" faculty in the new part-time faculty member's teaching area, have had some training in hiring protocol. This training is provided to faculty members who serve on screening committees convened for hiring full-time faculty. Applicants who have successful interviews are placed in a special pool of candidates pre-approved for hiring. The lead faculty and the division chair, in conjunction with the chief instructional officer, select from among those in this pool. Special attention is given to protected group member applicants within this pool. Policy allows for hiring of individuals who have not completed the selection process only in emergency situations.

At the **Community College of Aurora**, the chair invites two or three faculty members to review candidates' applications, they agree upon candidates to interview, and the chair conducts the interviews.

Cowley County Community College's candidates for part-time positions are interviewed by a site director and by the associate dean. Frequently, a full-time instructor serves as part of the interviewing team. All applicants must be approved by the division chair after a review of their applications before they can be scheduled for interviews.

Cuesta College described the selection/hiring process for part-timers as fairly collegial, involving faculty, chairs, and deans. A faculty screening committee reviews applications and interviews and screens applicants; however, a larger faculty committee confers about full-time candidates. Chairs and deans have sole responsibility for the final step in the hiring process.

The assistant dean of evening/weekend programs on each campus in conjunction with the division heads at **Cuyahoga Community College** is responsible for hiring part-time faculty. A program coordinator (a full-time faculty member with release time) assists with interviewing, hiring, and evaluating part-time faculty.

De Anza College's deans of instructional divisions hire the majority of part-timers, in conjunction with the department chairs. Many of the qualifications for these candidates are standard in all California community colleges. All deans receive some training in the hiring process.

At **Greenville Technical College**, department heads are given total responsibility for hiring. Effective fall 1994, there are biweekly sessions for new department heads that address the institutional policies for and concerns in hiring part-timers. Each applicant for a part-time position must submit a writing sample, which is evaluated as part of the selection process. The topic of the writing sample is the candidate's educational philosophy or some aspect of the technology of the discipline.

At **Hagerstown Junior College**, department chairs receive applications and interview applicants for part-time positions; the vice president of instruction reviews the outcomes of these interviews.

Kirkwood Community College has a special application that must be completed by part-time candidates; applications are sent to the various departments upon receipt, and the departments inform the candidates about the interview schedule and conduct the interviews. Most departments involve full-time faculty in the process of choosing part-timers; college officials reported, "It's not a complicated process, and it's really centered at the department level."

Lakeland Community College recruits and selects its part-timers on a decentralized basis. Once each year, the human resources department advertises in local newspapers, as well as minority-focused newspapers. Deans, chairs, and full-time faculty conduct the hiring process. A special session on legal issues, including hiring, was provided at a recent department chair meeting. There is no training for deans or chairs in the selection of part-timers. Most of those who hire have been trained on the job.

The personnel office at Metropolitan Community College provides minimum qualification screenings of all applicants, and applications are forwarded to the division chairs, who have responsibility for interviewing and hiring. Some involve full-time faculty in that process; some do not. There is considerably more faculty involvement in the hiring process when a selection decision does not need to be made immediately. Minimum qualifications vary from discipline to discipline, and technical fields require more experience with technology than is required in more general education courses. While the general education areas require the standard master's degree and some teaching experience, full-timers typically will be required to have more teaching experience than part-timers. There are no formal college policies for the hiring of part-time faculty, and division chairs have not received formal training for this hiring process.

At **Modesto Junior College**, faculty in each area conduct interviews, although the interviews are described as minimal when compared to those conducted for full-timers. Most of the hiring is coordinated by the division dean.

Nassau Community College is in the unusual situation of having two faculty unions—one for full-timers and another for part-timers. This affects the selection of faculty in an interesting way. Under the terms of the part-time faculty contract, part-time faculty who have ten or more terms of teaching have the right to be selected for a part-time teaching assignment before those who do not have at least ten. In addition, part-time faculty with ten or more terms of teaching have priority over the full-time faculty in cases where the full-time faculty want to teach an overload class. An overload class taught by a full-time faculty member is considered part-time employment with preference; under the terms of the contract, it goes to part-time faculty. College officials remarked that on the positive side this leads to continuity among part-time faculty. On the negative side, full-time faculty feel a "tremendous amount of antagonism" regarding the overload situation.

The part-time faculty and their union battled the college for several years on two issues: the union believed that selection and assignment should be made only on the basis of seniority (defined as number of terms taught) and that, once hired, one was a generalist and was qualified to teach any course (because it was "just a community college").

The result of the seven-year, college-union conflict was a contract that establishes a pool of part-time faculty with seniority. From that pool, the college can choose those who will be hired. (College officials observed that this seniority system complicates the college's concern about increasing the diversity of its faculty, as individuals with such seniority typically are not representative of ethnic diversity.)

And, finally, all summer courses and evening courses taught after 5:30 p.m. are taught by faculty under the terms of the part-time faculty agreement. Even full-time faculty who teach in the summer, or in the evening, teach as part-timers. This arrangement has led to different standards for selection, evaluation, and so on.

At **Rio Salado Community College**, the faculty chair identifies the need for a part-timer and contacts the college's personnel department; a search of the college's database provides the chair with a list of applicants and their résumés. Full-time faculty members evaluate the résumés and select candidates to interview; representatives of the personnel department are present for the interviews. In most situations, chairs make the final selection. While the college does not provide specialized training in hiring, chairs are instructed to look for a good understanding of the discipline, experience, and appropriate qualifications for the method of delivery.

Because Rio Salado specializes in the delivery of accelerated courses, distance learning courses, and custom courses delivered to business and industry, the people making hiring decisions must assess whether the candidate is qualified in method and content. The college provides training in weak areas, if necessary. Faculty chairs sometimes provide informal mentoring service in these areas.

Santa Barbara City College's department chairs are primarily responsible for selection and hiring; they receive training in hiring techniques, along with appropriate literature on diversity and affirmative action. Whenever interview schedules permit, additional full-time faculty in the department assist with the interviews.

At **Santa Fe Community College**, department chairs are primarily responsible for selection and hiring. Whenever schedules permit, full-time faculty assist with the interviews. Often, a part-time coordinator (a full-time faculty member with release time) is involved in the hiring process.

The assistant deans at **Schoolcraft College** are responsible for hiring part-time faculty at the college. Criteria by which part-time faculty are hired are the same as for full-time. Exceptions are made in vocational and technical areas, where a bachelor of science degree and extensive experience is frequently considered appropriate.

Program directors at **St. Petersburg Junior College** interview the candidates; sometimes the academic deans attend the interview. Background checks by human resources personnel are standard procedure. The search-and-screen process for part-time faculty is not entirely the same as for full-time—for example, the president interviews all potential full-time faculty. Training for program directors in interview techniques is being implemented now.

All candidates for part-time positions at **Tarrant County Junior College** must submit the same application as any full-time candidate, submit transcripts, and meet all academic and experience criteria set for their discipline; some exceptions are made in the technical areas. Basic responsibility for hiring rests with the department chairs. They receive no special training for this assignment.

Triton College's department chairs interview part-time candidates. The dean or the assistant dean reviews the candidate's qualifications and forwards the recommendation to human resources. There is no formal training for the chairs in interviewing and hiring techniques and procedures.

At **Valencia Community College**, department chairs have the authority to hire part-time faculty on the spot at their job fair (contingent upon their passing a background check and having satisfactory qualifications).

At **Vista Community College**, the selection process varies depending on the time available for a hiring process to occur. When there is sufficient time available for hiring, the dean or assistant dean and the department chair interview candidates and make selections. For last-minute hiring, the dean or the assistant dean is solely responsible. The process of interviewing is not formalized for part-time faculty; while interviewers use a series of questions in their interviews, the process has not been evaluated by the district's quality control process.

Westchester Community College selects candidates in two phases. Candidates are interviewed by the department chair. Then they are interviewed by the associate dean who determines if there is sufficient enrollment to justify the hiring and if the candidate meets the criteria for the course to be taught.

According to materials provided by all of the colleges, there is one notable exception to the general observation that department chairs are responsible for hiring part-time faculty. The English department at the Allegheny Campus of the four-campus **Community College of Allegheny County** attempts to follow closely the criteria for hiring full-time temporary faculty, as it considers part-time faculty excellent candidates for full-time temporary positions. From time to time, the department, depending on need, receives approval to hire someone for a one-semester full-time temporary position.

This selection process for part-time hiring begins with a part-time faculty coordinator, a full-time faculty member elected by the department faculty to serve for two years and to assist in the coordination, management, and evaluation of part-time faculty. The coordinator reviews all résumés and applications for part-time teaching positions, selects those that meet or exceed the minimum criteria, and submits them to the part-time faculty committee composed of full-time faculty who agree to serve. This committee reviews résumés and recommends to the coordinator the applicants it wishes to interview. The coordinator arranges interviews for each approved applicant with two to four members of the committee. The interview includes questions about the applicant's education, relevant to knowledge and application of contemporary composition theory and teaching experience. In addition, interviewees are required to grade and comment on a student paper and to explain the theory behind their comments and grading practice.

The full committee receives information from the interviews and votes as an entire body whether to admit the applicant to the part-time teaching pool, based on guidelines for part-time faculty. Then each approved applicant receives a letter informing him or her of the decision. The letter emphasizes that admission to the pool does not guarantee employment because the number of courses available to part-time faculty may vary widely from semester to semester.

To reduce the difficulty of hiring tasks for the department chair, the part-time faculty committee established a system whereby all members of the part-time pool are ranked according to established criteria. The purpose of the system, beyond helping the chair decide fairly and equitably which part-time pool members should receive teaching assignments and which should receive more than one assignment, is to ensure that sections staffed by part-time personnel receive the highest quality instruction available.

The committee, at the recommendation of the college personnel office, has established a procedure for ranking the part-time pool members:

1. Each current member of the part-time pool will be placed in one of three categories: highly competitive, competitive, and non-competitive.

2. New members of the pool will be assigned to a fourth category, new members/ not ranked, and will not be moved into any of the above three categories until they have taught at least one course on campus and submitted a portfolio for evaluation.

3. The committee will review the pool rankings each semester before assignments are made for the following semester. Faculty rankings may be changed by vote of the committee if an instructor's performance has changed as measured against the criteria.

4. When placing part-time faculty in the pool divisions, the committee will consider:

   a. Quality of course outline and the portfolio

   b. Adherence to college regulations and contract provisions

   c. Adherence to developmental review policies and practices

   d. Recommendation of department chair after review of personnel files

   e. Recommendation of developmental review coordinator

Elements that do not affect the placement of persons within the pool include student complaints regarding part-time instructors when no formal complaint has been filed with the department chair; participation in department and college activities (since not all part-time instructors have equal opportunity to participate); inability to accept a specific teaching assignment; and inability to accept any teaching assignment in a given semester.

The guidelines for screening part-time applicants include: a relevant master's degree with some graduate course work, some teaching experience (with a priority assigned to college-level basic writing and Composition I teaching), references, and anything in the applicant's credentials that do not fit in any other category but provide solid reason to consider the applicant seriously. While courses are to be offered only to individuals in the highly competitive, competitive, and new member categories, in situations where no one is available in those categories, members in the noncompetitive category may be offered a teaching assignment.

Most colleges do not require teaching demonstrations by part-time candidates. Three of the colleges, **College of the Canyons, Cuesta College**, and **Vista Community College** reported that potential part-time candidates are often asked to present a brief performance of technical expertise (specific to technical areas) or a teaching demonstration. However, only at College of the Canyons was the demonstration mandatory.

CONCLUSIONS

Procedures for recruitment and hiring of part-timers are less formal, less rigorous, and less advertised than those for full-time faculty.... In addition to providing no measure of quality assurance, loose recruitment and selection procedures may limit the cultural diversity of the instructional staff (Boggs, 1984, p. 15).

Unfortunately, the common strategies for recruiting, selecting, and hiring part-time faculty that were identified and assessed more than a decade ago have undergone few changes. While there are some notable exceptions, most college procedures and policies for hiring part-timers can be characterized as less rigorous and less thoughtful than those for hiring full-timers. Some colleges argued that spending similar amounts of time and energy to hire part-timers as was spent for full-timers was counterproductive, especially when the part-timer would likely spend very little time at the college, or when there were few applicants from which to select, and so on. They argued that they rarely had adequate time to make their decisions and that if they had the time and a qualified pool of professionals who had been previously selected, their procedures would be different. Others who invested more time and effort in hiring their part-time faculty argued that they must make every effort to find the most qualified professionals, whether they are to teach part-time or full-time.

Most hiring was decentralized to departments, and department chairs were the major keys to hiring; some were assisted in selection and hiring procedures by committees of one or more full-time faculty, but such hiring committees were usually considerably smaller than those that would have conferred to select a full-time member of the faculty. Formal training for these tasks was rare, and most reported that training occurred informally on the job.

We discovered that colleges' recruiting strategies were uneven with regard to expanding faculty diversity. Some colleges—primarily those in urban settings—identified some current strategies for increasing diversity, and others noted that statewide mandates regarding affirmative action guidelines had established standard practices. But most colleges did not offer their position on written guidelines, and some regarded strict attention to diversification as an added burden on an already laborious, time-consuming, and admittedly singular task. Yet, colleges have enormous opportunities for expanding the diversity of their faculty during recruiting. Even in those areas in which colleges have no difficulty in finding part-timers to hire, where applications are plentiful, recruitment cannot be overlooked as a powerful tool by which faculty diversity can be expanded.

Part-time faculty, by numbers and contact hours alone, have an enormous impact on the conduct of community college classes and programs. Most of the colleges we studied reported part-time to full-time ratios of 2–1 and 3–1. Some colleges reported even higher ratios. With three exceptions, these colleges did not require any on-site demonstration of teaching ability, and only one college required a writing sample. Some colleges observed that hiring individuals by reputation—for example, outstanding high school teachers and professionals in technical areas recommended by members of college advisory boards—provided at least some evidence of teaching performance. Colleges with an abundance of unsolicited applications rarely mentioned the need to look further than their current pool for qualified candidates. Colleges' major concerns focused on paper evidence that potential part-timers met at least minimum transcript and experience qualifications.

If good teaching is the hallmark of American community colleges, then colleges should bring serious attention to the critical steps of identifying those who can best deliver it. It is not possible for colleges to spend too much time or effort in choosing the people who have the colleges' reputations in their hands. Moreover, having made their decisions, colleges must put time and thoughtful efforts into orienting part-timers to their environment and into providing them with training for their professional growth and development.

CHAPTER 4

Seeing so much that is familiar, almost anybody can think she understands community colleges, although almost nobody does.
—McGrath and Spear, 1991, p. 9

ORIENTATION

Welcome to the Community

In his book *College: The Undergraduate Experience in America,* Boyer describes student orientation to traditional four-year institutions of higher education as an act of "affirming the traditions." He observes:

> The first few weeks on campus are critically important. This is the time when friendships are formed and attitudes about collegiate life take shape. And yet, we found during our study that new students have little sense of being inducted into a community whose structure, privileges, and responsibilities have been evolving for almost a millennium (1987, p. 43).

He continues that colleges and universities should give special priority to the difficult task of orienting part-time students, that if they are not integrated into campus life, undergraduate education in America increasingly will become simply a process in which part-time students "drift on and off the campus"; credits and credentials will be earned and appropriately recorded but "the most essential values of…education will be lost" (p. 49). Boyer's warnings about the importance of early introductions of part-time students to the traditions of educational communities apply as intensely to the part-time faculty who are also citizens of that community.

Orientation programs that provide information and resources as well as a view of potential support systems have helped retain new students and have helped them to succeed. Nadler (1992) and other researchers have observed that the same should happen for faculty orientation and mentoring programs (Boice, 1992; Kogler Hill, Bahniuk, and Dobos, 1989). While orientation requires tremendous expenditures of time and effort, "it can pay off in terms of future dividends in the form of increased productivity, greater employee satisfaction on the job, and great institutional identification and loyalty" (Biles and Tuckman, 1986, p. 132). Programs that promote mentoring of new faculty members and smooth their way into the institution are critical for faculty retention, productivity, success, and quality in their professional lives (Hall and Sandler, 1983; Jarvis, 1991; Schuster, Wheeler, and associates, 1990).

PART-TIMERS AS CANDIDATES FOR ORIENTATION

Studies of part-timers indicate that they have an array of responsibilities other than teaching part-time, which increases their need for orientation to the college. Part-timers often:

- have full-time jobs

- have less teaching experience than full-time faculty

- give primary allegiance to their full-time job

- prepare less for class than full-time faculty

- feel a sense of separation from full-time faculty

- are not acquainted with the basic teaching- and discipline-oriented philosophies of their employing institution

- are also teachers at other institutions (Biles and Tuckman, 1986, p. 128)

While Biles and Tuckman, among other researchers, observe that "academic institutions might benefit from clear-cut orientation programs specifically tailored to the needs of part-time faculty," they note that academic administrators are not always inclined to orient and develop part-timers to their institutions and programs (1986, p. 128).

WHAT WE KNOW ABOUT ORIENTATION PROGRAMS AND PROCESSES

In general, orientation programs "create a unity, an *esprit de corps,* a sense of community" (Twale, 1989, p. 161). Orientation provides some transition from one culture to another; orientation programs for new faculty, as well as for new students, are designed to help them begin a socialization process that acquaints them with their new campus. The initial socialization effort is more than a welcoming event; it is part of a well-developed plan for acquainting faculty with the culture of the institution, the norms of the institution, the expectations of the college, and the roles of the new members of the community.

The roles that community colleges expect their full- and part-time faculty to play offer increasingly complex challenges, and those challenges are particularly overwhelming to new faculty. Faculty members' introductions to college are complicated by the increasing diversity of the student clientele and the fact that most faculty who eventually teach in community colleges "did not embark on their careers with specific academic preparation to do so" (Hawthorne, 1991, p. 365). Yet, "to many faculty members' dismay, however, few community colleges offer formal new faculty orientation programs that address needs such as coping with role ambiguity and change" (Miller and Nadler, 1994, p. 441).

Gappa and Leslie (1993) discovered broad differences in orientation processes for part-time faculty. The processes often included familiarizing them with the college's mission, department curricula, and handbooks that described college services and where they could be found. They discovered that orientations ranged from "a sink-or-swim philosophy of benign neglect to elaborate programs that link orientation to instructional development and evaluation" (p. 181). Some colleges developed handbooks for new faculty (although these were not always up-to-date), and some included a social event at which college administrators would address the new faculty. However, especially at colleges where few new part-timers were hired each year, the responsibility for orientation was typically left up to the department chair. Gappa and Leslie discovered that some department chairs did a remarkably good job at orientation. They described one department chair's strategy for working with the twenty-nine part-timers teaching 40 percent of the department's sections:

> In math we are committed to working with adjuncts. All our faculty are involved in classroom observation. Our adjuncts are also involved in course and curriculum development. We have our first fall faculty meeting in the evening so the adjuncts can attend. We have a buddy system that pairs up full-time faculty with part-time faculty. We have meetings of course instructors to monitor student progress. We made space for adjuncts in the math lab. We have a full-time instructor serve as a course coordinator to keep everyone on the same schedule, more or less. When I hire an adjunct, I make sure [he or she gets] oriented to the syllabus, the schedule for the semester, the tests we use, and so on.... We coordinate the pace and sequence of instruction among sections. We involve adjuncts in curriculum change, invite them to workshops and faculty meetings. I am here from 5 to 7 p.m. with the coffee pot on. I encourage the adjuncts to come in and talk (p. 182).

Yet new part-timers not only want an orientation to the college; they have objectives in mind for that orientation. In a recent study to identify community college faculty's perceptions of the critical objectives for new faculty orientation programs, a random sample of 200 faculty out of a population of 665 employed by fourteen Nebraska community colleges responded to a questionnaire about twenty priorities for faculty orientation derived from the Council for the Advancement of Standards criteria for student orientation programs. Responses indicated that nearly twice as many faculty had participated in a new faculty orientation program as had not. Sixty-two percent of the respondents reported that their institutions offered a formal orientation program for new faculty. In prioritizing objectives for orientation programs, there was especially strong support for understanding the mission of the institution; transition to the institution; what the institution expects of new faculty; the technical aspects of scheduling and registration; and policies, procedures, and programs (Miller and Nadler, 1994). Faculty expected orientation programs to be transition-focused. "Faculty wanted to know 'What role do I have at this institution?' followed by 'How do I fulfill this role?' and, in time, 'What role do I have in this department?' " (p. 447).

Respondents to this survey indicated that they had ambitious goals for orientation. The full-time faculty responding to this questionnaire ranked in importance the following orientation program objectives:

- assist new faculty in understanding the mission of the specific institution

- aid new faculty in their transition to the institution

- help new faculty understand the institution's expectations of them

- explain the procedures for class scheduling and registration and provide trained supportive assistance to accomplish these tasks

- provide information concerning academic policies, procedures, requirements, and programs

- create an atmosphere that minimizes anxiety, promotes positive attitudes, and stimulates an excitement for teaching and research

- integrate new faculty into the life of the institution

- provide an atmosphere and sufficient information to enable new faculty to make reasonable and well-informed choices

- assist new faculty in developing positive relationships with other faculty, staff, peers, and other individuals in the community

- expose new faculty to the broad educational opportunities of the institution

- assist new faculty in determining their purpose in working at the institution

- provide opportunities for new faculty to discuss expectations and perceptions of the campus with continuing faculty

- help new faculty understand the department's expectations of them

- provide information and exposure to available institutional services

- provide information about the opportunities for self-assessment

- assist new faculty in understanding the purpose of higher education

- provide appropriate information on personal safety and security

- develop familiarity with the physical surroundings

- improve the retention rate of new faculty

- promote an awareness of nondepartmental opportunities (Miller and Nadler, 1994, p. 446).

Gappa and Leslie discovered several components that are common to the better-developed orientation programs:

- A social event of some kind is held.

- A general introduction to the institution is conducted, usually in the form of handbooks and other written information.

- An overview of effective teaching is provided.

- Linkages to department faculty are established, which sometimes means the assignment of a full-time faculty mentor (1993, p. 183).

And they observed:

> In our view, orientation programs are most successful when they are linked to more comprehensive professional development opportunities for part-time faculty. The initial "induction" sessions are valuable only when the expectations they establish are followed and reinforced by more substantial development activities in the ensuing weeks and months (p. 272).

A study of professional development practices, conducted for the League for Innovation in the Community College and reporting on the orientation of part-time instructors employed at some of its member colleges, discovered that while the responding colleges generally appeared to be orienting part-time instructors to the conditions of their employment, they should consider improving their pre-service orientation (Williams, 1985). The following recommendations were among those suggested by the results of direct survey responses and additional written responses. The colleges were advised:

- ...to devote more pre-service orientation time to explanations of policies and procedures, especially those relating to the grading system, academic standards, student attendance, class cancellations, and record keeping. In the words of one respondent, they need to know more about the "nitty-gritty."

- ...to provide . . . a concise orientation to the...college as well as a student profile. Both could be accomplished in handouts or a short film.

- ...to continue distributing the handbook...during pre-service orientation.

- ...to provide their adjunct faculty a thorough, well-organized pre-service orientation. Such a meeting should allow part-time instructors ample time to meet with supervisors and peers from their own departments. One of the most repeated written comments from respondents about pre-service orientation was the value they found in having an opportunity to talk to peers about the classes they were going to teach (pp. 106–107).

Biles and Tuckman (1986) provide a useful list of recommended items, adapted from a list provided by the Eastern Regional Center of the National Technical Assistance Consortium for Two-Year Colleges, that might be included in an orientation program and manual:

I. Introduction

- State the philosophy and objectives of the institution and how they relate to the part-timer's role.
- State the role of the institution in the community.

II. Administrative Information

- Clarify who will serve as administrative contact with the institution.
- Specify who in the institution is responsible for what functions. [Provide a list of administrative units and their key people.]
- State when and where academic materials such as syllabi, course outlines, reproduction work, etc., must be submitted.
- State the conditions of employment.
- State the pay periods and deductions.
- Clarify what the part-time faculty member is supposed to do when he or she cannot make a class.
- Specify the kinds of administrative support (e.g., secretarial assistance, office space, parking, and materials duplication) the part-time faculty member can expect to receive.
- Clarify who evaluates the part-time faculty member, along with how this should be done.
- Specify roll-keeping requirements.
- Specify institutional policies regarding classroom breaks.
- Specify where the part-time faculty member should obtain supplies such as chalk, slides, test booklets, etc.
- Clarify who the part-time faculty member should see to get answers to questions.

- Clarify the part-timer's teaching responsibilities.
- Provide the part-time faculty member with a general job description.
- Specify how a part-time faculty member can get classroom and building doors unlocked.
- Provide a school calendar (include social activities and pay days).
- Clarify how the part-time faculty members should handle drops and adds.
- Specify when classes start and end.
- Specify what the institution's student attendance policy is.
- Specify procedures for turning in grades.
- Provide a list of full-time faculty.
- Provide a list of institutional parking regulations.
- Provide a list of standing faculty committees.
- Provide information on policies and procedures regarding audiovisual equipment.
- Ensure that part-time faculty know the procedures for admitting late-registering students into classes.
- Ensure that part-time faculty know the policies for canceling classes because of bad weather.

III. Academic Information

- Provide information about who, if anyone, will assist the part-time faculty member with teaching techniques.
- Include information about teaching evaluation procedures.
- Provide hints about how to arrange for guest lectures and field trips.
- Clarify questions about part-time faculty office hours and space to conduct student conferences.
- Provide information about how to provide students with tutorial assistance.
- Provide tips on specific tasks that need to be completed during the first class (a checklist would be helpful).
- Clarify procedures for the part-time faculty member to contact a student at home or work.
- Clarify procedures as to how to obtain information about the background of students.
- Ensure the part-time faculty member knows institutional policies about grading and the system for turning in grades.

- Specify procedures to be followed if the part-time faculty member catches a student cheating.

- Give the part-time faculty member detailed information on library resources and ways to reserve books in the library for the short and long term.

IV. Emergency Procedures

- Provide information on how to reach campus security and campus medical facilities. Ensure that the part-time faculty member knows the procedures for obtaining emergency assistance.

- Provide a list of emergency telephone numbers (1986, pp. 130–132).

We asked our colleges these questions about orientation:

- Do you have an orientation program for new part-timers? (Describe the process.)

- Has your college developed a faculty/part-time faculty handbook? (Provide us with a copy.)

- Does your orientation program include a mentoring component?

- Is the orientation of part-time faculty a college/district level, or department level (or both) process?

In their responses, we discovered a variety of orientation processes and programs. Some orientation activities took place within the first days or even hours that the new part-time faculty were in contact with the college; essentially, they were intended to be little more than a "first look" at the college. Others were designed, initially, as short-term activities, but later developed in scope and required more faculty involvement over the teaching term.

Thus, we found that many orientation and staff development activities intersected philosophically, and drawing clear distinctions between orientation objectives and staff development objectives was often difficult. However, we had to somehow distinguish between the two for the purposes of this discussion. Therefore, in this chapter, we include primarily those orientation activities that were the first encounters between new part-time faculty and the college; in the descriptions of a few, we note that they have become full-blown, ongoing, established staff development activities that will be more fully described in the following chapter.

WHAT COLLEGES SAY ABOUT ORIENTATION
OF PART-TIME FACULTY

The part-time faculty coordinator at **Community College of Allegheny County** personally conducts a one-on-one orientation for each new part-time faculty member. This is a short-term mentoring association; however, it is considered adequate for establishing an appropriate relationship. Each new part-timer receives a handbook, along with other information such as community college student profiles.

Respondents observed that socialization and integration problems exist for those part-time faculty members who teach at off-campus sites. They do not come into contact with the core full-time and part-time faculty group on a regular basis and are somewhat isolated.

The centralized orientation at **Central Piedmont Community College** is a four- to five-hour session that is required of all new part-time faculty. Faculty are paid $30 for participating in the orientation. Sessions are held at the beginning of each term. Each person is given a handbook that reviews the basic policies and procedures of the college. A full-time faculty member assists with the session focusing on these policies and procedures. In addition, the orientation includes a session on identifying and supporting high-risk students. Profiles and characteristics of high-risk students are covered, and strategies to help them succeed are discussed. A photographic slide presentation provides a tour of the campuses; a physical tour is not feasible, especially at night with large numbers of faculty being oriented to the college at one time. The slide presentation has the advantage of being easily updated as facilities and key personnel change.

The entire orientation session is packaged as a self-paced learning module, available to those part-time faculty who are unable to attend the regular session. In these situations, an individual can view the slides and videotapes in the library media center and prepare a written report on the information he or she gathered. The report is reviewed by the staff development coordinator. On a more decentralized level, departments conduct additional orientations to focus on specific department issues.

College of the Canyons has a major orientation session at the beginning of the fall term and another mini-session in January. The fall session meets in two parts. In the fall orientation, everyone meets with the president, vice president, instructional assistant deans, program directors, and academic senate president; the first two-hour discussion features general college issues. In the second part of the orientation session, college officials discuss the college's expectations of adjunct instructors. The orientation session is not mandatory for adjuncts, but attendance has remained at about 50 percent of the total part-time faculty in the fall term. Many departments hold their own orientation sessions that focus on their specific disciplines.

While there is no formal mentoring procedure implemented currently, respondents noted that such relationships do occur informally between some full- and part-time faculty members.

A mandatory six-hour, new-faculty orientation session (for full- and part-time faculty) at **Community College of Aurora** occurs before anyone begins a teaching assignment. The college also puts on a second mandatory, three-hour session called "mid-semester problem solving." Faculty have an opportunity to talk about what has happened so far during the term. Also, the college has established a mentoring program in which experienced full- or part-time faculty are assigned to new faculty members to help them through their first semester.

New part-time faculty at **Cowley County Community College** must complete a six-hour orientation before they are allowed to begin their teaching assignments. During the orientation, college officials talk about the community college philosophy; share the college's long-range plans; and discuss teaching techniques, grading, and college expectations for part-time faculty in the classroom. This orientation is offered at the beginning of every semester and over two evenings for those who work full-time and cannot attend a longer session. The orientation is facilitated by the associate dean for continuing education.

> A lot of these folks come in and think they are going to lecture the old-fashioned way. They really aren't understanding the high-risk student, so we really focus on the high-risk student, and what they can expect to see in terms of behaviors that may be typical of those who need a lot of help (Dean of Instruction).

For the first semester, all new part-timers and full-timers are assigned a mentor by the associate dean for continuing education. The mentor is paid for providing this service. The college requires that the mentor have a pre-set number of contacts with their mentee; after the prescribed number of visits, the relationship becomes one of "if you need me, I'm here." The purposes of the mentoring program include coordination of course content, support to part-time faculty, and provision of a communication vehicle with the main campus program.

The college has established a Teacher Learning Consultant (TLC) program for adjunct and part-time instructors to support and strengthen the instructional program of the college by providing each part-time or adjunct instructor with a full-time instructor who can provide personal training, consulting, and counseling as needed. Part-timers are encouraged to use the TLC program whenever they need help or information. Full-time faculty may also use the consultants if they wish. Two faculty members are available to receive phone calls from any faculty member about difficult situations or college issues. The consultants' names, phone numbers, and brief resumés are included in the TLC information brochure. Calls to the consultants can be anonymous. "It's just someone who is there to visit about any problem that might be out there" (Dean of Instruction). The consultants are paid to serve and report that they receive an average of 15 to 20 phone calls a semester; however, as the dean reported, "that is 15 to 20 problems that didn't get big as a result." The TLC Program is described more fully in Chapter 5.

Cuesta College's mandatory, part-time orientation program includes an orientation workshop session (held one week before classes begin) and a mentoring program. During the initial orientation session, college officials discuss student characteristics as well as some key elements of successful teaching and learning, and conduct group exercises to get everyone involved. And, they provide an overview of key functions and reference materials that will help part-timers refer students to key systems in the college. A faculty orientation checklist for the first week includes such questions as: Is your class syllabus ready? Do you have keys for your classroom/lab? Where are the nearest restrooms to your classroom? Do you know the library hours? Do you have your class rollsheets? Has your evaluation been scheduled and are you clear on what to expect in the evaluation process? Orientation is conducted during the week prior to the beginning of classes.

Each of the department chairs assigns a mentor to the new faculty member. The responsibility of the mentor varies depending on the needs of the part-timer. Those part-time faculty who have never taught need more direction than those with experience who need little more than to learn the inner workings of the college. The mentor is there as a resource, as a backup, as somebody with whom to brainstorm. Mentoring must continue for at least one semester and sometimes continues for a year. To date, the college has relied solely on volunteers to serve as mentors.

Cuyahoga Community College has established a two-phase orientation process. The first phase, conducted by the office of the evening/weekend program, is an overall orientation to the college: a ten-minute orientation videotape; a part-time handbook including policies, procedures, support services, administrative staff, how to develop a syllabus, and what to do on the first day of class; a newsletter; and a discussion of grading, handling disciplinary problems, and who to contact for various concerns. Each department conducts an additional orientation, specifically regarding departmental issues.

A general orientation evening is conducted at **De Anza College**, and each department holds an orientation/welcoming session. The college orientation provides a general overview of the college—"who's who and what's what." A resource notebook containing easy-to-follow instructions about general issues and processes is provided to each participant. Respondents observed that the departments with more part-time faculty tended to be more aware of their concerns and that they did a better job of "welcoming them into the family."

A collegewide orientation is conducted at **Greenville Technical College** on the Saturday before classes begin each term. Saturday appears to be the most convenient time for most part-time faculty to attend. General sessions are conducted throughout the morning; there is lunch with a member of the division, and then there are division-level orientation sessions.

The college-level session includes an overview of the college, a review of the organizational chart, an armchair tour of support services, a discussion of classroom procedures for the first day, and other college policies and procedures. A part-time faculty handbook is distributed at the orientation and used as the orientation guide.

As part of the orientation, mentors may be assigned to new part-time faculty, if needed, to assist them through their first terms. Currently, the college is previewing a new adjunct faculty orientation program produced by **St. Petersburg Junior College** (described in this chapter) for possible inclusion in future part-time faculty orientation sessions.

Hagerstown Junior College has a two-phase orientation: a formal, general orientation meeting each semester, and separate orientation sessions with the division chairs. Approximately 70 percent of the part-timers attend the general meeting, a quasi-social event. A speaker is invited to make an address after dinner, and then the part-timers break into their divisions. Full-time faculty are invited to meet with the division breakout groups and the division chair to talk about divisional standards, behavior, and teaching expectations.

At **Kirkwood Community College**, all new and returning part-time faculty are encouraged to attend a half-day and evening activity that occurs before classes start. They come to campus and meet with others in their divisions and departments, and review department and college policies. Departments invite several full-time faculty to attend and talk about courses, syllabi, and expectations. Dinner is served in the late afternoon at the conference center, and an evening program begins shortly thereafter. Last year's orientation was conducted by a panel of full-time faculty, administrators, and one student, who reviewed general college issues and expectations; the year before there was a formal presentation. While attendance at the orientation is highly encouraged and well attended, it is not a mandatory activity.

Lakeland Community College holds a pre-service orientation workshop every quarter for new part-time faculty. The workshop reviews the policies and procedures that affect the part-time instructor, as well as areas of common concern to all faculty. In addition, veteran part-time faculty members present a brief overview of the experience of teaching at Lakeland. The dean of social science and public service technologies and the dean of counseling are the only administrators involved in planning the orientation session; part-timers work with them to plan the meeting.

The orientation is approximately three hours long; a dinner is included to create some informal interaction—"I think food facilitates an awful lot of comfortable interchange; they like to talk when they eat. I'm a firm believer that if you feed them they will come. And they do, and when we feed them they feel more comfortable" (Dean, Social Science and Public Service Technologies).

At nearly every session the president of the college and the vice president of academic affairs greet the new part-timers. They share their perceptions of the importance of part-time faculty to the college. Part-time faculty who have taught at other colleges comment that the president's and vice president's decisions to attend the session are especially impressive.

The program for the orientation session follows a theater format: "Teaching at Lakeland: A Class Act." At each level of the discussion, the program lists the page numbers in the faculty handbook on which the specific topic is addressed. The discussion about various topics is directed by the program, listed below:

Coming Attractions: Welcome to Lakeland
I.　The Printed Word (Sources of Information)
　　A.　The Lakeland Catalog
　　B.　The Lakeland Schedule
　　C.　The Part-Time Faculty Handbook
　　D.　The Student Handbook

Your Questions?
II.　Financial Backing (Pay and Benefits Information)
　　A.　Human Resources Requirements for Paycheck

B. Pay Schedule for the Quarter
C. Payment Options
D. Benefits

Your Questions?
III. Before the Show Opens (Preparing for Your Class)
A. Master Course Outlines
B. Importance of a Syllabus
C. Contents of a Good Syllabus
D. Duplicating Materials
E. Where to Obtain Supplies
F. Bookstore
G. Computer Availability

Your Questions?
IV. Opening Night (Meeting and Greeting Your Class)
A. Introducing the Syllabus
B. Class Lists
C. "Overrides"
D. The Drop-Add System
E. Withdrawal Policy
F. Warming Up the Audience

Your Questions?
V. Intermission and Dinner
VI. The Performance "Crew"
A. Library
B. Instructional Media Center
C. Counseling Services
D. Tutorial Services
E. Divisional Offices/Secretaries
F. Part-Time Faculty Office
G. Part-Time Faculty Activities
   1. Part-Time Faculty Advisory Committee
   2. Part-Time Faculty Professional Development Committee
   3. Professional Development Events
   4. Part-Time Faculty Recognition Dinner
   5. Adjunct Advocate

Your Questions?
VII. During the Run (Day-to-Day Concerns in Teaching)
A. Scantron Scoring Procedure
B. Food Service
C. Security
D. Class Cancellations

E.   Professional Relations with Students
F.   Teaching as a Performing Art

Your Questions?
VIII. The Reviews (Learning How Well You're Doing)
    A.   Classroom Assessment
    B.   Faculty Evaluations
       1. Divisional Evaluation Policies
       2. Student Evaluation Forms

Your Questions?
IX.   Final Performance (Turning in Grades)
    A.   Deadlines
    B.   Meaning of Grades
    C.   Informing Students

Your Questions?
X.   Campus Tour (Optional)

Collegewide orientation for new part-time faculty is held at the beginning of each quarter, in a four- to five-hour session at **Metropolitan Community College**. The orientation session was an optional activity until fall 1994; it is now a mandatory event. Topics covered during the orientation include the syllabus, meeting course objectives, using the selected textbook, managing the first class session, the differences between adult community college students and traditional college or high school students, incorporating media into classes, and using the services of the college.

A mentoring process has been implemented over the years; however, difficulties matching part-time faculty with full-time faculty at the beginning of every quarter created a need for an improved orientation system. Now, the mentoring process focuses on content-oriented issues that are specific to each department and course.

All new part-time faculty have mentors at **Modesto Junior College**. Typically, the mentor is a full-time faculty member from the part-timer's own discipline, but at times part-time faculty have been asked to serve. The college hosts all of the part-timers for dinner, and one or two administrators attend. Following dinner, there is an orientation to the college—described as the "nuts and bolts" portion of the evening. The following day, the majority of the divisions use their "flex time" (all part-timers are required to use this time for staff development) for a three-hour workshop, usually focusing on teaching techniques and classroom management issues.

Nassau Community College decentralizes orientation at the department level. Union requirements for hiring based on seniority have reduced the number of part-time faculty hired by many departments. Those that do hire part-timers conduct their own orientations.

A mandatory, three-hour orientation session is held for all new adjunct faculty employed by **Ocean County College**. The dean of instruction conducts the orientation sessions—"I consider hiring adjuncts important enough that [I] should conduct the orientation meetings." An hour and a half is spent on teaching techniques; additional topics include student self-concept, how to work with the high-risk student, the importance of the first day of class, and the philosophy of testing. He ends the orientation session with this summation:

> Nothing I've said, I hope, has given you the impression that the college expects you to mollycoddle your students or to lower your standards. Quite the contrary, we want you to expect high standards from your students, and then work your hardest to help them measure up. Students tend to be a lot like people. People tend to measure up to expectations. *No teacher ever got top performance from students by expecting less.*

Orientation for part-time faculty is mandatory at **Richland College**. Two years ago, Richland decided to begin changing the orientation process to accommodate both new and returning faculty instead of focusing exclusively on new faculty issues. The process now includes more faculty development focus on teaching and learning issues and is intended to reflect the culture of the college.

For years, the college provided orientation for new part-time faculty and, in many disciplines, there were meetings for part-time faculty to discuss curricular and procedural issues. But there never seemed to be a good way to address general teaching and learning issues and to build community among the 150 full-time and 450 part-time faculty. Recognizing this void, the Academic Council decided to initiate a Thursday evening faculty development session just prior to the start of the semester for full-time and part-time faculty beginning spring 1993. The program was so successful that it has been continued every semester since. Although the issues and format vary each semester, the session usually begins by introducing issues related to teaching and learning. This general session is followed by smaller group sessions that focus on issues raised in the general session. As an example, in the spring 1993 session, all participants read an article by Tom Angelo titled "A Teacher's Dozen: 14 General, Research-Based Principles for Improving Higher Learning in Our Classrooms," and facilitators then led groups in selecting one or two principles around which to discuss practices and share experiences. At these meetings, each faculty member was asked to choose a technique to use during the semester and report back to the group in a meeting later in the semester.

Santa Barbara City College encourages new part-time faculty to participate in a voluntary orientation program for which they are paid. The session addresses the basic college policies and procedures. Various full-time faculty are invited to talk about what new faculty can expect in the classroom and strategies to address the diverse learning styles of the students they are likely to have.

A mentor program has been established for part-time instructors who are working on master's degrees and wish to teach at the college. Participants in this program are required to work with a mentor during their teaching assignment. Other mentoring systems have been established in most departments.

Santa Fe Community College has tried a variety of approaches to orientation scheduling and implementation. At one time orientation was a collegewide event, with the president and vice presidents representing their various areas of concern. However, because of scheduling difficulties, this approach was not as effective or manageable as the planners had hoped. Finding a day that was convenient for all part-timers was impossible, considering that each department has a different schedule for interviewing and selecting them. The responsibility for providing orientation was given to officials at the department level.

For example, the English department has three orientation sessions: the first is the general overview needed by new hires prior to the start of a semester, and the two following sessions cover issues that arise during the semester. The department discovered that attempting to cover all of the issues and concerns in one session was overwhelming and not nearly as effective as having multiple sessions throughout the term. Part-time faculty are paid approximately $60 for participating in the initial six-hour session.

The first orientation session is held on a Saturday prior to the beginning of the semester. There are three general components to the orientation: 1) an overview of the college (including college policies, procedures, student support, faculty support, parking, and employment obligations); 2) departmental procedures; and 3) breakout sessions focused on specific courses, in which full-time faculty facilitate discussions on philosophy and approaches used in teaching various courses.

The second orientation session occurs approximately the third week of the term, to correspond with the collection of the first student papers. The session is approximately three hours long and is focused on grading standards. Actual graded papers are used as models, and the review is facilitated by full-time faculty and the department chair. This session is more effective at this point in the term rather than at the initial orientation session—since the focus is on that one, timely issue.

The third orientation session is held even later in the term and is focused on holistic grading. The department has a pass/fail final similar to the standard state test, and the orientation session addresses scoring procedures for this department test.

New hires who do not attend the orientation sessions do not get paid for those sessions. In those cases, the department chair will work with them individually to make up for the missed orientations. New part-time faculty hired in the spring or summer when there are no organized orientation sessions are assisted by the part-time faculty coordinator and the department chair who work with them individually to provide appropriate orientation.

Schoolcraft College uses a professional development video series on college teaching developed by a group of full- and part-time faculty members at the college. These faculty designed the video based on a consensus of the problems that new faculty are likely to experience, and they produced and acted out the numerous situations that featured problem solutions. New faculty are expected to view these videos in the context of a workshop session. The topics include such issues as student diversity, assessment beyond testing, managing the first class session, grading and scoring, and other topics.

In 1994, **St. Petersburg Junior College** published a series of videotapes and printed materials designed to orient, train, and support part-time faculty, titled Excellence in Adjunct Instruction. The college set out to develop a training tool that would address the specific concerns and challenges that part-time faculty face. Moreover, the college intended to design a system that could be integrated into a college's part-time faculty training program to be used in either a workshop setting or in individual and less-structured formats.

Two booklets and three videotapes complete the orientation packet. One of the booklets is used by the part-time faculty, one by the institution. The booklet prepared for the part-time faculty member begins with this letter:

To the Adjunct Instructor:

Welcome to Excellence in Adjunct Instruction.

You are part of one of the most powerful forces in community college education today: the rapidly growing ranks of part-time, or adjunct, instructors. Like your 200,000-plus colleagues throughout this country, you bring to the classroom a unique perspective that can enrich your students' educational experience in many ways.

The goal of the video series and this study guide is to help you succeed—both personally and professionally—in your career as an instructor. We've approached this goal in two ways: first, by providing basic information you need to help prepare effectively for the challenges of the classroom; and second, by offering some 'directional signposts' designed to stimulate your individual growth and development as an instructor.

This project grew out of one college's search for the best possible ways to prepare its adjuncts for successful teaching and learning in their classrooms. Because of that, you'll find this series takes a real-world approach to the questions, challenges and rewards of adjunct instruction.

We hope that you will take advantage of the self-assessment questions in this guide as well as the information provided in the videos to help you maximize the unique combination of skills, knowledge and experience you bring to your students. As a participant in the teaching/learning process, you have an exciting journey ahead of you. We wish you great success.

Excellence in Adjunct Instruction
Project Team

Part I of the booklet, "Adjunct Instructors—A Vital Educational Resource," provides an outline of the first videotape and a learning guide to be used in conjunction with viewing the tape. These materials focus on the mission, philosophy, and students of the community college, and on what makes an excellent teacher. Questions included in the learning guide, to be answered by the faculty member after viewing the tape, require the new instructor to apply what he has learned from the video to St. Petersburg Junior College. In addition, there is an opportunity to rank personal teaching practices according to the quality indicators discussed in the video, and to set goals for improving teaching and strategies for achieving them during the current term. Part II, "Preparing for Successful Teaching and Learning," also has an overview section and outline for the video; it emphasizes classroom and course management, plus teaching tips. It includes the following sections for faculty response after the viewing of the tape: specific information about the college, college officials, and policies; what the college, the students, and part-time faculty expect; planning for a course, calendar, and syllabus. Part III, "Responding to Diversity," follows the same format; the video outline is provided, and once the tape has been viewed, the learning guide directs the faculty member through a series of questions about cultural, ethnic, disability, and professional ethics issues.

The second booklet has been prepared for the institution and begins with this letter:

To the Administrator:

The Excellence in Adjunct Instruction program grew out of one college's desire to better orient, train and support part-time faculty. Recognizing the important role these instructors play in community college education—both at our institution and nationally—we set out to develop a training tool that would address the specific concerns and challenges adjuncts face.

At the same time, we sought to create a system that could be easily integrated into a college's adjunct training programs, either as a starting point or an enhancement of existing activities. As a result, these materials have been designed to offer you maximum flexibility. They can be most effectively used in a workshop format, but can also be used in less structured settings as your needs dictate.

In addition to offering guidelines for the use of the Excellence in Adjunct Instruction materials, this Institutional Guide also includes suggestions for creating and/or improving institutional practices related to recruiting, screening, hiring, orienting, supporting, and evaluating part-time faculty.

Given the forces we can expect to affect community college education in the coming decades, part-time instruction is unquestionably here to stay. The quality of instruction our colleges provide in the future is likely to depend more and more on the classroom performance of our adjunct instructors. That performance, in turn, will depend largely on the way our institutions manage the vast resource part-time instructors comprise.

It is an exciting challenge, and we hope this program will help you meet it with great success.

Excellence in Adjunct Instruction
Project Team

The Institutional Guide contains four major sections: Elements of Good Practice in Adjunct Recruitment, Employment, Orientation, and Support (an inventory offered as a guide to establishing the core elements of sound institutional practices); Eight Principles for Effective Use of Adjunct Faculty (guidelines offered for consideration as a basis on which to build sound principles and practices); Orienting Adjunct Faculty to the Legal and Ethical Responsibilities of Community College Instructors (questions to promote reflection and discussion at the institution level regarding (a) the quality of information on legal and ethical issues that is available to faculty at a particular institution, and (b) how effectively that information is being communicated to both full- and part-time instructors); and Conducting an Adjunct Faculty Needs Assessment (a survey to be used as a starting point for colleges to develop their own systems for obtaining feedback from adjunct faculty, including general information, legal issues, teaching techniques, and instructional preparation). The guide is distributed among selected administrators, other college officials, and department chairs; they respond to the various queries included in the issues sections; and their responses are returned to the person responsible for compiling the information for future assessment purposes.

This new series is used in orientation sessions for all new part-time faculty at SPJC and is available commercially. The series is managed by the departments and usually is shown in small workshop settings to encourage discussion and interaction.

SPJC has a manual for part-time faculty, complete with general, academic, student, and employment policies, as well as important phone numbers and maps. This manual is provided to each new part-time faculty member in a folder that also includes a variety of information brochures and leaflets—e.g., "Guidelines for Faculty: How to Deal with Academic Dishonesty."

Part-time faculty training and orientation are now more campus-based. The provost at each site coordinates the orientation program for all new part-timers. The dean of academic services at the Clearwater campus reported that the opening large-group session is becoming "more and more of an inspirational session." At the opening session, "we try to impress upon them the value they have to the college; we want them to feel a part of the school."

Program directors attempt to stay in good touch with part-time faculty. The third occasion on which the part-timer meets with a program director, after the pre-interview and the formal interview, is also a group meeting of new part-timers where they are each assigned a full-timer who serves as their mentor. College respondents observed that one of the best decisions the college made for getting orientation of part-time faculty off to a good start was establishing the mentoring program. All new full-time and part-time faculty are assigned a mentor for their first teaching term. The mentoring process is informal, but involves concerns and management activities that the part-timer may want to know more about. Departments on the various campuses choose their mentors differently. For example, at the Clearwater campus, three full-timers in a department volunteer to serve as mentors. No one reported a problem getting volunteers. The intent is for the process to be as informal and collegial as possible. "The name of the game in helping them get along is communication. They need to have access to information they need, and we try to provide them a means of getting it" (Dean of Academic Services, Clearwater campus). At the St. Petersburg/Gibbs campus, the mentors are selected and assigned to new adjunct faculty by the program directors. In larger programs with multiple sections of a particular subject (e.g., the science area), the program director will schedule discipline meetings, and one of the full-time instructors will become the lead instructor for that group. The leader will meet with part-timers and coordinate specific course requirements. For example, in communication, the lead instructor must meet with them to discuss holistic grading and specific outcomes required for the exam.

The reasons listed for continual communication include the inordinate amount of information that part-timers must absorb about the college and its policies, and the "one-on-one award for the adjunct" when program director and mentor remain involved. "When you value your people, you treat them well" (Dean of Academic Services, Clearwater campus). Program directors are encouraged to rotate their evenings on campus so that different part-timers will see them on a regular basis. "There is only one way for program directors to know what's going on with adjuncts, and that's to be there—whenever that is" (Associate Vice President of Educational and Student Services, District Office; former academic dean at St. Petersburg/Gibbs campus).

Orientation is conducted at the campus level and is department- and discipline-specific for part-timers at **Tarrant County Junior College**. The orientation includes meeting significant people in the departments—the department chair, subject-specific full-timers, and secretaries. There is no formal orientation process at the college level. Departments assign an experienced full-timer to act as a mentor for each part-timer, help with classroom management, and orient the part-timer to the campus and its facilities, providing the course syllabus, course information document, necessary textbooks, and other course materials. There is no part-time faculty handbook; part-timers use the general faculty handbook.

At **Triton College**, orientation occurs one evening before classes begin. A policy book, including teaching and grading tips, is distributed. The president and vice president of the college often attend this session and spend approximately three hours discussing information that part-timers should have.

Orientation is not mandatory. Many times the college cannot provide training because the part-timer has been hired literally the night before the class is scheduled to begin. In this case, the part-timer is mentored by a full-time faculty member who is compensated for this assignment, and the two meet several times to discuss course syllabus, materials, teaching methods, and grading procedures. An adjunct faculty evaluator/mentor checklist includes information to direct discussions, queries, and other evaluation procedures during the pre-classroom visit conference, the first classroom visit, the post-classroom visit, the review of the part-time instructor's student evaluations, and the second classroom visit.

Orientation is decentralized and conducted by each department chair at **Valencia Community College**. Each department conducts breakout groups that discuss various department-specific issues. The College Teaching Course is a major orientation and staff development program; a full description of this course is included in the following chapter. All part-time faculty members have a full-time faculty mentor.

Vista Community College has a faculty orientation at the beginning of each fall and spring semester for all full- and part-time faculty, continuing and new. Sometimes one of the full-time faculty members provides a special additional orientation for all new faculty. Full- and part-time faculty receive a faculty handbook, letters of welcome, and a phone and office hour list for all the administrators, with a list of appropriate college officials to call for various problems.

CONCLUSIONS

The current social and demographic changes that are most affecting community colleges—increasing numbers of new and retiring faculty, increasing student diversity, and expanding college missions—create a special incentive for embracing and involving part-time faculty early on as they enter into the life of the institution. The challenges that these three changes bring are magnified when seen through the lenses of the part-timer's viewfinder. Unless these challenges are addressed in some organized and useful fashion, unless the part-timer's role and responsibilities are clearly defined, and unless the expectations the college has for the performance of this growing instructional force are well-defined and well-described, part-time faculty will not become effective partners in the teaching and learning enterprise.

Yet, while community colleges appear to be more committed than other institutions of higher education to providing orientation for part-time faculty members, it is not a common occurrence. There are some exemplary orientation programs in community colleges, but evidence continues to suggest that most part-timers are not integrated into a college with a formal orientation experience at the majority of American community colleges.

CHAPTER 5

*You're all out in the wilderness now, away from your homes and
your roots, wandering around trying to spot where you can settle
down—you are trying to fit in.... The first thing you're going to have
to learn about... life after orientation is that there isn't any. No, you
are not going to die, but a lot of the time you're going to feel no one at
this school would really care if you did.*

—Komarovsky, 1985

FACULTY
DEVELOPMENT
AND INTEGRATION

Doing the Right Things for the Right Reasons

Teaching and learning are at the heart of this study because they are the heart of American community colleges, and faculty are the key to the student experience. It is curious that—in an environment where growth and development and learning are so highly prized—such a widely accepted notion can exist side-by-side with another that says learning could or should be one-sided, that it need occur only on one side of the teacher's desk. It becomes even more curious when we observe that there is so much to learn—not only about *what* to do but about *how* to do it. "The public, and especially the four-year colleges and universities, are shifting more and more responsibility onto the community colleges for undertaking the toughest tasks of higher education" (Newman, 1971). Not only have these tasks become even tougher during the more than twenty years since

these words were spoken, they are being addressed by a faculty increasingly unpre-
pared to deal with them—faculty who have their feet in more traditional instructional camps, who have not been trained or prepared for these challenges, who are
near retirement, and who are more likely than ever in community college history
to be part-time or new employees. Moreover, it will require the combined creative
efforts of all involved in the teaching and learning enterprise to meet the challenges
effectively: as Benjamin Franklin said to John Hancock, on signing the Declaration
of Independence, "We must hang together, else we shall all hang separately."

It is from that perspective that we put faculty development in a sharply abbre-
viated historical context, review some of the common characteristics of outstanding faculty as we know them, and focus on recognized faculty development objectives and the strategies that address the needs of all faculty. The terms *faculty, staff,*
and *professional development* are used interchangeably although some differences in
definition are recorded throughout the literature and in practice. In this study, we
differentiated between *faculty development* and *integration*. However, while some of
their subtle differences led us to address them separately, we acknowledge that
they are so often intertwined that it is impossible to separate them.

What We Know About Faculty Development

Professional development as a concept is not new, but the concept has changed
to reflect changing times. From sabbatical leaves of the early 1800s to expanded
enrollments in graduate programs in the 1970s (Eble and McKeachie, 1985), professional development was essentially a teacher- and scholar-centered activity, an
opportunity to expand one's knowledge in one's own field. Yet, in the 1970s, this
development took a different turn; it became obvious that student populations
were changing so dramatically that faculty had to move beyond merely acquiring
knowledge and keeping current in their field and had to learn more about their
clientele (O'Banion, 1981). There were calls for graduate courses designed to train
faculty for teaching, for on-campus pre- and in-service training programs to provide instruction in teaching strategies, and for establishing some common agreement about the community college role and function (O'Banion, 1981). It became
clearer that professional development efforts had to expand to serve a broad array
of needs.

Faculty development—defined here as systematic processes offered to groups
of teachers in response to organizational needs and designed to promote growth,
understanding, and improvement in the classroom (Gaff, 1983)—historically has
met with serious obstacles. Among these were the views that a teacher's performance is an individual and private matter, a reflection of distinct, unique personal
gifts and talents (Mauksch, 1980), that scrutinizing and evaluating these gifts and
talents too closely should be discouraged (Miller, 1987), that classrooms are the
"mystery boxes in education" (Cross, 1987, p. 5), that credentials signifying one's
possession of requisite knowledge in any discipline also signify one's ability to
teach this knowledge, and that teachers do not require support and training for
improving their teaching (Pickett, 1984). Teaching, in fact, "for all its endless ver-

balizing, is a silent, secret art," a "private practice," maintained as such by "academic traditions and superstitions…that the Ph.D. is a license to teach; that scholarly assiduity ensures good teaching or makes up for bad; that the popular teacher can't be profound and the profound one popular; that teaching can't be taught; and that, however deficient a professor may appear, he will turn out to be, for some student, some time, a superior teacher" (Eble, 1970, p. 3).

However, neither these arguments nor the paucity of evaluation affects professional development as seriously as does the lack of administrative and institutional support (Lindquist, 1979), which is tied directly to the realities of dwindling resources that have reduced faculty compensation and travel budgets (Schuster and Bowen, 1985). Yet, it is predicted that in the 1990s more than half of all currently employed college and university faculty will retire or otherwise leave the profession (Roueche, 1990) and that by 2000, between 30 and 50 percent of all community college faculty will retire (Jenrette, 1990). There can be little argument that while the stakes associated with increased demands and limited resources have always been high, observers of our current situation maintain that the stakes have never been higher (Roueche and Roueche, 1993a, 1993b).

Toward that end, the AACC Commission on the Future of Community Colleges recommended that colleges make a commitment to recruit, retain, and develop top quality faculty; develop a faculty renewal plan in consultation with the faculty; and set aside at least 2 percent of the instructional budget for professional development (1988). Yet, faculty development remains one of the least prominent budget items in the majority of American colleges and universities (Roueche and Roueche, 1993a, p. 114). When part-time faculty development is funded, institutions most frequently assign responsibility to the department chairs or to department members, which makes any faculty development program a victim of uneven interest and involvement (Gappa and Leslie, 1993, p. 202).

INVESTING IN THE COLLEGE'S MOST IMPORTANT RESOURCE

Many colleges had staff development activities in place long before they had developed rationales for offering them or requiring faculty to participate in them. However, since the 1970s, there has been increasing attention to staff development as an institutional response to changes in the colleges' environment. Observers of these changes noted a number of reasons why colleges must provide faculty with opportunities to adapt and change:

- Staff members need updating in their disciplines.

- Staff members need to keep up with new developments in education.

- There is a continuing need to help staff members become attuned and stay attuned to the special philosophy and commitment of the community college.

- All staff members should develop an appreciation and understanding of community college students and the changing nature of the student population.

- There is a special need to provide induction opportunities for those who come new to the institution, especially those who come from business and industry with no background in education.

- Staff development is necessary in creative institutions simply to provide opportunities for renewal for the weary and the worn out.

- A growing number of community colleges support staff development as the key for developing a sense of community in the college.

- Some colleges say that all staff development is for the purpose of personal growth and that personal growth leads to professional growth and therefore to better instruction and to better education (O'Banion, 1981, pp. 6–8).

WHAT WE KNOW ABOUT EFFECTIVE TEACHERS

Not all members of a faculty will flower as teachers in the most beneficent climate. Nor are all effective teachers dependent upon outside support to maintain their effectiveness. But whatever else an institution does to foster good teaching it should provide ordinary and accessible means by which a teacher can develop, and ordinary and effectively operating means by which he can prosper (Eble, 1970, p. 7).

"Healthy staff development cannot occur where it cannot impact the instructional environment in significant ways" (Roueche, 1982, p. 28). There is much evidence to support the notion that staff development programs should center upon their most important objective—to provide information and training that can be transferred directly into classroom practice, an optimal mix of teaching expertise and subject matter expertise (Cross, 1989).

Findings from numerous studies of teachers who have been recognized as making significant differences in the lives of their students indicate that it is what these faculty do even more than what they think, how they behave even more than what they believe, that distinguish them from less effective teachers (Wilson, Gaff, et al., 1975). They cause students to think differently about a subject, a task, or themselves.

Studies of teaching excellence have identified some common characteristics among effective teachers; in fact, research on excellent teachers has provided the literature with a rich display of descriptions of those who engage in exemplary teaching practices. The framework for this admittedly brief discussion is drawn from the Teaching for Success model, developed and described in *Access and Excellence* (Roueche and Baker, 1987, pp. 147–178); the model is built upon thirteen general teaching themes: commitment, goal orientation, integrated perception, positive action, reward orientation, objectivity, active listening, rapport, empathy, individualized perception, teaching strategies, knowledge, and innovation.

Commitment. Excellent teachers take the profession of teaching and its responsibilities seriously, and they are committed to sharing, expecting, and teaching responsible behavior. The centrality of faculty to student satisfaction and persistence is well-established (Pascarella and Terenzini, 1979; Pascarella and Wolfle, 1985; Terenzini and Pascarella, 1980; Toy, 1985). "Student-faculty interaction has a stronger relationship to student satisfaction with the college experience than any other involvement variable, or indeed, any other student or institutional characteristic" (Astin, 1977, p. 223). A survey of 944 two- and four-year colleges and universities concluded that the "caring attitude of faculty and staff" was the most important retention factor at an institution (Beal and Noel, 1980, p. 19). As representatives of the institution, faculty become the "caretakers of a trust" that students place in them (Toy, 1985, p. 387).

Goal orientation. Not only do excellent teachers set high standards and goals for themselves, they design their courses to encourage their students to identify, set, pursue, and achieve their own goals.

Integrated perception. Excellent teachers see the big picture—that is, how their course fits with other courses within their discipline, with other disciplines, and with life outside the college. They not only see it; they articulate it to their students, and they design their courses to incorporate all of these pieces into student experience. Integrated approaches to teaching embrace a full range of visual and spoken images that give students special help with removing the perceptual barriers that classroom walls can create (Roueche and Roueche, 1993a).

Positive action. Excellent teachers encourage their students to take chances and to try tasks that they have never attempted or never successfully completed. At-risk students, in particular, are frequently unwilling to try (Cross, 1976); they identify early with failure and must receive rewards early on for their successes (Roueche and Mink, 1980).

Reward orientation. Excellent teachers are spurred by what has been termed "psychic income"—a bonus that occurs when students learn something new and the excitement is shared between teacher and student (Futrell, 1984).

Objectivity. Excellent teachers can remain objective, even in the face of student behaviors that create confusion or disruption. They maintain a sense of fairness and an open-mindedness that allows them to address demonstrations of student problems without passing judgment on the potential and value of the student.

Active listening. Perhaps the most difficult skill to develop, listening has been listed as especially poorly developed among professionals in medicine and in teaching! Excellent teachers not only listen, but they create a classroom in which students are comfortable about speaking out and joining discussions.

Now to learn to think while being taught presupposes the other difficult art of paying attention. Nothing is more rare: listening seems to be the hardest thing in the world and misunderstanding the easiest, for we tend to hear what we think we are going to hear, and too often we make it so. In a lifetime one is lucky to meet six or seven people who know how to attend; the rest, some of whom believe themselves well-bred and highly educated, have for the most part fidgety ears; their span of attention is as short as the mating of a fly. They seem afraid to lend their mind to another's thought, as if it would come back to them bruised and bent (Barzun, 1959, p. 36).

Rapport. Belief systems influence behavior; medical research has identified a strong correlation between a patient's belief that he will be able to survive a critical illness and his eventual survival. Moreover, research in organizational development suggests that people who believe that good things will happen, who have a sense of humor and use it, and who encourage others to laugh and enjoy their work as well, draw others to them. People are drawn to others who are positive rather than negative, happy rather than sad. A recent study of humor in the workplace discovered that individuals with positive personality traits are most likely to draw their co-workers like bees to honey; the researcher observed that teachers who laugh with their students are more likely to be seen as approachable by their students (Philbrick, 1989). They are less threatening when they share their own weaknesses and their personal experiences in and out of the classroom in a disarming and engaging manner. Teacher personality is important in determining success with students.

Empathy. "Active empathy" is the highly developed ability to recognize, interpret, and act on the clues that others give (Klemp, 1977). Excellent teachers share their own experiences with students to let them know that they understand what problems and concerns they may have and that they are common responses to many problems that often students feel are uniquely theirs.

But there is more to live teaching than a manner: the manner must fit. Teaching is not a process, it is a developing emotional situation. It takes two to teach, and from all we know of great teachers the spur from the class to the teacher is as needful an element as the knowledge it elicits (Barzun, 1959, p. 43).

Individualized perception. Recognizing the individual differences among students demands a special eye for detail. Excellent teachers understand that students learn and respond differently to various teaching situations, and they adjust their teaching strategies to accommodate these differences.

Teaching at its best is a great art, and great art of any kind is rare. Engaged in as a mass enterprise, for faculty as for students, teaching has difficulty rising above a kind of middle level that hits the students somewhat above where they sit down and well below where they think (Eble, 1970, pp. 2–3).

Teaching strategies. Excellent teachers make students active participants in planning learning experiences and accomplishing learning objectives; they make them active partners in the teaching and learning process (McKeachie, 1978). For many people, doing is far easier than talking about it.

From which I conclude that the teaching impulse goes something like this: A fellow human being is puzzled or stymied. He wants to open a door or spell "accommodate." The would-be helper has two choices. He can open the door, spell the word; or he can show his pupil how to do it for himself. The second way is harder and takes more time, but a strong instinct in the born teacher makes him prefer it. It seems somehow to turn an accident into an opportunity for permanent creation. The raw material is what the learner can do, and upon this the teacher/artist builds by the familiar process of taking apart and putting together. He must break down the new and puzzling situation into simpler bits and lead the beginner in the right order from one bit to the next. What the simpler bits and the right order are no one can know ahead of time. They vary for each individual and the teacher must grope around until he finds a "first step" that the particular pupil can manage. In any school subject, of course, this technique does not stop with the opening of a door. The need for it goes on and on—as it seems, forever—and it takes the stubbornness of a saint coupled with the imagination of a demon for a teacher to pursue his art of improvisation gracefully, unwearyingly, endlessly (Barzun, 1959, pp. 20–21).

Knowledge. Excellent teachers not only want their students to gather new knowledge, they remain actively involved in gathering new knowledge for themselves. They are lifelong learners in the best sense.

Innovation. Seeking out opportunities for improving their own teaching performance, excellent teachers are often called instructional risk-takers and bring creativity—a rare phenomenon—to the college classroom (Boyer, 1987).

A teacher's effectiveness, if we would but admit it, is composed of the tricks of the trade, devices used spontaneously and regularly to attract and hold attention, or specific devices connected with helping students master particular concepts or skills....After we have gained that attention, then the trick is to provoke the learner to practice the acquiring of a skill or to search out the answers to questions or to imitate the acts of mind and muscle that have been set forth (Eble, 1983, p. 55).

WHAT WE KNOW ABOUT FACULTY DEVELOPMENT ACTIVITIES

Two overarching caveats are critical to any discussion of faculty development activities. Professional development must be regular, systematic, and continuous throughout the academic year, beginning with new faculty orientation; integrated into the fabric of the institution (Eble and McKeachie, 1985); and evaluated for its timeliness and value (Roueche and Roueche, 1993a). Built-in institutional mechanisms can make the most of even one-time activities, but without these mechanisms, long-lasting effects on individuals and institutions cannot occur.

Moreover, professional development efforts must have something in them for faculty—there must be mechanisms through which faculty are motivated, involved, and excited about participating. While it is difficult to explain the relationship between motivation and achievement, we do know that the relationship is important—if two people of the same ability have the same opportunity and conditions under which to achieve a goal, the motivated person will surpass the less-motivated person in performance and outcome (Wlodkowski, 1985). And, for faculty, who, as Cross notes, "are more likely than people who have chosen other careers to respond to intrinsic motivators" (1989, p. 17), the opportunity to discover new ways of teaching will lead to improving their performance as teachers. "Intrinsic motivation...will be bolstered if experiences lead people to feel more self-determination and confidence" (Roueche, Baker, and Rose, 1989, p. 195).

> Intrinsic interest rather than extrinsic demand is what leads individuals to seek improvement. Lasting change can best be brought about by stimulating, supporting, and reinforcing positive efforts of faculty members. When external motivation is used by instructional-improvement programs, the carrot—not the stick—is the most common form of incentive (Gaff, 1975, p. 7).

There are numerous examples of highly effective faculty development programs, and they are as varied as the faculty for whom and the institutions in which they are designed. Staff development programs reflect the internal and external political realities of their institutions, the level of administrative support and available funds, the institutional climate, and the staff's readiness for development. These variables in large measure will determine what each program's activities will be (O'Banion, 1981).

Providing extensive descriptions would not be particularly useful for our purposes here, but there is some value to providing a broad overview of some of the more common approaches to effective faculty development. A simple framework for discussion includes the major components of a college: the student, the teacher, and the institution. To address the needs of the student, we speak of instructional development; for the teacher, personal development; and for the institution, institutional or organizational development (Gaff, 1975). However, in reality, the pieces of the framework cannot be so easily compartmentalized; these approaches to development overlap and intertwine—in fact, the difficulties of separating them in any tidy way clearly reflect the complexities of the teaching enterprise.

Instructional development activities focus on improving teaching skills, such as planning, organizing, motivating, using technology, designing teaching strategies, and evaluating. They expand the faculty's understanding of the student experience, motivation, and learning differences (Brophy, 1987; Eble and McKeachie, 1985). Sometimes master teachers, faculty who have been recognized as accomplished in their art, can become teachers of teachers, demonstrating teaching and evaluation techniques in formalized settings (Bloor, 1987), serving as mentors for new teachers (Valek, 1987), or learning to use technology in the classroom (Paoni, 1990).

Some community colleges think of the staff development program as a curriculum, a set of designed experiences for the development of the staff. If the program is conceived as a curriculum, the primary work is to develop a series of courses, seminars, and workshops that will be attractive to the participants—electives that satisfy faculty needs and interests; classes that offer credit toward a higher rank on the salary schedule or toward promotion; or courses such as Introduction to the Philosophy of the Community College. Moreover, activities may be only indirectly related to improving teaching—that is, visiting other colleges to review innovative or exemplary programs; attending conferences and working off-campus; having access to faculty acting as internal consultants; participating in retreats; engaging in graduate study; and having access to professional libraries (O'Banion, 1981).

Personal development activities aim to help faculty develop their inter-personal skills and their ability to relate to students. While few data are available that describe the effects of the fully functioning adult teacher on a student's learning experience, "it is unlikely an immature faculty can lead students toward their own integration and self-development" (Cohen, 1973, p. 108). If the faculty is the college's most valuable resource, development programs "must focus on development or renewal of the individual" (Preus and Williams, 1979, p. 23).

Faculty can improve. Teachers are people, and their personal and professional needs intersect. This is not something the college should discourage: college students often respond better to instructors who come across as "real people." Most faculty are willing to try to improve if they know what is needed, they are not made to feel incompetent because they aren't perfect, and the approach is positive rather than punitive or threatening. Faculty development/growth must therefore be an individual, personal phenomenon; it cannot be achieved en masse (Preus and Williams, 1979, pp. 23–24).

> An individual's professional work is intimately connected with his personal life; the quality of his work may be affected for good or ill by events in his family, his health, and his personal habits. An...improvement program may require efforts to promote the personal growth of individuals as well as their professional development (Gaff, 1975, p. 7).

Professional development plans established by individual faculty members encourage ownership of the program and further encourage people to look closely at their individual needs and interests, and plan for personal and professional growth—"one of the most important incentives in any staff development program" (O'Banion, 1981, p. 149). Other incentives should not be overlooked—that is, release time, promotions, direct stipends, salary increases, institutional recognition, and paid travel. However, "there is very little agreement...among the various constituencies...as to which rewards produce the best results" (p. 150).

Institutional or organizational development activities also help faculty and the institution create an effective teaching and learning climate. Such activities may include special opportunities for innovation—e.g., developing interdisciplinary courses (Collins and Stanley, 1991; Greening, 1987; Recktenwald and Schmidt, 1992; Wranosky and Mitchell, 1987) and team teaching (Ortego, 1991)—for participating in training or retraining experiences off campus (Bloor, 1987).

> Teaching and learning are individual but not solitary activities; they occur within a social context. The climate of the institution, the relationships between faculty, administrators, and students, and the policies and practices of the school affect the character of teaching and learning. The

improvement of instruction requires attention to these social and institutional factors as well as to individuals (Gaff, 1975, p. 7).

EVALUATING FACULTY DEVELOPMENT PROGRAMS

The aim is to develop a program that is so integrated into the fabric of the college that staff accept as normal the opportunity to plan goals and carry out activities that help them improve their teaching, administering and counseling. When the rewards are clear, and opportunities are provided, staff members will choose to be innovative and creative. When staff members begin to grow and develop, the college will move toward increased potency and impact (O'Banion, 1972, p. 104).

Staff development programs should be integrated with evaluation processes to allow the individual and the college to determine progress; "they should not be 'seek and destroy' missions but should focus on development" (O'Banion, 1972, p. 104). If what we know about teaching excellence drives and is reflected in the activities that appear under the umbrella of development, then it becomes critical to measure what staff development should be accomplishing and how well it has been accomplished.

However, any attempt to list the instructor characteristics that drive instructional evaluation requires

walking a thin line between too much generality and too much specificity. On the one hand, it seems most unlikely that any one set of characteristics will apply with equal force to the teaching of all kinds of material to all kinds of students under all kinds of circumstances. On the other hand, it seems equally unlikely that teaching is entirely idiographic, that there are no principles that apply to a wide range of teaching situations (Doyle, 1983, p. 27).

While creating such lists is risky, primarily because no comprehensive and documented theory of teaching is available from which to draw, certain faculty teaching qualities and characteristics deserve serious consideration. Doyle (1983) lists nineteen important instructor characteristics from his analyses of experimental and correlation studies by such researchers as Gage and Berliner (1975), Gagné (1970), Wherry (1952), Doyle (1972), Hildebrand, Wilson, and Dienst (1971), and Cohen (1981). By way of setting the stage for the introduction of this list, Doyle reviews the specifics of these researchers' discoveries; some we include here for the same reason.

- Careful attention should be given to individual differences among students.

- Gagné's nine external conditions for learning (1970, p. 304) include three that are internal to the student and may be indirectly influenced by the teacher, and nine, listed below, that are external to the student and under the direct control of the teacher:

— gaining and controlling the learner's attention

— informing the learner about intended outcomes

— stimulating the learner to recall capabilities already achieved that are pre-requisite to the new learning

— presenting the learning stimuli

— guiding the progress of learning

— supplying feedback

— assessing performance

— making provision for transfer of learning to new situations

— taking steps to assure retention

- Achievement-producing teacher behaviors include:

  — structuring—using cues, giving verbal signals such as "this is important," and organizing communication through clear exposition

  — questioning

  — probing—which, along with questioning, prepares students to learn

  — rewarding—accepting student's ideas, and encouraging good behavior (Gage and Berliner, 1975).

- There appears to be a modest but significant correlation between tested student achievement and rated instructor rapport (McKeachie, Lin, and Mann, 1971). Students appear to achieve at higher levels for teachers they like.

From these and other studies, Doyle also compiled a list of instructor characteristics that appear to be "more closely tied to research literature on student learning and therefore may constitute a more valid measure of college teaching" (1983, p. 36). An effective teacher:

- helps students distinguish what is important from what is not

- helps students stay interested in learning

- tailors the presentation to the student's level of development

- tries to reach all the different kinds of students in the course

- works to keep students attentive

- keeps students aware of the course goals

- helps students bring prior learning to bear on new material

- presents the subject matter clearly

- provides the right amount of structure: neither too much nor too little
- guides students in their study
- provides helpful feedback
- helps students apply what they have learned to new situations
- is approachable
- respects students
- understands students
- keeps students challenged
- knows the subject well enough
- emphasizes what is important in the field

Strategies for evaluating faculty development programs range from the simple to the complex—from merely counting the numbers of participants in various activities to gathering and analyzing feedback from participant questionnaires; from external discernment of changes in faculty behavior that were the direct results of the development program, to self-reports in which faculty articulate changes in their knowledge, attitudes, and style that resulted from their participation, to even more formal measurement activities that identify relationships between the development of faculty and the development of students.

> In healthy institutions it is probably possible to integrate staff development and staff evaluation activities. It is a goal worth pursuing, since both activities obviously pertain to improving the personal and professional development of staff. But if such an integration threatens staff development programs so that participation is limited or creates cynicism, then the two programs should be kept separate and the separation made clear (O'Banion, 1981, p. 159).

WHAT WE KNOW ABOUT INTEGRATING PART-TIME FACULTY INTO THE COLLEGE

"Integration is our word for the effort institutions make to ensure that their part-time faculty members are successful, valued, and supported in what they do" (Gappa and Leslie, 1993, p. 180). It is the effort the college makes to connect and keep in touch with part-time faculty, and to help faculty feel that they are involved in the mainstream of the college's life. However, the research documents that part-timers have "strong feelings about whether they are or are not 'connected' to or 'integrated' into campus life. For the most part, they feel powerless, alienated, invisible, and second class" (Gappa and Leslie, 1993, p. 180).

What is…fairly obvious…is that part-time faculty members are put in a different academic environment than the one in which full-timers operate. Rather than being descriptive, it is proscriptive. Rather than being one which cultivates, it dominates. By failing to suggest that part-time faculty members are valued members of an academic family, such an environment sustains the image of part-time faculty as an expendable commodity which is allowed to circulate on the periphery but is not a wholly accepted member of the collegial world (Greenwood, 1980, p. 57).

As one department chair observed about this treatment for part-time faculty: "We are eating our seed corn by degrading this part of our profession" (Gappa and Leslie, 1993, p. 180).

Part-time faculty should not function in isolation. Places provided for informal contact and communication appear to be an important priority. Colleges could provide a central location where there is access to office services, telephones, mailboxes, and coffee (Gappa and Leslie, 1993, p. 188). Some observers have reported that when secretaries and librarians work flexible hours, they provide evening part-time faculty and students with valuable services that are more commonly available to full-time and daytime faculty and students. Listing part-timers in the annual college catalogue or in a separate publication about all faculty provides a visible indication that they are part of the college team (Tucker, 1993). Inviting part-timers to social events, to faculty meetings and retreats, and to workshops and other events at the college signals that part-timers are important players. Allowing them an appropriate voice in decision making makes them feel welcomed into departmental affairs. And, as one math department chairperson observed during an interview about part-time faculty:

We should make…gestures of appreciation. We should welcome them to the institution, write a personal thank-you note to each adjunct at the end of the term, invite them to ceremonial and festive occasions like awards convocations and commencement. I review all the student evaluation forms, and put stick-on notes beside especially complimentary comments with a congratulatory note of my own (Gappa and Leslie, 1993, pp. 188–189).

Mentoring is useful in retaining and inducting new teachers, rewarding and revitalizing experienced teachers, and increasing professional efficacy (Gehrke, 1988; Little, 1990; Reiman, 1988; Zey, 1984). A complex process, mentoring must be designed around the needs of new teachers and their mentors, the current teaching skills of the mentees, the helping skills of the mentors, and the specific characteristics of the institution (Head, Reiman, and Thies-Sprinthall, 1992). Observers of the mentoring process have noted that it is worth the effort and time required to do it well; it facilitates the learning of new strategies, provides access to the organizational culture, develops an informal network of communication for transmitting professional information, and increases professionalism and diversity in the teaching-learning environment (Luna and Cullen, 1992, pp. 133–138). In fact, many practitioners and researchers agree that teaching skills are acquired best "through personal development, observation and imitation, and shared experience" (Eble, 1983, p. 63).

> Thus, the best teacher training—a barbarous term, for training is what we give disobedient dogs and show horses—may be that of master and apprentice. By that means, too, we might be able to bring both master and apprentice to examine carefully and set forth clearly just what constitutes their skills. It is baffling that so many teachers are reluctant to articulate just what it is they do. Perhaps it is from a becoming modesty, or from a respect for the mysteries of teaching which analysis can threaten, or even from an unacknowledged disrespect that regards teaching skill as a secondary accomplishment not exact enough to be a science or sufficiently inspired to be an art (Eble, 1983, p. 60).

As do all good teacher/student relationships, the mentor/mentee relationship's success "depends on what mentors do rather than who they are" (De Jong, Hartman, and Fisher-Hoult, 1994, p. 43). Good mentors are also good teachers; they must be able to provide support, empathy, and relevant information in a comprehensible fashion (Head, Reiman, Thies-Sprinthall, 1992); they must be good listeners and invest the time required to develop the relationship, try out new ideas, and share concerns and problems (Gold, 1992; Kay, 1992); and they must be able to handle an overwhelming number of responsibilities and tasks (Reiman and Edelfelt, 1990). New teachers need the following services and activities:

- help in developing competence without the mentor's providing a "screening process"

- an on-site mentor skilled as a peer coach

- time to work with their mentor and develop skills

- opportunities to talk with other beginners in an evaluation-free setting

- orientation to the institution

- realistic teaching assignments, especially regarding the number and type of classes

- an understanding of the context in which they will teach, including the values of the institution, at-risk student issues, and minority student issues (Thies-Sprinthall, 1990).

As Boice (1990) and others have observed, mentors are made, not born; they must be trained to provide exceptional mentoring services. Training should include information about building a successful mentoring relationship by meeting regularly, models of good mentoring relationships, and the goals of the mentoring relationship. The mentor and mentee should decide upon ground rules and evaluation procedures for accomplishments, and the mentee should eventually become a self-sustaining faculty member, not necessarily in the image of the mentor but with his or her own style and instructional competencies. Finally, there should be incentives for encouraging potential mentors to consider these time- and energy-consuming tasks (Wolfe, 1992). These incentives can include release time, stipends, funds for professional development, funding for travel or confer- ence registration fees, other professional development opportunities, and public recognition (Whaley and Galluzzo and Craig, 1990; Odell, 1992).

We asked these questions about faculty development:

- Do part-timers participate in college faculty development activities?

- Are there faculty development activities specifically targeted at part-timers?

- Is participation voluntary or mandatory?

In addition, we asked these questions about integration:

- Is there any process designed to involve part-timers in college life (beyond orientation)?

- What are the formal processes for integration (e.g., department or college par- ticipation on committees, faculty meetings, faculty senates, advising)?

- What are the informal processes for integration (e.g., inclusion in social func- tions, lunch or dinners on campus, outside activities)?

- What types of organizational support are made available to part-timers (e.g., word processors, audiovisual equipment, office space)?

WHAT COLLEGES SAY ABOUT STAFF DEVELOPMENT FOR PART-TIME FACULTY

College of the Canyons has developed an Associate Program for Adjunct Instructors that fosters the sharing of teaching ideas and working together, and provides a tangible reward for the pursuit of teaching excellence. It is a series of workshops and activities exclusively for adjunct instructors. The Associate Pro- gram places an emphasis on the discussion, development, and practice of teaching skills rather than on the dissemination of information. There is no attempt to propagate the one best way, nor is the program in any way tied to the evaluation of job performance.

The program is implemented in three stages. The first stage is the completion of a Teaching Skills Workshop (TSW), which is based on micro-teaching tech- niques. Workshops are held on four weekend days during the fall term. The dates for the six-hour-a-day workshops are announced in the program information, and participants must be able to attend on all of these days in order to enter the pro- gram. Twelve participants work together as a large group, but they are trained pri- marily in groups of four. The workshop emphasizes specific, fundamental teach- ing skills, including the basics of an effective lesson, planning and preparing for a lesson, and time management. Each participant must present a series of fifteen-minute videotaped presentations. This feature of the workshop, along with the collegial feedback provided by the group, allows even experienced instructors to learn from these teaching fundamentals. Members of the full-time faculty have been trained to conduct the workshops. However, at times when training is not available, a comparable workshop on micro-teaching can be substituted. The workshop can be scheduled in a variety of formats that make it attractive for part-time employees; for example, it can be conducted at night or on weekends.

The second phase of the program is a two-day, twelve-hour Advanced Teaching Workshop (ATW). The ATW is designed to provide exposure to teaching topics beyond the basics introduced in the first workshop. The content of the workshop varies and has been based, in part, on the requests of participants in the TSW for additional coverage of specific teaching topics. Full-time faculty members presented workshops on questioning techniques, critical thinking in the classroom, and classroom research during the most recent ATW. This portion of the Associate Program is an opportunity to explore current issues of interest in greater depth with very few restrictions on format.

The third step in the program is a Teaching Analysis. During both the TSW and the ATW workshops, teachers are urged to explore and experiment with new skills and techniques. The Teaching Analysis is an opportunity for feedback about the real-world application of those skills and techniques. Each program participant, in cooperation with a full-time faculty member, designs an analysis that responds to his or her current concerns in the classroom. The analysis is a kind of classroom research, helping the teacher to see that he or she can investigate teaching problems, develop solutions, and come to logical conclusions about the effectiveness of those solutions.

Completion of the three phases of the program constitutes a prima facie case for advancement to Associate Adjunct status. Participants are paid a small stipend for each of the workshops they attend, and Associate Adjuncts are permanently paid at a 10 percent higher rate than other part-time instructors. The program selection process is weighted in favor of instructors who have the longest periods of employment with the college so that long-term employees have a greater opportunity to advance to higher pay. By this means, the college is assured that it is investing in those employees who are most likely to remain.

Instructors who have participated in the program say they were thirsting for opportunities to talk about teaching with other teachers. They appreciate how the program has helped them establish a network of full- and part-time associates on campus. In open-ended evaluations, participants unanimously agree that the workshops affected their teaching practices, sometimes within days or weeks. Both workshops are designed to provide specific, practical teaching methods that can be integrated into instruction with relative ease.

Benefits for the Associates, as listed in the program information, include:

- *Improved Teaching.* Since the program emphasizes the practice and analysis of teaching skills followed by comments and discussion, teachers at every level of proficiency profit from the program. Participants often find a direct and immediate application for their learning. In some instances, changes in the class-room occur within days or weeks of participation in the workshops.

- *Professional Advancement.* The TSW, the ATW, the teaching analysis, and the granting of Associate status are each concrete indicators of professional advancement. Completion of this program implies a significant broadening of one's teaching knowledge and skills and is emblematic of a devotion to pro-fessional development. College of the Canyons, and, it is hoped, other com-munity colleges, will be cognizant of those facts during the hiring process.

- *Higher Pay.* Instructors who attend the workshops receive a stipend of $100 for the TSW and $75 for the ATW. In addition, Associate Adjunct instructors are paid at a 10 percent higher rate than other adjuncts. Associate status typically can be earned in three semesters.

Participants are selected on the basis of a number of criteria. Some considera-tion is given to seniority; the basic philosophy is that instructors who have been with the college the longest should be rewarded for that tenure. An attempt is made to represent each division and as many disciplines as possible. There is con-sideration of the number of times that an individual has applied for entrance into the program. If someone is not accepted the first year, their chances increase con-siderably in subsequent years. This means there is an advantage to making appli-cation even if one's seniority is low. Application comments made by applicants and lead instructors are also considered. No single criterion may entirely override any other. Selections are made by members of the Associate Program Committee, which has representatives from several programs and disciplines in the college. Both adjunct and full-time faculty members are on this committee.

Completion of the program is a concrete indicator of professional improvement that the college believes will be particularly beneficial to those adjunct faculty try-ing to secure permanent teaching positions. Admittedly, some faculty members have been attracted to the program as a route to higher pay. However, anecdotal evidence indicates that participants are more concerned with learning about teach-ing than with salary enhancement and are most impressed that the college is acknowledging their significance. In either case, the program provides a vehicle by which the college can distinguish for pay purposes between part-time faculty who stay with the college over the long-term and those who are only there temporarily. Finally, the Associate Program provides a basis for improving classroom instruction while simultaneously addressing the concerns of adjunct faculty members.

Staff development activities at **Community College of Aurora** are designed to reflect the diverse needs of the faculty, as prescribed by CCA's developmental waves of teachers-as-learners model. The Faculty Development Program (FDP) is offered to all full- and part-time instructors; it received the 1989 Program of Excel-lence Award from the Colorado Commission on Higher Education, an award that has provided $1 million over a five-year period (Barnes, 1991). At the end of 1995, the program is expected to be fully integrated into college operations and will con-tinue with the support of institutional and other funding. In addition, the FDP has won two national awards. The president of the college noted that this development program, praised in the college's recent accreditation report, helped them receive the maximum ten-year accreditation status. The FDP includes:

- a faculty mentor program
- a new faculty orientation
- community college teaching effectiveness seminars
- educational topics and yearlong projects
- mini-grants for teaching and learning excellence
- individual teaching consultation
- independent study
- the Teaching Resource Center/Idea Bank
- a videotape production
- an annual international "Teaching for a Change" Conference and mini-conferences
- consultation with other colleges
- opportunities to facilitate seminars
- publications, including the quarterly *Teaching for a Change* newsletter, which has international subscribers

Mini-grants for teaching and learning excellence are offered to instructors who choose to attempt an instructional innovation that would not otherwise be funded. Four types of mini-grants are offered:

- Course—projects that involve students enrolled in a single course
- Program—projects that have an impact on students in several courses within a discipline
- Interdisciplinary—projects that involve students in courses in two or more disciplines
- Community—projects that bring community issues into the classroom or take the classroom out into the community

The first CCA mini-grant was awarded to a mathematics instructor to purchase graphing calculators for Intermediate Algebra. The math division developed a graphing calculator project through a mini-grant; as a result, the entire division now uses graphing calculators in its classes. Student retention has improved in classes using graphics calculators. Other mini-grants have funded a variety of innovative projects: a solarium for long-term study of a variety of flora, a college/community talent show, upgraded computer hardware, a feasibility study for using CCA as a wildlife rehabilitation site, a resource library of materials to assist faculty and staff in identifying students' counseling needs, and hand-held slide viewers for humanities classes.

The faculty mentor program helps instructors develop their teaching skills, particularly if they are new to teaching, new to teaching adult learners, or new to the community college environment. This program pairs new instructors with classroom veterans who have demonstrated their ability to teach adult learners effectively. The two instructors work together for one semester. During this time, the mentor observes the new instructor's class at least twice and works with the new instructor to identify specific strengths and weaknesses in the new instructor's instructional approach, establish an action plan for improvement, and monitor the new instructor's progress. The mentor suggests effective teaching strategies or makes referrals for additional faculty development training. The new instructor also observes the mentor's class, to see the mentor demonstrate effective teaching. At the end of the collaboration, both the mentor and new instructor summarize and evaluate the effectiveness of their relationship. Faculty development staff members conduct training seminars and serve as a resource for mentors.

Faculty development specialists are available to consult with faculty regarding their individual concerns, helping them solve particular problems and develop specific tactics or techniques. Faculty with special needs or interests can develop individual projects and activities in consultation with a faculty development specialist.

The Teaching Resource Center/Idea Bank is a collection of books, simulations, videotapes, audiotapes, software, and other resources that faculty may check out or use in the Teaching Resource Center. Instructors are also encouraged to contribute to the Idea Bank, a collection of activities and techniques that have proven successful in the classroom.

The FDP is producing a series of videotapes on topics related to teaching adult learners. The first in the series is titled "We Are Different; We're the Same." It is used in new faculty orientation to show the diversity of students at CCA and to suggest an equally diverse repertoire of teaching methods. Two new videotapes and accompanying workbooks are now available: "The Transformation of Professor Goodenough" and "The Transformation of Professor Goodenough, Episode II: Beyond the Lecture Frontier." The first video focuses on using the interactive lecture method, and the second on using small groups in the classroom.

New faculty are required to complete the college's six-hour new faculty orientation course, and there is a follow-up session in which instructors talk about classroom problems and deal with classroom issues. Teaching effectiveness seminars, offered throughout each semester, empower faculty to tailor course content to the needs and abilities of students, rather than force-fitting students to course content. Topics for these seminars vary; new offerings are added each semester to continually pique the interest of the instructors and to upgrade and update their skills. Current topics include:

- teaching adult learners
- interactive lecture
- topics in diversity
- syllabus preparation

- assessment/grading
- quality questioning
- learning styles
- planning classroom activities
- teaching for thinking
- handling difficult classroom situations
- cooperative learning

- writing across the curriculum
- study skills
- developing objectives
- advance organizers/mapping
- student-centered activities
- ethics of teaching
- library research

Many of these classes are offered on a rotating basis so that instructors who are unable to attend one semester will have opportunities to attend later.

A second series of courses, Educational Topics and Issues, are in-depth projects designed for more experienced faculty. Each semester, one or more Educational Topics/Issues are offered. In the courses, interdisciplinary teams of faculty:

- participate in training

- collaborate on content and process objectives for their courses

- plan, implement, and practice classroom activities appropriate for their students and subject area

- design evaluation strategies to measure and evaluate student performance

- coach each other through implementation and change

Through these activities, all of which incorporate and model collaborative learning techniques, faculty develop instructional skills and incorporate new skills into their courses. Therefore, they may only be involved with one Educational Topics and Issues project at a time. All staff development courses are published annually in the FDP schedule.

An outside evaluator of the FDP, seeking to determine if the faculty development program at CCA influenced teachers to foster learner-centered classroom experiences, drew a number of conclusions about the program, among which were:

- Experiences at CCA tend to be learner-centered.

- FDP activities foster a philosophy and practice of learner-centered interactions.

- The overall climate of CCA supported internalization of the philosophy necessary to create learner-centered practice.

Recommendations included a suggestion to increase efforts to improve department collaboration between the FDP and instructional divisions on the mentor training and peer observation programs.

The evaluator's report documented that full- and part-time faculty members valued the program and stated that it contributed to their personal growth as learners and to their professional improvement. A variety of faculty members—

including retired university professors, young parents with children, professionals, full-time members of the CCA staff with teaching assignments, and persons intending to be full-time faculty members—expressed their support for the outcomes of the program. Each member of this group saw the program as meeting his or her needs. Department leaders stated that the program allowed them to request and get help in the design of customized training packages to meet the specific needs of individual departments.

Faculty development program data record 1,947 enrollments in the past fifteen semesters; an average of 129 faculty (out of a total of 250) participate each semester. Of special significance is the fact that the part-time faculty salary schedule is linked to participation in the Faculty Development Program.

The FDP is a strength of the college; it clearly connects the part-time faculty to the institution, enabling CCA to maintain nontraditional staffing patterns while providing quality instruction to students. CCA's differentiated faculty staffing patterns, use of alternative teaching strategies, and exemplary Faculty Development Program enable the college to use discretionary funds to support the mission and purposes of the college effectively. In fact, some faculty and administrators have expressed concern that the advantageous position the college enjoys with regard to its full-time and part-time faculty staffing might someday be compromised by moving toward more traditional staffing patterns.

Cowley County Community College uses a part-time faculty pay scale that reflects faculty participation in staff development activities. Level I includes new instructors with three years or less of applicable teaching experience. Level II includes new instructors with more than three years of applicable teaching experience, and Level III includes current and returning instructors. To get to Level IV, instructors must progress upward, level-by-level, by completing three semesters of teaching at CCCC and participating in twelve clock-hours of approved staff development. Current or previous instructors who have completed three or more semesters of teaching may move up a level at the beginning of the semester after they have completed the required staff development time.

Movement up the pay scale requires that part-timers participate in college-sponsored and approved professional development activities. They either attend in-service programs provided for all full-timers during the fall and spring semesters or activities arranged primarily for part-timers and conducted on Saturdays.

Selected segments of CCCC in-service activities for full-time instructors may be used as a portion of staff development time for part-time instructors with prior approval. Certain department meetings may be used as a portion of the staff development time for part-time instructors with prior approval, particularly those meetings involving curriculum or instructional techniques and information. Graduate courses, specialized training, and seminars may be approved to meet a portion of the staff development hours. Prior approval is required. At least six hours of the staff development time must be earned in staff development activities developed or provided specifically for part-time instructors. Part-time instructors may participate in staff development activities and receive credit for staff development time during a semester they are not teaching.

Included among the more recent activities, usually two to three hours in length, are sessions on teaching strategies and the high-risk student, the college's long-range plan, TQM, sexual harassment, the Americans with Disabilities Act, and dealing with difficult and disruptive students. Often, full-time faculty and administrators act as directors and resource persons for the sessions. Each workshop attended provides two hours of service time toward the next level on the staff development and compensation plan. Approximately one-half of the part-time faculty attend two sessions of staff development activities each year.

In addition, the various departments within the college are developing course guides—comprehensive guides that will provide an improved, coordinated curriculum. These guides are developed with the assistance of the part-time faculty. The teams that create the guides usually consist of four or five full-timers and two or three part-timers.

The college is moving toward sending more part-time faculty members to the International Conference on Teaching Excellence, sponsored by the National Institute for Staff and Organizational Development, in Austin, Texas. In addition, plans are being developed for the college to organize a mini-NISOD Conference for both part-time and full-time faculty. All faculty will be encouraged to submit proposals for workshops and to make a presentation. Part-time faculty would earn three-quarters of a day of staff development credit by attending three breakout sessions and the keynote session.

Cuesta College's flexible calendar requires full- and part-time faculty to attend a minimum number of hours of staff development activities annually. In addition to the activities held by the college, teachers can customize their activities by attending conferences or other workshop experiences. Some development activities are designed specifically for adjunct faculty. The college's faculty development officer designs the workshops based on the results of an annual survey that asks faculty to evaluate the year's flex activities and make suggestions for the following year. The staff development committee, on which part-timers serve, meets monthly and helps direct the workshops.

The Cuesta College Foundation board of directors established the Faculty Grants Endowment Fund with an initial gift of $5,000. The board currently provides funds for faculty grants to recognize and support faculty projects that advance college goals; and support innovation in instruction and service. All faculty, including part-timers who are college employees through the period of the proposed grant, are eligible to submit a proposal to receive grant funds. Award amounts vary. A Faculty Grants Selection Committee reviews applications and selects grant recipients; the committee includes three faculty representatives, two representatives from the Foundation board of directors, and one college administrator.

Cuyahoga Community College conducts a series of Saturday morning staff development programs once a quarter. These programs start with breakfast at 8:00 a.m. and continue until noon. Three topics were addressed during the 1993–94 academic year: testing and assessment, the adult learner, and teaching strategies. Each topic was presented three times, once on each campus. While the workshops are voluntary in nature, the part-time faculty contract requires that they participate in at least one faculty development activity each quarter. Currently, CCC provides a benefit enabling part-time faculty and their dependents to take a course at the college at no cost during the quarter following their employment.

Gappa and Leslie featured Cuyahoga's Educators Peer Instructional Consulting (EPIC) program in their book, *The Invisible Faculty* (1993), and deemed it the "most thoroughly 'packaged' orientation and development program for part-time faculty among all the institutions [they] visited" (p. 208). Emerging from an initial small-scale pilot experiment that paired part-timers with full-time faculty mentors, the EPIC program now matches all new part-time faculty with full-time faculty members. The mentor receives the equivalent of one-half credit hour release time from teaching responsibilities to work with the mentee; moreover, mentors are allowed to accrue "banked" release time credits and use them for professional development activities at a later date.

The mentor and mentee meet at least three times during the first quarter, keep journals of their meetings, review the part-time faculty handbook together, review the part-timer's course syllabus, review various teaching strategies, identify available college resources, and discuss the students likely to enroll in the part-timer's classes. The mentor and mentee observe each other's classes, although the mentor's observations are not used for performance evaluation purposes. The program's director reports that journal data indicate that the program has successfully forged ongoing, valuable professional relationships. A participant in the EPIC program observed:

> I don't feel second class here. The full-time faculty and [evening/weekend dean] are doing it right. I was in the EPIC mentor program. This was a very good experience. The mentor helped me fit into the college. I was invited to dinners, to workshops, and to Saturday morning [faculty development] programs. We are made to feel like we are a part of the college and that we are welcome here (Gappa and Leslie, 1993, p. 210).

Part-time faculty are paid to attend the flex calendar staff development activities at **De Anza College**. In addition, part-timers take advantage of the instructional skills center workshops. Each March or April, various divisions in the college meet in a retreat setting for staff development activities, and as many of the part-time faculty as possible are included.

Hagerstown Junior College, in an attempt to improve instructional delivery by part-timers, is developing three training units. A group of six relatively experienced adjuncts have been trained to provide instructional development, a project currently under evaluation. The college is also designing a project, Environmental Equity, intended to create a positive climate for ethnic and gender diversity. Finally, the college plans to conduct training on blended instruction, which emphasizes application and instruction. HJC's goal is for all of the college's part-timers to complete all three training units. Once this goal has been achieved and evaluation data regarding the units' value to the college indicate that they should be continued, the college plans to develop a dual-step salary system that will reward part-time faculty members who complete the training units. Ultimately the training will be required for employment. "More and more we are going to be measured on the effectiveness of our instruction. And if we put certain tools in the hands of our instructors, regardless of whether they are full- or part-time, we're going to become a more outcomes-oriented institution" (Dean of Instruction).

HJC's current staff development model includes recruitment and orientation (addressed in earlier chapters), communication, support services, an instructional clinic, and evaluation. Once part-timers begins teaching, a new phase of the development model begins with a series of activities intended to reinforce the orientation process. The communication component of the model includes an evening duty calendar that identifies for part-timers the college administrators and counselors on duty for various evenings each semester to answer part-time faculty members' questions or meet with students. HJC mails a weekly bulletin to each part-timer containing announcements of general interest to the college community; part-timers are encouraged to inform students of announcements in the bulletin and submit announcements for publication. Reinforcing the responsibility that each full- and part-time faculty member has to the college and to each other, and underscoring the importance of part-time instructors to the college is critical to helping part-time faculty feel a sense of identity with HJC.

The support services component provides part-time faculty with the same instructional support systems it provides for full-timers: media center equipment, clerical assistance, office space, instructional materials, funds for audiovisual material rental, media center personnel who help teachers develop alternative instructional strategies, and individualized learning centers that accept student referrals. Providing easy access to services and materials helps part-time faculty focus on instruction within especially compressed time constraints. Moreover, access to the services sends the message that part-time faculty are regarded as valuable members of the instructional team.

An instructional clinic that was established in 1976 allows faculty to share and resolve instructional problems. The clinic, now known as the David Lee Teaching-Learning Center, seeks to improve instructional delivery by focusing on effective lecturing, listening, cooperative learning, and diagnosing teaching-learning problems. Part-time faculty are advised of all meetings and invited to participate.

Part-time faculty are invited to attend the all-faculty conference that officially begins the fall semester at **Lakeland Community College**. In addition, part-timers have their own reception during the opening week of the new school year.

Because full-time faculty do not organize their own staff development activities, they are invited to and do attend the events organized by the Part-time Faculty Advisory Committee's Subcommittee on Professional Development. This committee plans a series of quarterly professional development activities on campus, all voluntary. Examples of events include:

Working with Difficult Students, a participatory workshop focusing on the etiology of mental health issues, theories of causation, and methods of dealing with difficult students, directed by a licensed psychologist and professional clinical counselor with extensive experience in private practice.

Participants were encouraged to contribute specific case examples in order to discuss methods and techniques for dealing successfully with this type of student.

How to Use Classroom Assessment Techniques in Your Classroom: Examples for Technical and General Education, a participatory workshop that examines Cross and Angelo's classroom assessment techniques. The workshop was directed by a psychologist and an instructor of manufacturing technology.

The Art and Science of Grading, a roundtable discussion directed by an instructor of composition, literature, and language, and an instructor of business management.

Beginning in the 1993–94 academic year, the Part-Time Faculty Professional Development Committee provided part-time faculty with the opportunity to fulfill personal and professional goals by providing funds to support activities that otherwise would not occur. Professional development funding is authorized by the vice president of academic affairs through proposals recommended by the Part-Time Faculty Professional Development Committee (PTF/PDC). Guidelines for proposals are developed early in the academic year. PTF/PDC awards are intended to help support:

- participation as a presenter, panel member, or moderator at professional functions
- attendance at conferences, workshops, and meetings of recognized professional associations
- visits to other community colleges
- activities above and beyond normal teaching responsibilities

Part-time faculty at **Modesto Junior College** must participate in flex-time activities by contract agreement. At least 20 percent of the participants in the college's Great Teacher's Seminar have been part-time faculty, and they are further encouraged to tie into a telecommunications network that links them with full-time faculty on campus who serve as mentors and classroom assessment experts.

Staff development at **Richland College** is tied to orientation, which was recently redesigned as an extended staff development activity. Participation in staff development activities is expected. In addition to orientation, the college holds a retreat on teaching and learning issues each fall and spring term. The retreat starts on a Thursday afternoon and ends on a Friday afternoon. Thirty to thirty-five faculty members attend each retreat, and by design 50 percent of them are part-time faculty. Faculty are invited to attend based upon recommendations of the department chair. Programs are varied; sometimes recipients of the teaching excellence awards are asked to make a presentation, and sometimes a student panel is on hand to remind the faculty of student concerns and issues.

Rio Salado Community College encourages part-time faculty to participate in a training course on the keys to essential instructional skills. The course is offered throughout the year, and as faculty are hired, they are directed into one of these courses. Because faculty evaluations are based on the keys to instruction and faculty are informed of this when they are hired, they are further motivated to attend. To ensure quality instruction at the college, Rio Salado views this course as essential for new faculty members. Full-time faculty chairs conduct two hour-long workshops and follow-up activities. There are now plans to extend this course to include in-class observations of current faculty. The objectives of the course are to provide information and training. After completing the course, faculty will be able to:

- identify the instructional skills that most directly contribute to student achievement

- define and explain each of the key skills

- generate examples of each skill

- describe implementation of each skill in their teaching

- enhance their existing teaching techniques

Rio Salado publishes the following list of Standards for Instructional Excellence for part-time and full-time faculty:

- Implement the four instructional skills that Rio Salado has identified as keys to instructional excellence by:

  — providing a connection with previous learning

  — stating an objective for each instructional activity

  — continually assessing student learning and adjusting instruction when necessary

  — asking students at the end of each class session to summarize/synthesize what they have learned

- Be a role model for students by demonstrating subject matter knowledge and strong written, verbal, and interpersonal skills in the classroom.

- Provide a complete, quality syllabus with a course outline at the first class meeting.

- Clearly state course expectations on the syllabus and review them at the first class meeting.

- Teach to the established district competencies/outline for the course.

- Design appropriate instructional activities which are appropriate for the class situation and which accommodate different learning styles.

- Return tests, quizzes, and homework with feedback in a timely manner.

- Base grading policies on student achievement and competence rather than effort.

- Use the required textbook and instructional materials.

- Assume proactive responsibility for student retention.

- Seek ways to improve teaching performance continually through workshops, publications, networking, etc.

The following are included in the guidelines and expectations for all faculty:

- Use the faculty handbook as a resource.

- Have adequate material prepared to teach every session for the entire class period.

- Attend Rio "all faculty" meetings, discipline-specific meetings, and area meetings as requested.

Various instructional excellence workshops are held each semester. Titles during the fall semester 1993 included: "Total Quality Management in Instruction—Awareness Training," "TQM in Instruction—Process Improvement Training," "Teaching with Technology," "Accelerated Learning—from Dickens to Pink Floyd," and "Student Shared Responsibility for Learning." In addition, the district provides as much as $300 a year for any faculty member to attend any workshop that applies to his or her teaching or discipline.

All staff development programs are open to part-time faculty at **Schoolcraft College**. The participation rate varies, since many part-time faculty work full-time jobs during the times staff development activities are scheduled.

At the beginning of each year, outside speakers are brought to campus to provide staff development opportunities for all faculty. During each term, a series of computer training sessions are conducted, albeit focused on training for full-time faculty. Part-time faculty are not typically included in these sessions because participants receive a new computer and all the software they choose for their offices upon successful completion of the training courses. This reward for course completion is considered too costly to extend widely to part-time faculty—although some part-time faculty have been involved in this series in the past.

Sometimes a full-time faculty member is assigned to mentor a part-timer. For example, when a person is hired for his or her professional field experience, yet has little or no teaching experience, a mentor is assigned for the first semester of employment at the college.

Triton College's salary schedule for part-time faculty includes the opportunity for salary enhancement after the completion of four workshops, three to four hours in length, created expressly for the part-time faculty. The workshops focus on topics such as developing critical thinking skills, teaching strategies for today's students, history and philosophy of the community college, understanding cultural diversity in the classroom, and using Triton College's resources. Registration is required for the workshops, and space is on a first-come, first-served basis. Full-time faculty, administrators, adjuncts, and the affirmative action officer conduct the training. While not mandatory, completion of these workshops is required for movement up the part-time faculty salary schedule.

There is one alternative to workshop attendance: the adjunct faculty member must demonstrate through his or her transcript that the topic has already been covered in undergraduate or graduate work. This procedure is accomplished by writing to the Human Resources Office and enclosing copies of the transcript plus copies of the course descriptions from the college catalog. Additional information may be required.

As part of a Title III grant to develop a comprehensive faculty training program, **Valencia Community College** established the College-Level Teaching Course (CLTC), designed to train all new full-time faculty and part-time faculty in areas related to college structure and teaching. This occurred after a joint committee of adjunct faculty and department chairs recommended improving the working environment by providing additional training and eliminating many of the distinctions promoted by exclusive part-time meetings and a separate part-time faculty handbook. Faculty are hired with strong content knowledge but may not have as much in-depth knowledge about college teaching. The CLTC consists of five three-hour sessions presented over a one-semester period. Included in the course are such topics as instructional methodologies, assessment and evaluation, learning styles, learning theory, testing and test design, classroom management, legal issues in higher education, cultural diversity, history of community colleges, and the role of community colleges. The sessions are held in the afternoons or evenings and are rotated among the different campuses. Fifteen to twenty-five faculty are typically enrolled in each section; most are part-time faculty as there are few new full-time faculty being hired currently.

The office of instructional affairs at Valencia, from which faculty training is coordinated, has its own budget that is largely funded from a federal Title III higher education grant aimed at improving the articulation between the college and the University of Central Florida. This articulation grant provided the seed money to develop the training and implement the system for training adjuncts via the CLTC. The grant paid for full-time staff and some part-time faculty to develop such programs as the CLTC, building a shared on-line transcripts databank, transfer student orientations, and other training and development projects. The University of Central Florida (UCF) was a partner with Valencia in acquiring and sharing this grant.

The pilot program for the CLTC was conducted with all full- and part-time math faculty from both UCF and Valencia. While the grant was not specifically designed to develop part-time faculty training, the CLTC's success has engendered a commitment to continue and extend the training to all adjuncts at Valencia. Any adjunct who wishes to receive associate status must pass through the CLTC and then be nominated by his or her chair as the one adjunct to receive associate status from that division that year. The associates are then listed by name and status in the college catalogue and provided with $300 in staff development funds for any staff development project they wish to undertake. All adjuncts are paid $15 per hour to participate in the CLTC. As part of the three-year plan to achieve tenure, all new full-time faculty must attend the CLTC, but they are not paid. College officials report that many adjuncts have commented that they would have participated for no pay. Many of the full-timers suggested that the CLTC "should be mandatory, especially for adjuncts."

The table of contents of the course syllabus describes the major components of the CLTC:

- Valencia Community College, University of Central Florida, and public higher education

- History and philosophy of higher education in America

- Role of community colleges in America

- Organizing the learning

- Lecture

- Teaching with discussions

- College teaching

- Student learning

- Classroom feedback

- Educational technologies and learning resources

- Creating and administering tests

- Academic and classroom issues

- Using an overhead projector in the classroom; transparency design and production

- Technologies for effective teaching

The college grants associate faculty status only to those adjuncts who (1) have successfully completed the CLTC training program, (2) have taught at Valencia for two of three terms per year for three consecutive years, and (3) are recommended by their department chair. The adjunct faculty member and the department chair must complete a confirmation in writing that the granting of such status should not be interpreted by either the college or the adjunct faculty member as the creation of any mutual expectation of continued employment. Associate faculty status provides access to limited tuition reimbursement benefits to enable associate faculty to participate in externally sponsored professional development activities, including graduate courses in their teaching disciplines. Associate faculty who use this benefit must agree to teach at least two more sessions at Valencia as an adjunct faculty member after a three-credit graduate course or equivalent training, if requested by the college to do so.

In addition, training sessions are offered to full-and part-time faculty, referred to as General Faculty Development Workshops. They include computer literacy workshops, including WordPerfect, Lotus 1-2-3, and Windows; and general teaching development workshops, including test design, classroom feedback, gradebook software, critical thinking, CLAST reading skills, and writing math equations using WordPerfect. These training sessions are offered at different times and days throughout the semester and at various sites and campuses. Other activities have included a bus tour of the campuses and centers, and workshops on collaborative learning, student services, critical thinking, gender and ethnicity in the classroom, and writing to improve critical thinking.

Part-timers are eligible for all staff development activities except sabbaticals at **Vista Community College**. The California System's flex-calendar allows colleges to provide staff development to all faculty and requires all faculty to participate in the flex-day staff development activities in a proportion equal to their teaching load. For example, part-time faculty members who teach six units—a 2/5 load—must participate in 2/5 of the flex-day hours of training that full-time faculty participate in. If they do not, they are not paid for the days they missed.

Greenville Technical College, Kirkwood Community College, Santa Barbara City College, and **Santa Fe Community College** invite adjuncts to all general staff development activities. Part-time faculty have been involved in computer and instructional techniques workshops offered monthly at GTC, the faculty enrichment program at SBCC, and the on-campus workshops with speakers and consultants at SFCC. At Greenville Tech, adjunct faculty with extended service have been given funding to assist with professional development, especially at professional conferences.

What Colleges Say About Efforts to Integrate Part-Time Faculty

Central Piedmont Community College has established a part-time employee merit award program. Part-time faculty may be nominated by any college employee via a brief paragraph that describes—with specific examples—the nominee's flexibility, dedication, dependability, productivity, competence, and involvement. Additional documentation from students, employees, and supervisors is encouraged and will strengthen the nomination document. Once a nomination has been submitted, it is valid as a review document for four consecutive quarters, excluding the summer quarter. During this extended period, the nomination may be updated to note subsequent accomplishments or to provide additional information. Award recipients receive $200 to apply toward any professional development activities they choose. In addition, an annual merit award provides a $1,000 cash bonus and includes a personal interview as part of the selection process.

Centralia College has established a core faculty component within its part-time faculty ranks. Faculty in this core group are identified as part-timers who have taught approximately 75 percent time over a number of years, after which they are given a 65 percent time contract, which provides a salary based on the full-time faculty salary schedule, rather than on an hourly basis. Currently, only three of the college's seventy part-time faculty are in the core group.

In the Allegheny Campus English department at **Community College of Allegheny County**, part-time faculty are invited to monthly department meetings, and they hold positions on all faculty committees except for the Part-Time Faculty Committee, which oversees selection and evaluation. They are involved in department activities such as selecting textbooks, reviewing curricula, identifying topics for developmental student exit exams, and developing departmental syllabi. The department hosts a professional development meeting once a semester, primarily for faculty of developmental courses to commiserate and exchange ideas about teaching issues. This meeting involves a meal, and if there are any new faculty, they are heartily welcomed.

The department, by encouraging part-time faculty to participate in professional and social activities, seeks to eliminate some of the communication barriers that occur when little time is spent together. However, the department is aware that it must avoid implying any permanent status for part-time faculty or creating any expectations of continuing employment.

Community College of Aurora encourages part-timers to submit articles about educational issues for publication in the *Teaching for a Change* newsletter. Part-timers serve on committees, meet with students, serve as student advisors, and participate in a wide variety of institutional services. Many part-timers attend the college's Teaching for a Change Conference.

The dean of educational development/faculty services observes: "We get high levels of participation because we ask for it…there is an expectation that people will do it." Moreover, part-timers are paid for their participation by means of a supplemental contract for extra service. For example, when part-time faculty members serve on college or department committees, the college provides them with an estimate of the hours they should plan to serve, and then they are paid for the service once it is provided.

In addition, the dean notes that early in the history of the college, there were no full-timers employed, only part-timers. And, while the college now operates with thirty full-timers and about 200 to 250 part-timers, it has maintained a different paradigm than other colleges with regard to part-time faculty because of its early days. "We think of our part-timers as our faculty. What we do, we do for all faculty. What we do works in part because of our faculty development program."

Part-time faculty have no rank, but the college does provide a salary scale based on part-timers' participation in professional development activities. Part-time faculty who consistently receive outstanding evaluations are most frequently offered the first available positions, although this is not a formal agreement of employment between part-time faculty and college administrators.

Part-time faculty are represented on the college council and all standing committees at **County College of Morris** if volunteers are available to serve. Part-timers are invited to all college socials and department functions, honored with service pins at a college reception, and provided with limited office space.

Cowley County Community College invites part-time faculty to serve on cross-functional college teams, and one part-time faculty member serves on the collegewide curriculum committee.

Part-time faculty at **Cuesta College** are actively involved in campus governance; they serve on committees and in the academic senate. A committee to address the concerns of part-time faculty has been created within the academic senate body. Part-timers are included in all department and division meetings and are invited to all informal college socials. The vice president of educational services observes that the college's small community strengthens relationships between full- and part-time faculty, and that its informality eliminates a number of communication barriers that are more likely to be created in large urban college settings. "The greatest strength of this program is the integration. We make them feel like an active part of the college and not like a side bar."

Moreover, "there is a high level of expectation at this college that people will not just teach and leave. I find that because of that, the long-term part-timers serve as role models for the new part-timers." The college does not require that part-timers keep office hours, but the examples set by full-timers spending time on campus and holding office hours reinforces the expectation. Currently, part-timers must share offices with full-timers; however, "people just cooperate here." In addition, part-time and full-time faculty have the same access to secretarial support.

Flexible staff development days are considered important opportunities for full-time and part-time faculty to interact at **De Anza College**. Part-timers are active in the faculty senate and on numerous college committees. There is no formal office space provided for part-time faculty, and they are not paid for office hours. However, they are invited to all college activities and, while attendance at graduation is not part of a formal agreement, they are always actively involved in this activity, as well.

The vice president of instruction observes:

> I think there are two groups of part-timers. One is the group that would not want full-time status if you gave it to them. They are professional people who merely enjoy teaching or who have another job. The other group are those who...desperately want a full-time job. They have a lot to contribute and are starving. And whenever [discussion] comes to salary increments or benefits, the professional people are "trotted out" as an example of how part-timers don't need [increments or benefits]. So, I think these two groups often get played against one another. At some point, we need to start thinking of various categories of our part-timers.

Greenville Technical College relies upon department heads to conduct any integration activities for part-time faculty, although part-timers are invited to all college social functions and department meetings. The President's Advisory Council, which is the faculty senate, and the Academic Council do not include part-time representatives. Part-time faculty in divisions such as arts and sciences and developmental education—where there are large numbers on campus during the day—are especially involved in college activities beyond their classroom responsibilities. Part-timers who teach in technical areas and at night are less involved because most are employed during the day in full-time positions outside of the college. The college pays part-time faculty to keep office hours to encourage part-timers to stay on campus and be more actively involved with other faculty and students. Faculty mentors are available to those faculty who request them.

Hagerstown Junior College involves part-time faculty in all divisional and institutional activities, including the development of common course syllabi. The college provides mentors for part-time faculty who either demonstrate a need for or request formalized instructional support. For example, a part-time instructor who has never taught but whose expertise in a highly technical computer field makes him a valuable resource to the college will receive a mentor. The mentor, a full-time faculty member, will meet with this instructor at least three times during the term. In addition, part-time faculty who are required to provide distance learning almost certainly will be assigned a mentor for the first teaching term. Other strategies for mentoring include a college-produced video that describes and demonstrates how a business applications course, for example, should be taught.

The communications division—with approximately fifty full-time and approximately 130 adjunct faculty—at **Johnson County Community College** undertook a process in 1993 to identify some creative ways to meet the needs of the adjunct faculty in that division. The process began when the dean of the division asked two full-time instructors, both of whom had previously been adjunct instructors for more than four years, to write about their perceptions and experiences in moving to full-time positions after being adjunct instructors. Their essays were used as a springboard for ideas in an adjunct/full-time committee. Although the committee was charged with finding ideas that could be undertaken within the division, the committee also analyzed other relevant questions:

- What is the real difference between being a full-timer and a part-timer?

- What could the college do to give adjuncts a better sense of satisfaction?

- What can members of a division do to retain the best adjunct faculty?

- How can we improve adjunct faculty morale and eliminate their sense of isolation?

From these questions and the collected responses and discussions, the committee members evaluated practices now in place and made recommendations that the college improve program-specific training and professionalism among adjuncts by:

- requiring as a condition of employment for all new adjuncts a teacher training program to acquaint them with writing syllabi, program policies, various assignments, etc., as practiced at JCCC. This training could possibly take place during in-service.

- providing contacts for an informal mentoring process by having the program director or adjunct committee members introduce each adjunct to a full-timer or experienced adjunct with similar office hours. Introductions would occur during the early days of the semester.

- continuing to make adjuncts aware of opportunities for professional development, such as the Master Teacher Workshop, special grants, and professional conference opportunities.

The committee also recommended that the college improve communication among adjuncts by:

- forming an adjunct instructor committee that meets regularly to address adjunct concerns and plan adjunct activities. The committee might include two full-time ex officio members to serve as intermediaries. The committee would report concerns to the program chair and report on activities of the program/division meetings.

- creating opportunities for monthly meetings of adjunct instructors in the conference room. The agenda might include formal presentations by experienced faculty or informal get-togethers to discuss a suggested topic. Consideration should be given to defining optimal times to allow more participation despite diverse schedules.

- providing a division bulletin board dedicated to adjuncts and their accomplishments.

The committee said the college should improve communication between adjunct and full-time faculty by:

- creating opportunities for adjuncts and full-timers to socialize or discuss professional issues.

- forming an ongoing voluntary mentor program, perhaps on a one-to-one basis—an adjunct paired with a full-timer.

- encouraging exchange of teaching observations between adjuncts and full-timers, possibly as part of a mentoring process.

- publishing an adjunct and full-time faculty division directory listing names, addresses, phone numbers, years of employment at JCCC, degrees and institutions, hobbies and special interests, etc. This would help faculty identify each other and offer an opportunity for faculty with common interests to seek each other out. Information could be compiled by individuals entering their own data directly into a database program.

- encouraging adjunct instructors to participate in program meetings through presentations, personal invitations.

Finally, the committee recommended improving adjunct morale and the working environment by:

- moving division storage cabinets and other superfluous furniture, etc., from the adjunct room, freeing space for adjuncts to have desk space and file drawers as space becomes available.

- adding another telephone, perhaps in the conference room. Having the phone in the conference room would provide opportunity for a private call.

- recognizing long-time adjuncts with a professional title.

- allowing long-time adjunct instructors to participate in decision-making regarding textbooks, course outlines, etc., by giving them a vote that counts— if not a whole vote, at least a partial one.

- presenting length of service awards to division instructors.

- creating a Meet-Your-Colleagues Day, early in the semester, hosted by full-timers with refreshments provided by the division. Two of these events could be held, one for Monday-Wednesday-Friday instructors and one for Tuesday-Thursday instructors, with refreshments provided throughout the day. The event would extend into evening hours to accommodate part-timers with different schedules.

- rewarding outstanding teaching with an Adjunct of the Semester award and publishing the announcement in the faculty newsletter.

- equipping the adjunct room with basic office supplies, including staplers, scissors, a dictionary, a thesaurus, tape, etc.

In the communications division at JCCC, most of the above recommendations have been implemented, while others are still under consideration (Bethke and Nelson, 1994).

Although there are no formal agreements in place, **Kirkwood Community College** involves part-time faculty on departmental committees and in special projects within departments. Part-time faculty share limited office space and have secretarial support within their departments. The college provides a chili supper for part-time faculty at mid-term each semester to encourage them to interact socially and professionally with other faculty, deans, and department chairs. There is no planned program; the event lays the foundation for building the professional relationships that are critical to part-time faculty teaching for the first time, as well as to others who are returning to campus. Kirkwood has also established a part-time faculty advisory committee to represent each academic department. Representatives are appointed by the department, and they examine professional development and orientation, teaching and curriculum, compensation, working conditions, and departmental involvement.

Lakeland Community College has established an advisory committee of part-timers representing each of the academic divisions. These representatives, appointed by the deans of the divisions, currently meet twice a quarter. The committee began as a task force to look at part-time faculty conditions and concerns, gathering information from other colleges and survey responses from their own part-timers. This generated a list of recommendations for the administration, focusing on college issues that part-timers felt were important. As a result, the college began to make changes. For example, the college provided extra parking spaces for part-timers who teach at night when the parking lots are more crowded, created an automatic deposit system for faculty paychecks, and renovated the part-time faculty office to make it an inviting center for professional activities by providing desks, mailboxes, and a small lounge area with artwork and comfortable seating. This center has become a gathering place for work and conversation with other faculty and students. The dean of social science and public service technologies observed, after receiving thank-you notes from approximately twenty-five faculty members, that part-timers appreciated "a place to work, to feel at home, and to socialize with each other." The *Adjunct Advocate,* a newsletter written for and by part-time faculty, also evolved from the work of the part-time advisory committee.

Metropolitan Community College has established a mentoring program for newly hired part-time faculty. Program coordinators match each new part-timer with a colleague on the same campus; division chairs are often consulted about potential mentors. Throughout the term, mentors and part-timers meet on selected occasions, and a final documentation of the events and contact outcomes is recorded.

Two part-time faculty members are included in the academic senate at **Modesto Junior College**. Part-timers have responsibility for managing a teaching resource center, and they serve on the flex-activity planning committee.

Ocean County College publishes a monthly adjunct newsletter. Part-time faculty frequently comment that the newsletter helps them feel a part of the college and that it has initiated discussions of good ideas for professional development. The dean of instruction noted that the full-time faculty of the business and computer science department have an informal custom of mentoring new adjuncts, providing collegial support, and conducting informal classroom observations.

A focus group study of several issues at **Richland College** identified a need for more part-time and full-time faculty interaction. One strategy for increasing that interaction has been to involve part-time faculty in the fall and spring semester retreats on teaching and learning issues. These biannual Adult Resource Center retreats are held for a limited number of full- and part-time faculty and administrators. Of the thirty to thirty-five faculty members at each retreat, one-half are part-time. The off-campus overnight retreats promote teaching excellence by exposing faculty to the innovative ideas and techniques of their Richland colleagues in an informal setting.

During the 1993–94 academic year, the college experimented with teaching/learning teams in the reading/writing program. Each semester, four teams of four to six faculty each were created from interested full- and part-time faculty in the departments of English, developmental writing, developmental reading, and English as a Second Language. The purpose of the teaching/learning teams was to share strategies for teaching reading and writing, interact about classroom problems, and discuss current literature in the field. The teams provided an interactive process by which faculty could gain a better understanding of program philosophies and could help each other improve teaching and learning. The process includes an orientation, team meetings, visits to each other's classes, and an end-of-semester process evaluation. This project is continuing in 1994–95 with some changes based on the evaluation process.

Richland College's Evening and Weekend Division Office for part-time faculty operates with four full-time staff members. Part-time instructors' mailboxes, lockers for storing materials, tables and carrels, computer terminals, electric typewriters, a copier, a machine for making transparencies, and a Scantron are located in this office. Four small rooms are available for teacher-student conferences, for study, or for grading papers and tests. All part-time faculty have access to the districtwide electronic mail system. The dean of student resources is housed in this division and is available to the part-time faculty during daytime hours. The vice presidents and deans have evening duty assignments, working approximately once every three weeks in the division office to be available to part-time faculty and students during evening classes.

Positive results of these programs include more long-term interaction among full- and part-time faculty, a greater sense of involvement in the college by part-time faculty, improved knowledge among faculty of teaching and learning issues and possibilities, a willingness among part-time faculty to try new methods, and a greater inclination among part-time faculty to ask for help and to offer their services. Part-timers are eligible for teaching excellence awards, and they receive special recognition if they stay at the college for ten or twenty semesters.

With only twelve current full-time faculty, **Rio Salado Community College** employs part-time faculty department chairs. In large program areas, part-time faculty mentors assist the faculty chair by working with other part-timers in the department.

Santa Fe Community College tries to "create a balance where [part-timers] feel welcome but [committing additional time to the college] is not required, and it won't be held against them in later hiring decisions if they cannot participate" (English Chair). Each part-time faculty member receives the correspondence, memos, and reports that all full-time faculty receive; they are provided office space in the same areas as full-time faculty. They are eligible to serve on planning and implementation committees if they wish, but they do not have a vote on policy issues.

A committee of full- and part-time faculty has been established by the faculty senate to explore several part-time faculty issues: creating a permanent part-time classification, improving benefits, and expanding part-timers' opportunities to choose textbooks and design curriculum.

While office space is almost nonexistent for part-time faculty at **Schoolcraft College**, word processing services and media support services are amply provided. A mentoring system is not formalized or required, but is available to part-timers with little or no teaching experience or who have special instructional needs.

The union contract calls for preference points, based on seniority, for part-timers. An accumulation of a predetermined number of preference points results in a promotion from part-time to adjunct status. Once they achieve adjunct status, these faculty are eligible for travel funds and more costly professional development activities.

Tarrant County Junior College provides some office space for part-time faculty, either shared or alone. In an effort to increase the number of student contact hours outside of class, the college requests that part-time faculty keep office hours, for which they are paid. Part-timers are always invited to professional development activities, and their participation is voluntary.

Part-timers are not included in the faculty senate, and they typically do not serve on college committees. Pay differentials are based on longevity and educational degree attainment. The college is currently discussing providing an increase in salary for each year of part-time employment.

While various departments at **Triton College** already employ strategies by which to integrate part-timers into the life of the college, new ideas are being discussed: inviting part-timers to monthly department meetings, involving them in making policy decisions, acquainting them with full-time faculty, and providing office space within departments in order for students to meet with them. One part-time faculty member is included formally in the academic senate to provide insight from the part-timer's perspective.

To promote the notion that "faculty are faculty" at **Valencia Community College**, the part-time faculty handbook was eliminated and replaced with a handbook for all faculty; collegewide and department meetings, graduation, and other college events and activities are open to all full-time and part-time faculty. In addition, full- and part-timers are eligible for teaching awards.

Part-time faculty are identified by a two-rank system: they are either regular part-time or associate faculty. To become associate faculty, they must have completed a fifteen-hour training session, taught three consecutive years at the college, and been nominated by the faculty. As associate faculty, they are eligible for additional training funds for graduate courses, travel, and other purposes, and have their names in the catalog along with regular full-time faculty.

Part-time faculty members can be elected as department chairs at **Vista Community College**; they can serve on all college committees and are eligible for staff development funds. The faculty senate has co-presidents—one is a contract, full-time faculty member, and the other is part-time. All faculty are members of the senate and have voting power.

They are dedicated faculty members who put out for this college. So I think the senate decision to have co-presidents was a reasonable reflection of the commitment the part-time faculty have shown to the college. I hear suggestions [out there] that institutions suffer academically when they employ part-timers. There is some strange notion that part-time faculty are not committed to teaching or that they cannot form cohesive departments, and I have to say that at least at Vista Community College, it is our part-timers that form the cohesive departments. It is our part-timers, for the most part, that have been elected department chairs. And, I think our

institution benefits because the part-time faculty clearly, given their working conditions, are people who are quite devoted to teaching and to excellence (President of the college).

At **Westchester Community College**, the assistant dean for evening programs serves as an advocate for part-time faculty on the president's cabinet, giving them "a voice at the highest level" (Vice President and Dean of Academic
Affairs). A committee of part-time faculty meet and discuss their affairs with the
dean. Social events such as evening suppers are arranged, and coffee sessions are
held periodically to maintain good communication between part-time faculty and
the college administration.

Part-time faculty members are invited to all activities on campus, are eligible
to attend department meetings, have two representatives in the faculty senate,
may attend all faculty senate meetings, and may serve on committees to search
and screen applicants. The "Westchester Community College Adjunct Faculty
News and Views" bulletin is published in the fall and spring terms. Although part-
time faculty are not required to keep office hours because offices are not available
for them, many do so, on their own, in the library or elsewhere on campus. After
nineteen semesters of teaching at the college, part-time faculty members are
placed on a priority list for teaching assignments and are allowed to select the
courses they prefer to teach before others in the part-time faculty pool are allowed
to choose.

> If money were no object, I would have a place for adjuncts. I'd like to have
> them hold office hours (that we would pay them for) and have them
> involved in orientation and pay them for that, as well....Unfortunately, we
> cannot afford this now, and I do not see any light at the end of the tunnel
> (Vice President and Dean of Academic Affairs).

CONCLUSIONS

You can define good teaching any way you like. Simply take any outcome,
process, or quality that seems desirable, and then define good teaching as
whatever something called a teacher does to bring it about efficiently. Even
a cursory fishing in the literature will net such definitions by the dozen.
Good teaching has been defined as what the "teacher" does to produce
inspired pupils, excited pupils, interested pupils, creative pupils (Broudy, as
cited in Lewis, 1975, p. 19).

Peters and Waterman, in *In Search of Excellence* (1982), contend that excellent
companies are characterized by an ability to incorporate change into their
institutions. Excellent organizations identify the behaviors that will improve their
performance and their bottom line, and that will move them toward standards of
excellence, and they encourage their employees to grow toward the new standards. In education, "excellence characterizes a school or college that sets high

expectations and goals for all learners" (Pickett, 1984, p. 31). And, in community colleges, which regard themselves as premiere teaching institutions, high expectations of faculty should be accompanied by efforts to train and retain excellent teachers.

> The staff of a college is its single greatest resource. In economic terms, the staff is the college's most significant and largest capital investment. In these terms alone, we affirm that it is only good sense that the investment should be helped to appreciate in value and not be allowed to wear itself out or slide into obsolescence by inattention or neglect (Yarrington, 1973).

More than forty years ago, Klapper wrote: "Generally speaking, the actual achievement of a college, an undergraduate institution, does not rise appreciably above the level of classroom performance" (1949, p. 228). He was addressing both teacher and student performance, and nothing has occurred in the interim to change that notion. "We contend that learners sit on both sides of the teacher's desk" (Roueche and Roueche, 1993a, p. 120); moreover, we agree with Boyer's warning that "if faculty and students do not see themselves as having important business to do together, prospects for effective learning are diminished" (1987, p. 141).

All faculty, part-timers included, should be provided with the means to grow and develop as teaching professionals, to be involved in "continuing efforts to help [them] shape their teaching to the needs and goals of the institution and focus on achieving the learning outcomes considered important. By 'continuing' we mean efforts that usually begin during the part-timers' orientation and extend well into their first year of teaching or beyond" (Gappa and Leslie, 1993, p. 204). They should be integrated into the college community and recognized as increasingly important players in the teaching and learning process in the interest of providing quality instruction to the growing number of full- and part-time students who will sit in their classrooms, in the interest of appreciating the investment value of the part-time faculty, and ultimately in the interest of establishing and maintaining the college's reputation for teaching excellence.

CHAPTER 6

Good teaching is at the heart of the undergraduate experience.
The evaluation of teachers is...the mark of a good college.

—Ernest Boyer, 1987

INSPECTING THE EXPECTATIONS

Conducting Faculty Evaluation

The dire predictions of the growing underclass of academically underprepared and underserved individuals who will seriously weaken the structural supports for our social and economic future have created a widespread interest in assessment of the processes of higher education that are designed and conducted, for all intents and purposes, to provide this society with a literate workforce and an educated citizenry.

In all fairness, it must be said that we in higher education have not been totally inattentive to these predictions. We have, however, delayed so long in responding in any serious and significant way that the love affair Americans have had with higher education, and surely with public education, has all but ended, and there are clear signs that even the tenuous friendship has cooled (Roueche and Roueche, 1993b, p. 14).

The quality of love affairs and friendships is determined, in large part, by the level of commitment brought to sustaining them. In the face of increasing community concern that colleges are not demonstrating high levels of commitment to their work—as demonstrated by students' performance in and out of the institution— political winds are blowing toward more assessment and accountability. The Student Right-to-Know Initiative, launched in 1990, required postsecondary institutions to disclose persistence and graduation rates; this initiative, and others demanding that public schools and colleges disclose potentially embarrassing data to their communities, was spawned by evidence that even when colleges identify their deficiencies, they sometimes are not remedied. There were signs that these legislative efforts to gather information about educational institutions' value to the community were but warning shots before "more decisive, centralized, and intrusive enactments" (Ewell, 1991, pp. 16–17).

Colleges have ample evidence to support internal initiatives to assess the quality of their services. Some states are moving toward minimum competency testing and outcome measures, others to performance-based funding strategies. Florida was one of the first states to mandate minimum competency skills testing, beginning at the high school level and, in 1984, extending into college. Currently, all sections of the CLAST (College-Level Academic Skills Test) must be completed successfully by any student wishing to receive an associate's degree or to enroll in upper-division classes at a four-year institution in the state (Rogers and Steinhoff, 1991). In 1981, Tennessee became the first state to apply academic performance criteria to funding decisions for state colleges and universities (Banta, 1985). Institutions were eligible for funding increases or supplements based on their ability to demonstrate the quality of their academic programs according to five standards. Texas is considering results-based components for state funding allocations using scores on the Texas Academic Skills Performance (TASP) test, which measures college preparedness levels in basic skills, and student outcomes for measuring program effectiveness (Texas Higher Education Coordinating Board, April 1992).

The unbelievable variety of program assessment strategies reflects the controversies that surround the who, what, why, and how questions about evaluation. These controversies have proven themselves to be long-lived. In a general sense, evaluation has never been particularly welcome as a guest at the educational table (Roueche and Roueche, 1993a, p. 203). Evaluation of educational programs has triggered criticisms of narrowness, irrelevance, and unfairness (Weiss, 1983). Such evaluation has been accused of creating anxiety and immobilizing faculty and staff (Guba, 1969). And, as many critics and researchers have discovered, "few people want their programs evaluated, but everyone wants to know what works" (Hanson and Kerker, 1991, p. 211). However, as Boyer warns: "In the current climate, there is great danger that politicians, not educators, will shape the process as funding formulas are linked to narrow yardsticks of assessment.... Such efforts often measure that which matters least" (1987, p. 262). And, he further observes that colleges must search for appropriate ways to evaluate their work:

If they fail to take more seriously their responsibility for evaluation, do not become, for example, far more articulate about goals, do not become much more knowledgeable about their students and their growth, nor become more thoughtful about the coherence of their academic programs, major decisions will be taken out of their hands (p. 262).

It is difficult to imagine that teachers might be constrained so narrowly by the decisions of outside entities, that good teaching will be defined and evaluated in narrow, limited ways that bypass the individual teacher. However, unless colleges have clear goals and create standards against which they can measure their performance, they cannot reliably evaluate themselves or their faculty.

Accountability means relating objectives sought to ends achieved. Precise accountability requires some systematic means of gathering, analyzing, and evaluating data, hence demands for improved methods of evaluating faculty performance can be expected—especially from state legislators (Miller, 1974, p. 3).

EVALUATING TEACHING PERFORMANCE

It is the personalities, the competencies, the philosophies, the commitments, and the behaviors of people who teach and administer programs that make them successes or failures. Program evaluation, at its core, reflects the performance of the key figures in the teaching enterprise—the faculty. "If teaching is to assume the status it deserves, the performance of each teacher in each classroom should, we believe, be formally assessed" (Boyer, 1987, p. 155).

Yet the problems implicit in measuring teacher performance are many, ranging from identification of appropriate criteria against which teachers can be evaluated, to the selection of valid methodologies that measure teacher performance, to compiling a comprehensive set of teacher performance variables, to identifying the sources from which measurements must be collected (Borich, 1977). While there is an abundance of research about faculty evaluation over the last sixty years, the research is uneven in quality and sometimes contradictory. There is much to learn about the concepts that underpin teacher evaluation and the problems inherent in the evaluation process. The literature abounds with conceptual frameworks for evaluation systems and perspectives for planning and implementing them.

The conflict surrounding evaluation processes and products is fierce. At the root of this conflict is the argument that human beings cannot be quantified by formulas or inflexible tools. However, as Miller observed:

We live in social contexts and we are judged according to some standard and by someone. While evaluation has developed very rapidly during this half of the twentieth century, it is conceivable that the "final" system of evaluation will not be developed in the foreseeable future, considering human complexities. Yet research and development have moved the field of evaluation much closer to respectability in terms of reliability and validity. Some fairly firm conclusions can be drawn from evaluation, and reliability can be determined. The alternative is much less desirable: it is the rejection of what we do know about research and evaluation in favor of second-hand and/or intuitive judgment. In an age of science, the "art" of teaching must be respected, but the "science" of pedagogy is becoming more sensitive, adaptable, and precise (1972, p. 74).

In the final analysis, one must admit: "It is difficult to know when you have arrived if you have never been certain where you are going" (Roueche and Roueche, 1993a, p. 205). Colleges must choose their modes of transportation and arrival carefully. And, yet, evaluation designs cannot be drawn in an inflexible fashion; there are no hard-and-fast rules for their development, just as the designs themselves are not carved in stone. In fact, as Popham observed, "a detailed dissection of many evaluation models would reveal, as was true with Dr. Frankenstein's monster, that they were built from the remains of others" (1988, p. 23). For our purposes, we will limit the discussion to a presentation of some common threads that have been woven throughout many descriptions of the complex fabric of evaluation. Perhaps in so doing we will provide a broad framework of issues that will pique interest in further reading and research.

WHAT WE KNOW ABOUT EVALUATION OF FACULTY

"Willingness to change is inversely proportional to proximity" (Miller, 1974, p. 12). The closer to home evaluation comes, the more resistance individuals, departments, and institutions create. Arguments include: good teaching is impossible to define; peers and administrators are good judges of teaching, but students are not; and evaluation should be limited to classroom performance (Addy, 1981). Yet, while we are likely to argue the relative merits of particular forms of evaluation and the specifics of evaluation—the who, what, why, when, and how issues—there should be no argument about whether or not it should be conducted.

"A good beginning point [is] to develop a clear statement of purposes for faculty appraisal" (Hammons, 1981, p. 48). Outstanding scientists and researchers of evaluation strategies agree about the purpose of evaluation: "The overriding purpose of faculty, administration, and institutional evaluation *must be to improve the instructional program*" (Miller, 1974, p. 8). "Appraisal data, whether applied to diagnostic, formative, or summative purposes, should serve not only to evaluate but also to improve teaching performance" (Borich, 1977, p. 43).

- Effective assessment requires *clear purposes,* as well as reasons why the goals ought to be *assessed* and the uses to which the information will be put.

- Meaningful assessment is dependent upon *long-term commitment* and requires *unusually long timelines* for development.

- Sustained assessment requires a *constituency*, and "information" alone provides an insufficient basis for sustaining it (Ewell, 1991, pp. 16–17).

However, in addition to providing colleges with directives for designing valuable evaluation systems, researchers also offer admonitions. Colleges are warned against collecting purposeless data—they should have clearly defined goals for data collection. Student success must be the main indicator of teaching effectiveness:

- "Data-driven" research projects produce information of limited usefulness; organizing data projects around problems, issues, or decisions to be made produces information of much greater value (Kinnick, 1985, p. 97).

- "An appraisal system must rest on the assumption that the teaching behaviors measured relate to meaningful pupil change. Yet...few strong empirical relationships have been identified between teacher-process and pupil-product variables" (Borich, 1977, p. 139).

- An evaluation of a teacher is not equivalent to determining the teacher's instructional competency, i.e., the ability to effect desired changes in learners. Defensible decisions concerning teachers rest on many kinds of data. However, it is essential that among these data appears valid information about teacher competencies. There is evidence that this latter kind of information is now overlooked in favor of subjective impressions of the teacher which are concerned primarily with the teacher's personal attributes and instructional techniques. Effectiveness in teaching is best evidenced by criterion measures which detect pupil growth as a result of the teacher's instruction (McNeil and Popham, 1977, p. 198).

The following observations about the evaluation of part-time faculty are woven throughout two decades of literature of research and experience.

- The evaluation system must begin at the time of employment. Part-time faculty must be made aware of the institutional commitment to evaluation and development during the intake interview.

- An institutionally developed instrument has several advantages. It takes institutional needs into account. Also, the group that develops it has a commitment to its implementation and effectiveness. Finally, it is easily revised to meet changing institutional conditions. There are, however, questions of reliability and validity.

- A comprehensive evaluation design...should be multidimensional: self-, supervisor, and student assessments should be used...implementation should be structured and regular...confidentiality is important.... It helps to ensure that respondents provide an honest assessment...timing is important.... Application should occur far enough into the course so that students can respond accurately, yet not so late that they respond more to grade threat than to instructional content (Frey, 1976).

- Part-timers should have some input into the use of evaluation results (Parsons, 1985, p. 25).

Behrendt and Parsons recommend using a commercially developed system—the Instructional Design and Effectiveness Assessment (IDEA)—to validate any in-house evaluation instrument. The IDEA provides a database against which to compare local college findings. They describe an experiment with this instrument: "All full- and part-time faculty were evaluated using the IDEA system. The IDEA institutional summary was compared with the college's frequencies and percentages summary. No significant differences emerged.... Given the lack of divergence the college staff accepted that their instruments were valid.... As a result of the design used with the IDEA experiment, it was possible to distinguish between full- and part-time faculty on the IDEA summaries. Again, no significant differences emerged between the two groups" (1983, p. 39).

Clearly, evaluation cannot be limited to a single measure. Faculty evaluation must have a purpose beyond simple vague notions of accountability or faculty development. The purpose, for example, can be tied to a clearly articulated plan for the college by using faculty evaluation as a measure of college productivity. It can provide an index of progress as faculty and administration work toward accepted goals, cultivate the college's human resources, develop new standards of performance, focus attention on the elements of successful teaching, and determine how these elements might be shared to improve the overall quality of the teaching effort. "The task of a truly effective evaluation plan is simply to describe what the faculty member contributes to the productivity of the college" (Ratcliff, 1984).

If student success is the central mission of the college, then the central question for evaluation may well be: "Has the teacher effectively caused learning to occur?" Yet, that question alone will raise a number of specific, related questions: e.g., what are the definitions of success; what impact has the teacher had on the institution regarding improving retention efforts; who should be involved in the evaluation? Whether judging program outcomes or the performance of individuals, the legitimacy of success depends on the criteria used to make the judgment.

Criteria used to make these judgments about success are the double-edged sword of evaluation. Questions that are neither broad nor deep can provide criteria that reflect only superficial indices of success: for example, if a teacher's effectiveness is defined by the number of students completing a course with a passing grade, what is to be said when those same students cannot negotiate a follow-up course successfully? If the questions develop criteria for success that include student demonstrations that they can negotiate subsequent courses and eventually graduate, then the evaluation design becomes more complex, but it is a significantly more realistic appraisal of teaching success. Asking and answering only the easy questions creates a false sense of success; an evaluation design so created will collapse eventually under the weight of its own shortsightedness.

In a survey of 250 community colleges in a nineteen-state region, 88.6 percent of the colleges indicated that their college had an evaluation system for part-time faculty in place; 41.2 percent indicated that they were "not satisfied" with their evaluation efforts (Erwin and Andrews, 1993, p. 559). Of the more common components of these systems, these methods of evaluation were performed in the following order by responding colleges: evaluation by students (n=204); evaluation by supervisor (n=160); evaluation by faculty (n=50). The response totals indicated that many of the colleges used a combination of methods in their evaluation systems.

The most common forms of evaluation of teaching performance are described here. One less common evaluation tool—the portfolio—is described in great detail, primarily because current literature and several interviews cite this tool as deserving of special attention in future discussions of evaluation systems; one college requires portfolio production of its part-time faculty. All of the colleges described one or more of the most common evaluation strategies, but, as expected, colleges implemented them in considerably different ways and in a variety of combinations.

CLASSROOM OBSERVATIONS

Classroom teaching is the arena in which most part-timers are evaluated, although some programs include service to the college and community and professional development activities. Useful data can be provided by classroom visitations. Miller offers these guidelines:

- The visiting team should be composed of two individuals: one in the teacher's discipline and one outside it, and respected...faculty members.

- Members of the team should be selected by the dean, in consultation with the department chairman.

- Planning for the visitation should include the teacher who will be visited.

- The date of an initial visit should be set primarily by the teacher, and a synopsis or outline of the session should be distributed to the team at least one day before the visitation.

- A standardized appraisal form should be used.

- A postsession with the teacher should take place no later than three days following the class visitation to discuss the observations and tentative conclusions of members of the observing team, provide the teacher with an opportunity to respond, and prepare a final report.

- The final report is filed with the dean, department head, and the teacher, who should have an opportunity to respond in writing (1974, p. 21).

Assessment of the quality of materials and procedures is another criterion in the total evaluation package. Miller suggests that while judgment of this criterion should rest with colleagues who are familiar with the content and purposes of the course, assessment might be done by someone other than a colleague teaching the same subject, perhaps by a teacher outside of the discipline who looks at all materials and makes some judgment about their timeliness, academic soundness, and relationship with the course objectives (Miller, 1974, p. 26).

PEER REVIEW

Common patterns of peer review included: assigning or inviting peers to sit on classroom observation teams, assigning full-time faculty to mentoring roles that include classroom observations whose results are shared only with the instructor, and using full- and part-time faculty to assess course materials.

SELF-ASSESSMENT

—Tell me, good Brutus, can you see your face?
—No, Cassius, for the eye sees not itself
But by reflection, by some other things…
(Julius Caesar, Act I, Scene II).

While many of us would prefer to judge our own performance, human nature places limitations on this evaluation strategy. Self-evaluations have not been researched well or long, and the results of research findings are inconclusive about relationships between self-ratings and student ratings (Miller, 1974). Self-evaluations, however, are important vehicles with which teachers can confront their own weaknesses and recognize their own strengths—two critical steps in an evaluation process. Miller suggests that a teacher self-evaluation should include gathering student appraisals near the beginning of the term to identify weaknesses or areas that need attention and begin improvement efforts, and again at the end of the term for comparing the two appraisals and assessing teaching effectiveness; and conducting face-to-face class evaluations. Furthermore, he suggests that teachers should be allowed to answer such questions as:

- What are my teaching accomplishments during the academic year?

- What are my greatest academic strengths?

- What aspects of my overall college contribution should be considered? (1974, p. 28).

STUDENT EVALUATIONS

Research findings have established that student evaluations are a valid measure of teaching effectiveness, particularly when student achievement is considered the outcome of good teaching (Abrami, D'Apollonia, and Cohen, 1990; Callahan, 1992; Cohen, 1981; Marsh and Dunkin, 1992). "Those who oppose use of student appraisals deny the single most important data basis for judging teaching effectiveness" (Miller, 1974, p. 3).

While faculty beliefs as to the qualifications students bring to the evaluation process vary widely (Dent and Nicholas, 1980; Ory, 1991), evidence that student evaluations are reliable assessments is clear and consistent. Although there is not as much evidence about the validity of student evaluations (Miller, 1974), studies indicate that student-rating scales are valid procedures for assessing the quality of teaching (Hildebrand et al., 1971; McKeachie, W.J., 1979; McKeachie et al., 1971).

Feldman (1988) analyzed thirty-one studies regarding student evaluations and discovered that rank ordering in importance of twenty-two instructional characteristics between faculty and students "were in fact more similar than different" (p. 314). There was strong agreement among students and faculty about the importance of enthusiasm, preparation, organization, fairness, and concern for students. They also agreed that clarity of course objectives and requirements, the teacher's personality, and the teacher's research activities were not important in the assessment of teaching. But students placed "greater emphasis than faculty on teachers being interesting or stimulating and lesser emphasis on their being intellectually challenging" (p. 312). Many faculty may contend that extraneous variables, such as gender, class size, rank and experience of the teacher, teacher's personality, and time of class, influence student evaluations and therefore do not provide valid conclusions about the quality of their teaching (Aleamoni, 1987; Miller, 1972, 1974). However, most studies do not support this contention (Barnes and Barnes, 1993; Cashin, 1988; Centra, 1973; Feldman, 1992, 1993; Smith and Cranton, 1992).

Choosing Forms. The literature has little to say about choosing instruments for student evaluations, and while it can consume many hours in the total time spent on developing a faculty evaluation system, many researchers indicate that the form itself is one of the least important factors in the entire evaluation process. Miller (1974) provides a useful description of several still current forms; Borich and Madden (1977) present a detailed and exhaustive review of numerous instruments, with helpful evaluative comments and a further reference section. While numerous commercial forms are available and widely used, many colleges choose to create their own. Most researchers agree that if adequate time and thought go into the process of creating forms, then the product may be more acceptable and the information it produces more credible to those being evaluated than a commercially available form.

For those colleges that choose to create their own forms, researchers and test developers suggest adapting existing instruments to avoid completely reinventing the wheel. Halstead (1970) indicated that an adequate rating scale should contain four components: an underlying theory of instruction or a model of the instructional process, a translation of the theory or model into one or more operational definitions, development of a rating scale consistent with operational definitions, and assurance that student raters understand the criteria. Colleges can start by defining good teaching and evaluating various rating scales based on how well the items on each scale relate to the various dimensions of the definition. Asking faculty to list possible items to include on a rating scale and ranking them to create a list for comparisons is also a strong start. Miller (1974), having made these observations, also reported that such "dragnet" lists created by faculty vary little from the lists derived from more conceptually derived statements (pp. 35–36).

Whatever the form, the student evaluation should be brief and easy to administer. Moreover, it should be administered consistently. If the teacher is to be out

of the room during the assessment time, proctors should administer the evalua-
tion, and all teachers in all classes should absent themselves during this time.
Finally, the results should be fed back to the teacher within a two-week period
(Borich, 1977; Miller, 1974).

THE PORTFOLIO

"A portfolio is nothing but a folder, a pouch—an emptiness: a collection device
and not a form of assessment. But portfolios lend themselves to assessment,
and for assessment they have enormous virtues and dangers" (Elbow, 1994, p. 40).
The portfolio, while relatively new to the faculty evaluation scene, has been an
increasingly common method of evaluating English composition students for
more than two decades. Even more recently, it has been used to evaluate visual
arts students—albeit with uneven levels of acceptance among faculty even within a single discipline. Portfolios offer the evaluator a look at process and product
at once; they provide a better picture of what has actually happened over the
course of time than would any single criterion, and they are a more accurate
reflection of strengths and weaknesses than any single test.

The difficulty posed by portfolios, however, is that they "do *not* give us a better picture of 'how good' a writer someone is, if what we have in mind is a number.... Readers will differ according to their values" (Elbow, 1994, p. 45). Elbow
observes that portfolios may best be scored with one of two holistic scores—either
Excellent or Poor/Unsatisfactory—since scoring studies have determined that
most raters have difficulty agreeing on the middle-range of performance. Portfolios reflecting middle-range performance would be dismissed. "Many portfolios
soon disqualify themselves by having too much weakness to be excellent or too
much strength to be terrible" (p. 49). The strength of portfolios lies in their ability
to show us the complex range of individual differences. "Surely most of us have
learned that we don't so much help people improve as persons by giving them
constant diagnosis of strengths and weakness. We help them improve by engaging
with them in serious and felt relationship" (p. 54).

Faculty evaluation systems have focused over time on instructional evaluation
systems, emphasizing the delivery of instruction rather than the responsibilities
of the instructor as a subject matter expert. The relationship between process and
product is, by and large, ignored; researchers advise that the evaluation of instructional delivery should be combined with assessment of faculty roles in curriculum,
instruction, student advisement, and community service in order to provide a
more comprehensive view of faculty performance (Ratcliff, 1984).

In the search for evaluation strategies that take into consideration this broader
view of the faculty member's role, several community colleges have turned to the
use of portfolios for determining promotion and tenure for full-time faculty.
Miami-Dade Community College, in establishing the policies and procedures
for faculty advancement, has developed what it considers to be a fair, equitable,
and consistent assessment of faculty performance. The performance portfolio is
principal among the sources of evidence used to assess candidates for advance-

ment. The portfolio is compiled by the individual faculty member seeking advancement, but additional information is brought to committee deliberations from the chairperson/immediate supervisor, the associate dean or equivalent, the dean and campus president, and student and other clients.

A chronicle of career activities, the Miami-Dade portfolio seeks to compile official documents and original work that attest to the quality and consistency of the candidate's performance; it illustrates the ways in which the faculty member has fulfilled the requirements of the advancement he or she seeks. *A Guide to Assessing Performance Portfolios* (Miami-Dade Community College, revised February 1994) describes the components that are to appear in the portfolio. The following details are adapted from this assessment guide, with appropriate inserts from *Faculty Advancement Policies and Procedures,* which is referenced in the guide. The complexity of the procedure, for both assessor and the faculty member being assessed, is obvious from the following description. Many of the college officials we interviewed cited the enormous amount of time and effort required on both sides of the evaluation process as major drawbacks for using portfolios as an evaluation tool, especially for evaluating part-time faculty. However, we present this rather lengthy description because several other colleges expressed an interest in using portfolio evaluations.

Faculty Job Description. The job description helps establish the context in which the faculty member fulfills his or her responsibilities. Understanding an instructor's primary professional responsibilities will help determine if the other documentation is appropriate and adequate. It also will help assess whether activities are components of, or go beyond, professional expectations.

The Portfolio Narrative. The portfolio narrative is a description of how the faculty member has met the criteria for continuing contract, promotion, or the endowed chair, as described in the college's *Statement of Faculty Excellence.* Candidates answer the following seven questions, which are designed to explain how the documentation illustrates both the quality and consistency of their performance:

- What challenging goals have I set for myself, and what progress have I made towards attaining them?

- How do I motivate students or others whom I serve?

- How do I interact positively with colleagues and students?

- How do I create a climate conducive to learning?

- How have I updated my own knowledge, professional skills, and resources to make my instruction or service meaningful?

- How do I meet or support the individual learning needs of students?

- What information do I have that shows my students' achievement or the effectiveness of my service?

In addition, the narrative lets the candidate explain which documents illustrate the attainment of which criteria. Aspects of the documentation that are not self-evident will be explained in the narrative. Writing style and form will vary and should not be a consideration in evaluating the portfolio.

Documentation. Candidates for continuing contact, promotion, and the endowed chair must demonstrate excellent performance as described in the college's *Statement of Faculty Excellence.* Candidates for promotion and the endowed chair must demonstrate active participation in activities that support the mission of the college as well. The documentation section of the portfolio serves as a major source of evidence that the required criteria have been satisfied. Materials may be presented that are creative and attractive, but that should not be their sole worth. All documentation is judged only by the evidence it provides that the candidate has met required criteria for the next appropriate advancement step. The documentation section of the portfolio contains the following:

- *Annual Performance Reviews.* The annual performance review is prepared by the faculty member's immediate supervisor, who comments on the faculty member's performance within four categories identified in the *Statement of Faculty Excellence.* The immediate supervisor responds to the faculty member's self-assessment in this section. In some instances, the commentary serves as evidence that a requirement has been met. In each annual performance review, the immediate supervisor comments on the individual's progress toward a continuing contract or promotion. An assessment of endowed chair candidacy is not required in the performance review. Performance reviews for the preceding three years are a necessary component of the portfolio and should reflect a pattern of professional growth and excellent performance. Performance reviews, when used with other evidence, including recommendations by the chairperson/immediate supervisor, associate dean, and dean, should verify what a candidate for continuing contract or promotion has said in the narrative.

- *Self-Assessment.* In the self-assessment, the faculty member responds to the same seven questions required for the portfolio narrative. By reviewing the annual self-assessments in chronological order, the pattern of growth required as a criterion for advancement may emerge. The supervisor, in the performance review narrative, may specifically reference statements made by the faculty member in the self-assessment by referring the portfolio reader to the self-assessment itself, rather than by restating the information contained. The faculty member is in the best position to report attainment of a number of criteria. A supervisor's concurrence with a faculty member's self-assessment ensures validity; no other evidence is required in most instances.

- *Student/Client Feedback.* Student/client feedback also contributes to the annual performance review. Students are the best source of documentation for some aspects of faculty roles, and their feedback on performance is required. The collegewide student feedback process is not standardized at the present time. Data from a standardized procedure will not be required until both have been adopted by the Faculty Senates and the College Executive Committees; however, some kind of student/client assessment of performance must be included. Many faculty members have departmental or personally developed feedback forms. The faculty member explains results as necessary within the documentation section. In addition to formalized feedback forms, applicants may choose to include unsolicited feedback from students when it clearly documents specific aspects of their performance.

- *Additional required documents.* Other required documents include one initial handout or other course handout from each of the most recent three years; one test or a description of some other assessment procedure from each of the most recent three years; examples or descriptions of teaching strategies used during each of the most recent three years; and one example or description of student achievement from each of the most recent three years. Through these documents faculty members demonstrate how they carry out their primary professional responsibilities. Evaluators should expect great variability among portfolios in this area.

- *Optional documentation.* Some portfolios contain only required documentation. Candidates for promotion to the higher academic ranks and endowed chairs, however, usually include optional materials. Because the endowed chair program is highly competitive, endowed chair portfolios normally include a variety of optional materials. The determination of how much and what to include is strictly at the discretion of the individual faculty member. These materials may include:

  — *Peer review.* Aspects of performance or the quality of participation in activities may best be substantiated by peer review. Colleagues who have observed teaching either as members of a teaching team or as independent observers, who teach sections of the same course, or who have worked with the candidate on a project or in departmental activities are qualified to present evidence of an applicant's performance. Peers are aware of contributions to curriculum development and of a willingness to share methods and materials. Those who receive students from prerequisite courses can testify to the preparedness of the students they receive. Honors or recognition received from peers can be used as documentation as well. In many instances, peer review, while not required, may enhance the portfolio.

  — *Activities congruent with mission of the college.* Applicants for promotion or the endowed chair must provide evidence of involvement in activities congruent with the mission of the college. Faculty members must be excellent teachers, but they must also contribute to the department, division, campus, and college in a manner consonant with the rank they seek. While candidates for assistant professor and associate professor are required to be involved in activities at the department, division, campus, and college levels, candidates for senior ranks, such as associate professor, professor, and senior professor, must be substantively involved in such activities. Substantive involvement implies that the individual contributes, plays an active role, and is influential in achieving the goals of the activity. Any applicant may, in addition, choose to document professional involvement outside the college in activities that are congruent with the college mission.

The guide also provides the following checklist to help evaluators review the portfolio:

- Are all required performance expectations and criteria addressed?

- Are the sources of documentation for a specific criterion appropriate?

- Are they current?

- Is the evidence adequate?

- Have multiple sources of information been used?

- Is student-centeredness apparent?

- Is continued professional growth apparent?

- Is student or other client feedback included?

- Is the appropriate number of self-assessments included?

- Is the appropriate number of performance reviews included?

- Has the immediate supervisor commented favorably in the performance reviews?

- Are administrative recommendations included? (This criterion is not required for endowed chair candidates.)

- Are the administrative recommendations consistent with one another?

- Are the sources within the portfolio consistent with one another? Are they consistent with the administrative input?

- Has evidence been put forward for involvement in activities beyond those required by primary professional responsibilities?

- Is the evidence for involvement in activities appropriate for the level of promotion sought? (Required for promotions candidates only.) (adapted from *A Guide to Assessing Performance Portfolios©*, Miami-Dade Community College, 1994)

LINKING EVALUATION TO PROFESSIONAL DEVELOPMENT

"An appraisal system, regardless of its objectives, must incorporate training opportunities...or alternative instructional resources...if it is to have any lasting effect in the classroom" (Borich, 1977, p. 43). Hammons and Watts (1983) suggest that prior to making other decisions about an evaluation system, a college should "determine what role the part-timer is to play in the institution and what responsibilities will define the role" (p. 19). "Formative applications of appraisal data...are prescriptive rather than evaluative" (Borich, 1977, p. 37). The following formative objectives, proposed by Behrendt and Parsons (1983), describe the part-timer's role and the responsibilities that define it:

• to arrive at a mutual understanding of the general institutional goals as well as specific instructional goals

• to foster an understanding of how the part-time faculty member fits into the achievement of these goals

• to help individual adjunct faculty members improve their teaching performance

• to promote communication among administrators, supervisors, and adjunct faculty members

• to increase the effectiveness and efficiency of all adjunct faculty as a team, as well as achieving parity between full- and part-time teaching staff (p. 35)

Gappa and Leslie (1993) observed that teaching evaluations should be used to help part-time faculty improve their performance by tying evaluations to development strategies that would help them develop their teaching skills. Behrendt and Parsons' (1983) summative objectives lend themselves to data collection and implementation strategies for designing a faculty development program:

• to gather information to make personnel decisions on retention, salary, promotion, and so on

• to maintain an inventory of adjunct faculty resources for subsequent use by the institution or possible reassignment or retraining

• to gather data to conduct research on the factors related to the effectiveness of part-time faculty members

• to gather information to inform internal and external audiences on the effectiveness and worth of adjunct faculty

• to use this information to help determine the needs for staff development activities (p. 35)

Summative assessment is particularly useful in making decisions involving merit and reemployment of teachers. If training and feedback have been provided as a result of formative assessments, then the summative use of data serves as a means by which the teacher's performance can be certified as adequate or not. It can, in fact, be predictive—being used to predict success in a specific teaching assignment (Borich, 1977).

RECOGNITION

A study of part-time faculty services at community colleges in a nineteen-state region uncovered few merit recognition programs. Of the 250 responding schools, outstanding part-time faculty were formally recognized by only 13.2 percent. In contrast, 60 percent reported that full-time faculty merit recognition programs had been established at their colleges (Erwin and Andrews, 1993, p. 560). The researchers observed that many of the recognition and evaluation systems were underdeveloped. These systems were described as "just getting started," "in need of systematic improvement," or "nonexistent or weak." As would be expected, colleges with no firmly established evaluation system found it difficult to recognize outstanding faculty (p. 560).

BENEFITS OF EVALUATION

The primary focus of evaluation should be positive; it should provide a basis upon which teaching and learning can be improved. Behrendt and Parsons provide a useful checklist of the benefits of evaluation. They note that evaluation benefits part-time teachers through:

- integration into the college's intellectual community and the establishment of psychological ownership of the college's mission

- improvement of individual teaching effectiveness

- increased enjoyment and satisfaction in teaching

- development of potential as a teacher

- improvement in their full-time job performance, since faculty normally teach subjects closely related to their full-time occupation.

Evaluation benefits an institution by:

- supporting better teaching performance, leading to more satisfied customers through effective learning

- creating a more stable pool of part-time teaching faculty

- providing the information necessary to make personnel decisions

- integrating a teaching faculty that understands the objectives of the institution

- increasing cooperation with local businesses and industries that generate support and act as a recruitment source for the community college

- helping evaluate program effectiveness (1983, pp. 40–41).

In our interviews, we asked college officials the following questions about the evaluation of part-time faculty:

- What are the components of the part-time faculty evaluation process at your college (or in your district)?

- What are the modes of evaluation (e.g., student evaluation, portfolios, administrative/faculty observations)?

- How often are part-time faculty evaluated?

- Do the part-time faculty receive formal recognition (e.g., teaching awards, merit increases)?

What Colleges Said About Evaluation of Part-Time Faculty

Beginning in fall 1992, **Community College of Allegheny County**'s Part-Time Faculty Committee in the Allegheny Campus English department required that each part-time faculty member have one course portfolio on file. The following items must be included in the portfolio:

- a course outline and list of assignments

- copies of at least three writing assignments

- a written rationale for one of the writing assignments

- a one-page summary of the instructor's philosophy for teaching writing

All part-time instructors are required to submit a course outline for each course they are teaching, based on the department syllabus. New part-time instructors who have not previously submitted a portfolio must prepare the above materials and submit them in a manila folder by the due date. If the course outline is already on file, as it should be, they need not submit another copy. Part-time instructors who have submitted a portfolio are not asked to submit another. They may update their materials as they wish, including current course outlines, and add to the portfolio on file any of the above items that are not already in the folder. Instructors will be invited in future semesters to update or add to materials on file. Typically, portfolios are compiled after the first year of teaching, then updated each semester or as requested.

When all materials have been received, two or three members of the Part-Time Faculty Committee review the portfolio. Each portfolio receives one of three ratings: excellent, satisfactory, unsatisfactory. If the portfolio is excellent or satisfactory, this will be recorded in the folder. An unsatisfactory rating indicates that the committee feels that improvements to the portfolio are warranted, and the coordinator notifies the instructor in writing of the requested changes. The instructor then has the opportunity to make changes and additions to the portfolio. Once revisions have been made, the portfolio will be re-evaluated. If the instructor does not respond to the request for changes or improvements in the portfolio, a copy of the request for improvements will be placed in the instructor's folder, indicating that the changes were not made. Criteria for evaluation of portfolios are completeness and thoroughness; conformity with college regulations and contract stipulations; conformity with department policy and syllabus; conformity with developmental course and review requirements; and consistency with department syllabi, developmental course requirements, and the instructional level.

The evaluation process at **Central Piedmont Community College** includes several procedures. The department head or a full-time faculty member designated by the department head observes all new part-time faculty in their first quarter of teaching. Following the classroom observation, the department head and the part-time faculty member hold a conference. They review performance and discuss needed changes. After the first quarter, each part-time faculty member is observed every fifth quarter through the duration of employment. In addition to observations and conferences, each faculty member is evaluated by students using a student opinion survey form. This is a computer Scantron survey, and results are compiled and sent to the faculty member and department head. In cases where the student opinion survey indicates a consistent pattern of concern, additional conferences are held.

Adjunct faculty at **Centralia College** are evaluated by their students during the seventh week of every quarter. Full-time are evaluated once a year. The results are sent to the faculty member and the appropriate division chair, and a copy is put in the personnel file in the instruction office. The division chair may prepare a written evaluation of the part-timer's performance; the evaluation could be drawn from a class observation or the part-timer's departmental involvement. Part-time faculty who wish to apply for extended studies funds must complete a self-evaluation.

At **College of the Canyons**, students evaluate part-time faculty, and faculty conduct a self-evaluation that reviews accomplishments since their last evaluation and sets goals to be accomplished before the next evaluation. A conference is held with the department chair to discuss the evaluations. Additionally, one person conducts a class observation. This person is usually a full-time faculty volunteer chosen by the department chair.

At **Community College of Aurora**, students evaluate part-timers every semester for several years, but the number of years over which evaluations are conducted varies among divisions. After several years, the part-timer is evaluated once a year; long-time faculty are evaluated approximately every other year. Faculty development officers receive the results of these evaluations and design training for all part-timers based upon this information. For example, if student evaluations indicate that faculty, in general, are having problems with lesson planning, development officers design and put on a workshop on that topic. Classroom observations are also conducted. The college has decentralized the review systems, and individual divisions design their own review policies and procedures.

Adjunct faculty members who have been employed at **County College of Morris** in their present rank for at least five years, have taught during at least ten sessions, and meet the education requirements for promotion may submit applications for promotion to the next higher rank to their department chairperson and to the associate dean of academic services. The chair reviews promotion applications and, in consultation with the associate dean of academic services, makes a recommendation to the division dean. The division dean then makes a recommendation to the vice president of academic affairs, who forwards a recommendation to the president. The president sends recommendations for promotion to the board for consideration. Faculty members whose application for promotion in rank have been considered are notified of the outcome by their department chairperson. The purpose of the adjunct faculty evaluation is to improve the quality of the educational process, develop the teaching potential of all adjunct faculty members, and provide reasonable academic criteria for granting promotion and reappointment. All adjunct faculty members are formally evaluated during their first session and at least every third teaching session for at least five years. Those who have taught at CCM for five years are evaluated at least once every ten teaching sessions or five years, whichever comes first. The college reserves the right to evaluate adjunct faculty members more frequently than indicated in these guidelines. The evaluation procedure includes administrative and student evaluations. A self-evaluation is incorporated into the application for promotion, but it need not be submitted for each evaluation period. Once yearly a classroom observation occurs. All aspects of the evaluation procedure are considered when the college makes a promotion decision.

The administrative evaluation is based upon criteria such as teaching effectiveness, departmental service, administrative effectiveness, and professional growth. The department chair, or a designee, conducts the administrative portion of the evaluation. Any written evaluation reports are presented to the adjunct faculty member at the evaluation conference. If an adjunct faculty member has applied for promotion, the chair evaluating this promotion request sends an exact copy of the completed recommendation form to the faculty member prior to its being forwarded to the division dean. The adjunct faculty member signs the final evaluation report, signifying that it has been read and reviewed in consultation with the department chair. At the evaluation conference with the department chair or someone designated by the chair, the adjunct faculty member is given a copy of the final administrative evaluation report, and the faculty member is given the opportunity to respond in writing.

The student evaluation, titled the Student Opinion Report, asks the student about teacher preparedness, teaching style, and organization of the course. More unusual questions include: "Why did you take this course?" "Approximately how many hours did you devote to this course per week outside of class?" and "What is your opinion of this questionnaire?"

Cowley County Community College uses a three-pronged approach to part-time faculty evaluation. The first semester an adjunct faculty member teaches at the college, the dean of instruction, or one of the two associate deans, observes an entire class session. After the first semester, part-timers are observed by the director of the instructional center once a year. The observation is less evaluative and more developmental, designed to promote more interactive instructional strategies. Students evaluate part-time faculty every semester; each class taught by the part-timer is evaluated—for example, a part-timer teaching Composition I and Composition II will have two evaluations. Evaluations are kept on file, and copies are returned to the instructor.

Cuesta College has a threefold evaluation process for part-time faculty members—student, peer, and self-evaluations with an administrative review. All evaluative processes occur at least once during the first semester that a part-timer teaches and every other year afterwards, unless there is some indication of a problem that would justify more frequent evaluations. The dean of instruction and division chair oversee the evaluation process. We describe these processes here in their entirety because, while other colleges' handbooks or policy materials described one or more of these processes, they were typically described in less detail; this rather lengthy description is included here to provide a representation of others that were mentioned in the interviews.

The purpose of the faculty evaluation process is to assist faculty in becoming more effective by identifying aspects of performance that meet district standards and developing a plan for improving those aspects of performance that fail to meet district standards. The division chair holds a preconference with the instructor prior to administering the evaluation instruments. The preconference includes:

- for new instructors: a review of evaluation procedure and examination of instruments to be used; examination of course handouts, including course information, grading procedures, attendance, assignments, and readings; and a determination of the objectives of the current evaluation

- for continuing instructors: a review of stated goals from the preceding evaluation; a determination of progress made in areas that needed improvement; a review of evaluation procedures and examination of evaluation instruments to be used; an examination of course handouts; and a determination of the objectives of the current evaluation

The instructor is required to bring to the preconference responses to the following:

- What do you perceive as your teaching strengths?

- In what areas would you like to improve, given the opportunity?

- In what way do you feel you are contributing to the accomplishment of the Cuesta College plan?

- Do you make a contribution to shared governance at Cuesta College?

- What are your long-term goals as an instructor?

- List an immediate goal to be accomplished this semester.

- How do you propose to accomplish it?

The self-evaluation questions include:

- What are the principal activities involved in performing your job? (Be specific.)

- What are your immediate and long-term goals? To what degree do they support unit and college goals?

- How do you intend to achieve them?

- How do you evaluate your effectiveness in achieving these goals?

- In what respects have you been particularly successful? What are your strengths?

- In what areas have you been dissatisfied with your performance? What specific plans for improvement have you considered?

- How could the district assist you in improving your effectiveness?

- Additional comments, if desired.

A classroom evaluation visit is scheduled, and prior to the visit, the instructor completes this plan by responding to the following:

- Describe course content to be discussed/activity to be performed.

- Describe the methodology that is planned to convey the above content/activity.

- Briefly outline the time schedule planned for the class session.

- Attach copies of any handouts/course materials that may be useful/helpful to the observer.

A student evaluation form includes responses (in a range of excellent to unacceptable) to the following statements and questions.

- The relationship between course objectives and what is actually taught.

- The use of methods and materials which are challenging to students and appropriate to the subject matter.

- The relationship of the exams/methods of evaluation to subject matter.

- The grading procedure for this class.

- The instructor's organization of this course.

- The instructor's use of class time.

- The instructor's consistency in beginning and ending this class on time.

- The instructor's demonstrated knowledge of the subject matter for this course.

- The instructor's encouragement of students to appreciate different perspectives and/or approaches to relating to problems and issues pertinent to this course.

- The instructor's interest and enthusiasm for the subject.

- The instructor's ability to communicate subject matter to students.

- The instructor's ability to create a classroom atmosphere which promotes learning.

- The instructor's speaking ability.

- The instructor's sensitivity to the different ways in which students learn.

- The instructor's patience, fairness, and promptness in evaluating and discussing student work.

- The instructor's respect for the diverse cultural backgrounds of students.

- The instructor's respect for the confidentiality of information from and about students.

- The instructor's availability for consultation during scheduled office hours.

- What do you believe your instructor has done especially well in teaching this course?

- What do you believe your instructor could do to improve his or her teaching of this course?

- Is there anything specific, positive or negative, not previously noted you would like to add concerning this class, or other conditions in this class which affected your opportunity to learn?

- Do you feel that the classroom instructor presented this evaluation process without attempting to influence your response? (If no, please explain.)

Peer evaluation occurs within the first year for each new employee and every three years for each continuing employee. Division chairs/directors schedule and arrange peer evaluations for all certificated part-time staff. The team of evaluators may be chosen from any of the full-time certificated staff, preferably from the division of the person being evaluated. The division chair/director appoints one committee member, and upon formation of the committee appoints a chairperson of the team; the faculty member to be evaluated appoints one committee member; the division chair/director and the faculty member to be evaluated mutually agree on the third committee member.

The evaluation committee and the instructor hold a pre-evaluation meeting one to two weeks in advance of the main evaluation meeting. At this meeting, they review the self-evaluation instrument and identify objectives, class structure, syllabi, instructor's teaching style, and updated course outline. They also review the instructor's additional activities, such as committee participation, professional activities, and leadership experiences. The person being evaluated chooses an observation pattern—a specific hour for the team to visit the work area or a one-week period for drop-in visits. The person to be evaluated also selects one of the following peer/student evaluation instruments: peer observation of instruction and Cuesta's student evaluation instrument, a non-classroom peer evaluation instrument produced by each educational service area, or a small group individual diagnosis (SGID) method, a five-step process involving the course instructor, students in the instructor's class, and a faculty colleague trained to act as a facilitator. The committee and the instructor also review the peer and student evaluation instruments and schedule a follow-up and post-evaluation meeting time.

At the post-evaluation meeting, ideally held one to three days after the evaluation, the chair of the team informs the person being evaluated of the peer review results. The completed evaluation is then placed in the official personnel file, along with self- and student evaluations. An opportunity for the person being evaluated to comment is provided on the final post-evaluation document. The file is made available to the dean/director/division chair for use in completing the administrative review.

The peer observation of instruction uses a rating scale from "unable to assess" to "very good" and includes the following major areas: clarity (method used to explain or clarify concepts and principles); interaction (techniques used to foster students' class participation); organization (ways of organizing or structuring subject matter); and disclosure (explicitness concerning course requirements and grading criteria). In addition, the peer observer must rate course subject matter competence, utilization of a comprehensive grading procedure, and provision of effective overall instruction. Additional comments and suggestions are encouraged.

The division chair compiles the data once all evaluation instruments have been completed, prepares a summary and analysis from the results, notes areas meeting or exceeding district standards, and identifies areas that are below district expectations. In a postconference with the instructor, the division chair reviews the results; the instructor receives a review copy of the report prior to the conference. The instructor is allowed to react and respond to the evaluation report and its implications; the division chair provides constructive criticism based on the evaluation report; and the division chair and instructor can mutually develop objectives to be achieved by the next evaluation.

The process of evaluation of part-timers is similar to that for full-timers at **Cuyahoga Community College**. Part-timers are evaluated during the first quarter of employment and afterwards on an annual basis. Evaluation is a combination of classroom observation and student evaluation. Faculty have a pre-observation meeting with the evaluator, and a post-observation meeting is also held. Full-time faculty are paid to assist in the evaluation process for part-time faculty. The record of the evaluation goes into the part-timer's personnel file.

At **De Anza College**, an agreement between the Faculty Association and the district calls for evaluation of part-time faculty members at least once within the first three quarters of employment. The evaluator may be a dean, a division chair, a department coordinator, or a full-time faculty member designated by the administration. This evaluator visits the class and collects the student evaluations as well. Ordinarily, the evaluator visits the part-timer's class and writes an account of what happened during the visit on an official evaluation form. The part-timer is required to sign the evaluation before it is placed in the personnel file. Signing the form does not indicate that the part-timer agrees with the contents of the evaluation—only that it has been read. If the part-timer disagrees with some part of the evaluation, he or she may write objections on a separate piece of paper that is attached to the official evaluation and placed in the personnel file. No evaluation or any other material is added to the personnel file unless the part-time faculty member is informed of the addition.

The administrative and peer evaluation form includes both objective and narrative data. The rating system requires responses of satisfactory or better, satisfactory but needs improvement in specific area(s), unsatisfactory, N/O (not observed), and N/A (not applicable). Section I evaluates the following professional qualities:

- *Professionalism.* Keeps current in discipline. Demonstrates cooperation and sensitivity in working with colleagues and staff. Accepts criticism. Submits required departmental reports/information. Maintains adequate and appropriate records. Observes health and safety regulations. Attends required meetings. Maintains office hours and is accessible to students.

- *Professional Contributions.* Contributes academically to the discipline, department, and district. Participates in special assignments, committees, projects, research and development areas as needed in the discipline, department, and district. Shares in faculty responsibilities.

Section I ends with narrative comments on professional qualities specifying areas of excellence and areas requiring improvement.

Section II evaluates job performance and includes four assignment areas—classroom faculty, counselors, librarians, and resource faculty (e.g., health professionals). Only the assignment area of classroom faculty is featured here.

- *The teacher:* Uses current materials and theories. Employs multiple teaching approaches when applicable. Uses materials pertinent to the course outline. Teaches at an appropriate level for the course. Communicates ideas clearly, concisely, and effectively. Paces classes according to the level and material presented. Maintains a student-faculty relationship that is conducive to learning. Demonstrates sensitivity to differing student learning styles. Stimulates student interest in the material presented. Tests student performance in fair and valid ways. Uses class time efficiently. Provides students with a written explanation of the evaluation process, expectations and requirements, assignments, course content, relevant dates, and other information. Demonstrates sensitivity in working with students of diverse racial and ethnic backgrounds, sexual orientations, and physical and mental disabilities.

Section II ends with narrative comments on job performance, based on observation, or evaluation visits. These comments specify areas of excellence and areas requiring improvement. Section III is the evaluator's comprehensive summary statement, which may include, in addition to an overall evaluation, professional activities not previously mentioned, suggestions for further growth, and professional contributions to the district. Section IV is reserved for the faculty member's comments.

At De Anza College, part-time faculty have hiring preference, which is defined as hiring rights with the college. The greater the number of terms a part-timer has been available to teach a class, the greater the rights to the next available assignment. A college official noted that "it is sort of an elaborate hiring order." If the part-timer's evaluation is poor, he or she is not placed on the preference list or is not hired for the next semester. Thus, the first evaluation determines whether part-timers are placed on the preference list; those on the preference list are evaluated at least every three years. Consistently positive evaluations make a part-time faculty member eligible for re-employment preference.

Department heads at **Greenville Technical College** visit classrooms and observe each new part-time faculty member twice during the first term of employment. One of these visits is announced. After the first term, there is one unannounced visit each academic year. New full-time faculty are visited three times during the nine-month probationary period; the department head visits twice, once unannounced, and the dean visits once, announced. Two visits annually, one announced, continue after the probationary period has ended. Student evaluations are conducted for every class for the first two terms of the part-timer's employment. Students respond using a five-point rating scale from "strongly agree" to "not applicable" or "do not know." The first four statements address student characteristics and plans:

As a student, I...

- was prepared academically to take this class.

- attend this class regularly.

- study adequately for this class.

- would take another class from this instructor.

A conference is held with each new part-time faculty member prior to the first classroom observation to review the purpose and method of the observation. Within a week of the observation, a conference is held with the instructor. All classroom visits are documented by an observation instrument developed by the Academic Council for collegewide use. The Academic Council is an advisory team of faculty representing all divisions of the college.

At **Hagerstown Junior College,** part-time faculty evaluation includes a supervisory visit and student surveys, conducted the first time the part-timer teaches and every third course thereafter. The results of the student surveys are provided to the instructor; a computer analysis provides the institutional average so that each instructor can determine item by item his or her performance in comparison to others in the college. Letters accompany the evaluations that indicate whether or not the performance is acceptable; another letter highlights any specific problems and identifies resources and the person to call to review the problem. If a serious problem exists, the letter identifies who will be contacting the instructor for further discussion. Any student comments that are included on the survey form are typed and presented to the instructor. The department chair and the vice president of instruction review the comments.

Part-time faculty evaluation at **Kirkwood Community College** occurs every semester of the first year's service. A class observation is conducted by the department head, and a meeting is held with the instructor to review the results. The observation report is a modified version of that used at **De Anza College.** Currently, there are no firm policies regarding evaluation procedures; however, after the first year the college encourages evaluation every other year. The instructor is required to administer student evaluations for each class.

Evaluation at **Lakeland Community College** is decentralized, although the college is working now on an integrated process. Students evaluate all part-time faculty each quarter and, in many departments, department faculty or the division dean carry out in-class observations. Most part-timers are observed during the first two quarters of service.

Originally, the division representatives at **Metropolitan Community College** conducted once-a-year classroom observations; but increasing numbers of part-timers created a scheduling problem that was partially relieved by adding to the number of observers. Student evaluations also are used and reviewed by division representatives.

Part-time faculty evaluation at **Modesto Junior College** is decentralized and division-specific; however, the college plans to move toward a new system within the next two years. Currently, part-timers are evaluated through an observation by an administrator and by student evaluations once every six semesters. Evaluation is required for every new faculty member, but after the initial evaluation, the state mandates a cycle of only once every six semesters. Some divisions independently conduct regular evaluations.

The Evaluation Committee consists, at minimum, of one peer and the immediate administrators. Peer review means involvement in the process of at least one full-time faculty member who is mutually agreed upon by the person being evaluated and the administrators. The peer evaluator(s) and the immediate administrator make at least one performance observation, meet with the Evaluation Committee to summarize findings, and meet with the person being evaluated to discuss these findings. The college encourages student and self-evaluations.

The primary criterion for evaluation is the quality of performance of professional responsibilities. A set of criteria for evaluation of faculty has been developed by the Yosemite Faculty Association and the Yosemite Community College District. The written criteria are given to faculty by their immediate administrator. Faculty members scheduled for evaluation are given a current description of their assignment by the immediate administrator prior to beginning the evaluation process. Evaluators must have knowledge of the rights and responsibilities of the district and of the faculty member being evaluated. Administrators and faculty involved in the evaluation process are trained in the use of faculty evaluation procedures provided by the Yosemite Faculty Association and the Yosemite Community College District.

Richland College is experimenting with a new way of conceptualizing the evaluation process, with the goal of tying evaluation to the faculty development process. The recent acquisition of a Title III grant has allowed the college to establish teaching and learning teams across the developmental reading and writing, English, and English-as-a-Second-Language disciplines. The motivation for implementing these teams was a reading and writing program review report that recommended that the part-time faculty evaluation process be improved. The teaching and learning teams include one full-time faculty member and several part-time faculty. The teams decide what they want to work on as a team to improve teaching and learning, visit each other's classes, and make recommendations to each other for improving teaching. This holistic process is considered to be an improvement over the former process in which a classroom observation was made by a department chair, followed by a consultation between the chair and the instructor.

Each new part-time faculty member at **Rio Salado Community College** is required to have three successive evaluations, beginning with the first term of teaching; two of the evaluations must be in-person peer evaluations; the third can consist of student evaluations. The faculty chair and mentors evaluate the quality of the four essential instructional skills identified by the college as keys to instructional excellence:

- introduction—providing a connection with previous learning

- focus on topic—stating an objective for each instructional activity

- assessment and adjustment—continually assessing student learning and adjusting instruction when necessary

- content summary—asking students to summarize/synthesize what they have learned at the end of each class session

Prior to the observation, the instructor completes a self-assessment form and has it ready for the observer at the observation time.

A follow-up conference occurs between the faculty chair and the part-time instructor after the observation. The part-timer receives the evaluation by mail, along with the appointment time for this conference. Often, these conferences must be held by phone. The evaluation form must be signed by the observer and the observed, and the observed faculty member may include his or her comments as well. Signing the form does not signify agreement with the content. The college is trying to make the evaluation process a mentoring experience.

At the beginning of each semester, faculty chairs receive a list of all instructors, the number of evaluations each has had, when they occurred, how many more evaluations they must have, and whether the evaluations should be done by peers or students. Student evaluations are given in each class, but they are not included in the formal evaluation unless they are necessary for reaching an appropriate number of evaluations.

The college is moving toward higher-level evaluation techniques that look at teaching techniques as well as student outcomes. A portfolio system has been tested, but was not successful. Those involved in the pilot project learned that faculty needed training and evaluators needed to use several levels of evaluation to make the portfolio a useful tool. Asking a beginning faculty member to put a portfolio together is requiring too much, but asking an experienced faculty member to do so is appropriate. Faculty are developing a model for advancement through training that corresponds to advanced levels of evaluation and pay. With this system, one should be able to look into the database, identify the training that a faculty member has completed, receive the evaluation results, and determine what the next steps should be.

The current evaluation system at **Santa Barbara City College** is a two-tiered process. Student evaluations are conducted in every class each semester; the survey results are reviewed by the department chair. All new certified part-time instructors are observed by the department chair or a designated full-time certified instructor once a semester for two consecutive semesters. Department chairs give a written response to the instructor following each visit and submit a copy to the vice president of academic affairs. After the first year's probationary period, part-timers are evaluated every two years. Faculty are encouraged to administer student surveys every semester, but they are required to do so only once every two years after the first year of teaching. Department chairs have the authority to require a formal evaluation of a part-time instructor at any time.

Part-time faculty at **Santa Fe Community College** are evaluated according to the same teaching criteria as full-time faculty; however, full-time faculty are required to submit a portfolio/report on teaching, learning, curriculum scholarship, and service. Part-timers may participate in curriculum development, scholarship, and service; but they are not required to do so and are not evaluated on these activities.

Department chairs observe at least one class taught by each part-timer during the first semester of teaching. After that, the adjunct coordinator or the chair observes at least one class during the second semester and one class each following year. In addition, course materials are submitted for review, and student evaluations from every class and every term are reviewed by the department chair. Also, part-timers are provided with college data that allow them to compare retention and drop-out rates, GPA, class size, and other variables of their classes with college norms. Evaluations are not formally used in making hiring decisions, in the sense that part-timers are not guaranteed employment beyond the semester for which they are hired. The evaluation system is considered a a tool for improving teaching and learning during that semester only, not a process to support continuous employment.

At **Schoolcraft College,** students evaluate part-timers in every course they teach, every time they teach it. If these evaluations are above the college-determined cut-off score, no other evaluations are conducted by college personnel. When student evaluations fall below the college-determined cut-off score, full evaluations are conducted. The department chair or a full-time faculty designee conducts classroom observations, and a full report is generated. A negative evaluation terminates the employment of a probationary part-timer. Non-probationary employees are given support to correct deficiencies. If subsequent evaluations are negative, employment is terminated.

Program directors at **St. Petersburg Junior College** observe part-timers' classes during their first term of service. Student surveys are used, although the results of these surveys are not part of a formal, annual evaluation process. The results of the student surveys are given to the individual faculty members after the completion of the term.

Evaluation of part-time faculty is identical to that of full-timers at **Tarrant County Junior College**: they are observed by their supervisor and evaluated by their students. The appraisal package includes an instructional visit appraisal, a professional responsibility appraisal, a student appraisal, a self-appraisal, an evaluator-instructor conference, and an appraisal summary memo. A copy of the appraisal package must be completed during the first year of employment for full-time faculty and preferably during the first semester for part-timers. One package must be completed each year during the first two years of employment, preferably during the first semester, for both full- and part-timers. A minimum of one appraisal package is completed once every two years for all full- and part-time instructors in their third and fourth years of employment. After the fourth year, a minimum of one appraisal package is completed once every three years for all instructors. Student evaluations must be administered each year for all faculty regardless of the years of service.

At **Triton College**, the department chair and the full-time faculty member who has been assigned to mentor the part-timer are responsible for the evaluation process. The mentor submits the evaluation to the chair, who then recommends that the dean either rehire or not rehire the instructor. Student evaluations are included in the evaluation process.

All part-time faculty at **Valencia Community College** are evaluated by students in every class they teach. The chair and faculty member review student evaluations as a part of the chair's formal evaluation. All part-timers are observed in class by the department chair or a designee during the first two successive terms of employment. If part-time faculty continue to be hired for additional terms, the frequency of classroom observations becomes the same as that for full-timers. These evaluations are reviewed by the faculty member and the chair. Observations are made only by those who have been specifically trained in classroom observation. Formal evaluations are conducted by the department chair on an annual basis, but no later than the second successive term after initial employment. The chair's formal evaluation considers whatever information the chair and faculty member wish to include, and is not limited to student evaluations and classroom observation sessions. Part-timers who have been determined to be deficient in any area of instruction are frequently required to enter a program designed to provide development.

There is no part-time faculty evaluation system currently in place at **Vista Community College**; college officials observe that efforts by the unions to link evaluation efforts to job security have resulted in no formal system being developed. Evaluations that do occur are described as intermittent, sporadic, and informal efforts.

At **Westchester Community College**, new part-time faculty are observed for the first two semesters they teach. If both evaluations are satisfactory, instructors are observed either every semester or periodically thereafter, depending on the number of part-time faculty in the department. For example, the math department, with seventeen full-timers and fifty part-timers, probably would choose not to observe each part-timer each semester. In addition, part-timers are required to submit copies of their midterm and final examinations for review by the department chair.

WHAT COLLEGES SAY ABOUT RECOGNIZING PART-TIMERS

The majority of colleges whose officials we interviewed did not have formal recognition programs for part-time faculty. Some indicated that they had no formal recognition plans for either full- or part-time faculty. And some indicated that future plans included special recognition categories and ceremonies that would include part-timers. One college official commented that full-time faculty at his college had gone on record opposing teaching awards for part-timers, although they had approved of providing awards for service to the institution.

Cuesta College has a process of making faculty awards, and on some occasions part-timers have been recipients. The primary selection criterion for the M'May Diffley Award for Faculty Excellence is excellence in the role of a faculty member at Cuesta College. Other criteria include community and/or campus activism, involvement in the arts, and the ability to motivate science students. Full- and part-time faculty may nominate one candidate, describing in detail how the nominee meets the primary criterion, and describing in detail how one or more of the additional criteria apply. An ad hoc selection committee appointed by the Academic Senate President includes four faculty members and at least one past Diffley award recipient. The selection committee must reflect the variety of academic clusters and segments, and it may include one part-time faculty member who is a current member of the Academic Senate. A cash award from the endowment earnings of the M'May Diffley Award for Faculty Excellence is given to the recipient. In addition, there is a faculty grant program for which part-timers are eligible to apply for teaching and learning training. The funds are raised by the college foundation; both full- and part-time faculty are eligible to apply.

Cuyahoga Community College, Kirkwood Community College, and **Richland College** recognize part-timers for years of service. Cuyahoga Community College recognizes part-timers for twenty and twenty-five years of service by awarding a plaque at the annual campus convocation program. The college also has proposed that a Teaching Excellence Award, including an honorarium, be given annually to a part-time faculty member on each campus. At Kirkwood Community College, this recognition is made at five-year intervals: after five years, instructors receive a walnut paper weight, after ten years a desk pen, and after fifteen years a plaque printed with their name and years of service to the college. One part-time faculty member has been with the college for twenty-two years.

Greenville Technical College's You Make a Difference recognition program is held twice a year for all employees who have "gone beyond the call of duty." Each department/division has a successful nominee; each employee recognized receives a "You Make a Difference" mug or T-shirt. Part-time faculty members have won this award on several occasions. The college has established another reward system that recognizes outstanding performance. Boxes of Cracker Jacks tell faculty that they are "crackerjack" instructors, and PayDay candy bars accompany notes that say, "You deserve an extra pay day."

Lakeland Community College has no established teaching awards. How ever, discussions are underway to provide longevity awards for part-time faculty. Each spring the college hosts a part-time faculty recognition dinner, giving service awards for serving on part-time faculty committees. The president of the college, the vice president of academic affairs, and the chairman of the board of trustees make remarks about the important role of part-time faculty at the college.

Metroplitan Community College, Richland College, and **Valencia Community College** have established teaching excellence awards recognition programs. Part-time faculty are eligible for these teaching awards.

Rio Salado Community College is studying the feasibility of a salary schedule based on staff development, performance, and other criteria. A brief recognition ceremony for faculty is held at graduation. Faculty chairs name the faculty member to be recognized, and one person is recognized from each area. Each recipient is given a certificate, a letter from the president, and has his or her picture taken with the president. Part-time faculty are eligible for this recognition, which is determined by student input and evaluations as well as input from other faculty members based on their observations and discussions with students.

CONCLUSIONS

Recognition of good teaching is not only a matter of giving continuing attention to it, but of trying to increase the worth of doing it well. Although there are many means of recognizing and valuing teaching within both the individual's and institution's grasp, ultimately we are facing the values abstractly held by the profession and given concrete form in institutional and individual practices (Eble, 1970, p. 3).

The admonition is old and the source unknown, but the advice is sage and clear: "To achieve a goal, you must inspect what you expect." If good teaching, as Boyer observes, is at the heart of the college experience, then the college that wishes for its students and, ultimately, its community to hold it in high regard, to respect the work that it does and the services it provides, must examine that work and those services. If a college expects its teachers to cause learning to happen—an apt definition of teaching—then it should regularly inspect the processes and the products of the classroom experience. Yet there are significant indications that unsatisfactory performance by a part-time teacher is not and may never be detected; they teach at odd hours, often away from campus, and without direct supervision (Boggs, 1984). Most studies report that evaluation does not occur or needs radical revision before it can be used to provide any assurance that quality teaching is occurring (Bonham, 1982; Hammons and Watts, 1983; Leslie et al., 1982; Scheibmeir, 1980). Others report that most evaluation plans are poorly implemented, are inconsistent, are too cumbersome, have inadequate follow-up, are conducted too late in the semester, are conducted too sporadically, do not distinguish between good and bad teachers, and are generally too weak or incomplete. Moreover, there are too many part-timers and too few evaluators for fair and competent assessment (Erwin and Andrews, 1993, p. 560).

Another adage comes to mind: "If a task is worth doing, it is worth doing well." The difficulties associated with faculty evaluation must be addressed; part-time faculty cannot be left out of the evaluation loop because programs are too unwieldy or poorly designed. Part-timers represent too large a cadre of responsible instructional figures to ignore their performance and their impact on students and the reputation of the institution. Faculty evaluation should occur regularly, fairly, and productively.

Part-timers should know what the standards are, should have opportunities to demonstrate that they can meet them, should be able to rely upon consistent processes that will evaluate their performance, and should be allowed opportunities to improve based upon feedback from the evaluation process. The primary use of data generated by evaluation should be to help faculty become more effective teachers. As Gappa and Leslie (1993) observe, "it is far sounder to invest in expanding the capacity of people than to discard more or less capriciously anyone who does not measure up from the very beginning" (p. 275).

Program evaluation and faculty evaluation occur when colleges take seriously their responsibilities for helping students achieve their educational goals. While individual faculty members should not be expected to assume total responsibility for meeting all of each student's needs, they should be identified as critical pieces in a mosaic of responsibility. Even when responsibility for student achievement is collective, that responsibility does not reduce the responsibility of individual faculty or the importance of singular classroom experiences. The only danger, as Boyer observes, lies "in systems in which all are said to be responsible" but in which "none can be held accountable for what happens or does not happen" (1987, p. 158).

Finally, the recognition of outstanding teaching and teachers reinforces the best of what we are:

> Teachers teach, students learn, in bad weather as well as good. Some measures can be taken...that might increase recognition of teaching, both in its visibility and in rewards....Teaching comes into prominence to some degree as departments, colleges, and universities examine their criteria for good teaching, their procedures for reviewing it, and their stated expectations with regard to faculty performance. Such examination is necessary if reward is to follow recognition and if a college community as a whole is to perceive the high place of teaching in the reward structure (Eble, 1970, pp. 5–6).

CHAPTER 7

It behooves one to adapt oneself to the times if one wants to enjoy continued good fortune.

—Niccolo Machiavelli

CREATING THE MOSAIC FOR A COMMON CAUSE

Putting the Pieces Together

We opened the discussion of this study of the employment and integration of part-time faculty in American community colleges with one of Gappa and Leslie's (1993) observations—that arguing about the place of part-time faculty in colleges and universities is a useless exercise. Positioning ourselves for or against their presence in these institutions is a futile activity. Part-time faculty are a reality in American institutions of higher education. Research data indicate that part-timers have increased steadily in number over the past twenty years, that they represent increasingly larger percentages of the total number of all college faculty, and that they will play a major role in teaching for the foreseeable future. Their numbers are swelling as increasing demands on higher education and declining funding combine with impending waves of faculty retirement and the resulting faculty shortages. Colleges must change the way they think about providing educational services in the future. Although the arguments surrounding instructional quality continue to polarize observers of this phenomenon, there is no doubt that part-timers will have an extraordinary impact on the ways in which community colleges respond to these challenges.

Yet, even within the maelstrom created by these challenges, this study reveals colleges thoughtfully exploring and addressing their practices, policies, beliefs, and assumptions surrounding the use of part-time faculty. These colleges and their leaders are investigating and changing what numerous researchers and writers define as the building blocks of their organizational "cultures" (Schein, 1985, 1992; Trice and Beyer, 1993).

In *The Cultures of Work Organizations,* Trice and Beyer (1993) refer to practices, policies, legends, myths, stories, and organizational hierarchies as the *forms* of the organizational culture. However, beliefs, values, assumptions, expectations, and ideologies are the deeper, underlying, and intangible *substance* of the culture—sometimes evidencing and sometimes contradicting the cultural forms. While a business may have "Customer service is job one" in its mission statement (cultural form), the treatment of its clients by employees might demonstrate a different sort of value (cultural substance). The tension between form and substance constantly changes; an organizational culture develops over time as the organization and its leaders face the problems of internal integration and external adaptation.

In this research, we directly explored the cultural forms—the policies, practices, and procedure—and indirectly observed the cultural substance—the values, beliefs, and assumptions—of community colleges that have focused on the part-time faculty issue. The consensus of those we interviewed was that part-time faculty would be hired in greater numbers in the future and that colleges must find better ways of integrating them into the life of the institution. Important challenges will shape the cultures of our community colleges. From the responses to our interview questions and the written descriptions of successful programs and services, we offer the following recommendation to colleges striving to improve their use and integration of part-time faculty: **Colleges must take serious steps toward improving the utilization and integration of part-time faculty.** To design a viable utilization and integration plan, colleges should consider the following implementation strategies:

All part-time faculty should be recruited, selected, and hired with clear purpose and direction. A college should clearly define what it wants to accomplish with part-time faculty. Gappa and Leslie recommend that colleges think about what they can do with part-time faculty and what they cannot do without them (1993, p. 234). It is important to know how many part-time faculty are employed, what roles they are asked to play, how well they play these roles, and whether or not the roles are appropriate. Answers to these questions will help colleges assess whether the numbers and assignments of part-timers are justified and whether the additional students institutions are able to enroll as a result of increased use of part-timers put too serious a strain on the institutions' infrastructure. Affirmative action guidelines should be used as vehicles for increasing diversity at the institution, initially in the ranks of the part-time faculty and eventually within the ranks of the full-time faculty. Finally, the protocol for the hiring of full-time faculty, especially when that protocol includes a mandatory teaching demonstration, should be followed in the hiring of all part-time faculty. As a general rule, department chairs primarily make part-time hiring decisions; in circumstances where this practice will continue, chairs should be given formal training in selection and hiring practices. Other personnel, such as program directors and full-time and part-time faculty, also should be involved in the selection and hiring processes, and they, too, should be trained in appropriate hiring protocol.

All part-time faculty should be required to participate in substantial orientation activities and provided with faculty support structures. Orientation for part-time faculty should be a mandatory activity that covers a broad array of institutional priorities. However, part-timers' introduction to this new environment should not be limited to a single session on college practices and expectations but should be continued with a carefully planned series of opportunities to familiarize the part-timer with the college and the expectations it has of its faculty, its students, and its services. Moreover, orientation programs should be tied to the college's ongoing professional development activities, helping faculty keep up-to-date in their disciplines and develop successful instructional strategies, articulating college expectations, and creating and sustaining faculty collaboration activities such as mentor relationships within and between disciplines. Part-time faculty report that their most valuable staff development activities are occasions during which they can share teaching experiences and innovations with other teachers in their discipline. Finally, a college handbook, designed for all faculty, is an important guide to the college, its students, and its services and support centers; a handbook should be provided to each part-time faculty member.

All part-time faculty should be required to participate in professional development activities. Well-informed and instructionally accomplished faculty are essential to student success. Today, at increasing numbers of colleges, part-time faculty represent more than 50 percent of the total faculty, and they represent the total faculty for many students who enroll in the institution. The college should expect the same level of teaching performance of part-time faculty as of full-time, and part-time faculty should have the same advantages and opportunities to improve their teaching as do full-time. Part-time faculty should be required to attend professional development activities that are scheduled conveniently for those with nontraditional teaching schedules, and they should be strongly encouraged to attend others that are available to all faculty. They should be required to engage in a mentor relationship within their own discipline area with either a more experienced part-time faculty member or with a full-time faculty member for at least their first full teaching term at the college. Colleges that require participation in professional development activities and include compensation for professional development, compensate the part-timer for participation in various activities, or require participation for continued employment, report improved relationships between part-time faculty and full-time and higher evaluations of the teaching performance of part-timers.

All part-time faculty should be integrated into the life of the institution. Part-time faculty should not be expected to exist as a separate community, as shadows on the periphery of the institution; chroniclers of the part-time faculty experience report that they too frequently inhabit a much different world than that of their full-time colleagues. Part-timers should be invited to attend all college activities, to participate in faculty meetings, and to serve on department and college committees, especially those considering curriculum design or student development. The same array of support services that full-timers enjoy should be available to part-timers as well. Moreover, colleges should establish part-time faculty organizations to provide opportunities for part-timers to meet with other part-time colleagues, allow part-timers to add to faculty governance discussions, evaluate the conditions under which part-timers work, and identify potential vehicles by which part-timers can contribute to the academic community.

The performance of all part-time faculty should be evaluated. Part-time faculty should be evaluated as seriously and consistently as full-time faculty. Moreover, evaluation should be tied to professional development; part-timers should be provided with the same opportunities to improve as full-time faculty. Evaluation should not be conducted for the sole purpose of deciding to continue or terminate employment. There should be clear objectives for the evaluation process, and the process should be standard across the college. Finally, part-time faculty should receive equitable consideration in the college's formal activities that recognize and celebrate teaching excellence.

Part-time faculty should have equitable pay schedules. While we did not seek out specific information in our interviews about salaries for part-time faculty, our survey responses provided some evidence of widespread, general pay inequities between full- and part-time faculty; and the literature expresses concerns about inequities as well. We agree with Gappa and Leslie (1993) that whatever the system a college chooses to set salaries for part-time faculty, it should be fair—it should provide "equitable compensation for the work performed" (p. 256). We hasten to note that "equitable" does not necessarily mean "equal." Gappa and Leslie further recommend that the approach an institution takes to part-time faculty pay be "rational, clear, and based on the traditions and practices the institution has established for setting salary policy for other employees" (1993, p. 256). They recommend that if full-time faculty have the benefit of a merit pay system, a cost-of-living adjustment, and an opportunity to move up a pay scale, so should part-time faculty. We second these recommendations.

The equity issue has fueled persistent arguments; and, no doubt, it will continue to do so. On average, colleges' expectations of full-time faculty are decidedly higher and broader than are their expectations for part-timers, for they reflect an array of responsibilities and duties that extend beyond their classroom assignments. In those cases where part-time faculty responsibilities outside their classroom assignments are limited or nonexistent—as is currently the case at most community colleges—then part-time faculty salaries should not be closely tied to those paid to full-time faculty. However, there are solid arguments that compensation to part-time faculty for their teaching and any additional service to the college should more realistically reflect the value of their contribution to the institution.

> Some means of rewarding the [part-time faculty] must be derived. It may be necessary and desirable to define a faculty member's workload in terms of something other than teaching, thereby creating a rational way of paying...part-time faculty for work on college committees, for advising students, and for other activities that go beyond the classroom but are clearly activities that should be performed by professionals (Vaughan, 1991, p. 112).

CONCLUSIONS

Successful colleges assess the value of their actions by one overarching evaluative criterion—Is it good for the student? Students' opinions about the institution and the quality of their academic experiences rest in the hands of teaching professionals with whom they spend the majority of their time at the college.

> People make the difference in achieving exemplary status for an institution. Excellent teaching thrives best in an environment which supports and fosters shared values focused on the central purpose of learning. Taken together, specific attitudes, approaches, policies, and decisions produce an achievement-oriented climate which is conducive to success among students and to high morale among staff (Roueche and Baker, 1987, p. 188).

Part-time faculty make critical contributions to teaching and learning in the higher education enterprise—educationally, socially, and economically. For the contributions and the extraordinary potential they bring, part-timers should be acknowledged and treated as valuable citizens of the academic community. Part-time faculty are sleeping giants; their sheer numbers and their impact on college instruction cannot and should not be ignored. The issues that have divided full-time and part-time faculty, the issues that have separated part-timers from the larger academic community, will not go away. They will be addressed, or they will maim higher education.

Furthermore, colleges must identify for themselves the strategies that will most effectively promote their own use and integration of these new citizens, these strangers, into their communities. The colleges that have developed an array of these strategies report that they are reaping the benefits of their increased and enhanced inclusiveness. Perhaps what these colleges have shared will be helpful to other colleges.

Finally, our findings have encouraged us. We have confirmed, firsthand, our belief that many community colleges are capable of making good on their decision to create communities of learners. They have recognized the strangers in their company and have drawn them in. We conclude with this observation that embraces the array of challenges we have described in this study and targets the major challenge of the future:

It is time for cooperation and for making common cause. That common cause is academic excellence, which can only be ensured when the best faculty members, both full- and part-time, are working closely together (Gappa and Leslie, 1993, p. 285).

APPENDICES

A p p e n d i x   A

National Part-Time Faculty Utilization Survey

We would appreciate your sharing with us as much of the following information as possible. This information will assist us in preparing a state-of-the-art report that will be shared with all community colleges. If you wish for the data you provide to be kept anonymous, please let us know by checking the space below this paragraph. Also, in answering these questions, please use information from fall 1993. If for some reason data from another term and year must be used, please indicate the term and year below. Thank you for your cooperation.

Please keep data anonymous._____

Term and year if *different* from fall 1993 _____

District (name and state) _____

1. How many part-time faculty did your district employ in fall 1993?_____

2. How many full-time faculty did your district employ in fall 1993? _____

3. How many credit hours of instruction were delivered by each of the following?   _____ part-time   _____ full-time

4. How many non-credit hours of instruction were delivered by each of the following?   _____ part-time   _____ full-time

5. What is your average per course salary for part-time faculty (not including benefits)?   _____ per course

6. Are part-time faculty members eligible to receive benefits?
                    _____ yes   _____ no

7. If the answer to #6 is *no,* skip to #9. If the answer to #6 is *yes,* indicate the minimum credit hour load qualification that **part-time** faculty must seek to receive benefits and the average dollar value of the package.

_____ credit hours   _____ avg dollar value of benefits

8. In fall 1993, how many **part-time** faculty in your district received _____ benefits?   _____ received no benefits?

9. What is your average beginning level compensation for one year, without benefits, for a new full-time faculty member with minimum qualifications?

_____ per year

What is the dollar value of this same position's benefits package?

_____ benefits

What is the average number of credit hours this beginning faculty member would be expected to deliver?   _____ credit hours

10. Based on your experience with adjunct/part-time faculty, share with us your ranking of the following issues *in order of importance* in utilizing part-time faculty, with 1 being most important and 7 being least important.

_____Recruiting part-time faculty

_____Selecting/hiring part-time faculty

_____Orientation for part-time faculty

_____Involving part-time faculty in college life

_____Staff development for part-time faculty

_____Evaluating part-time faculty

_____Retaining part-time faculty

11. In general, characterize your support services for part-time faculty (e.g., wordprocessing, office space, access to college information): (Check one)

_____centralized—handled mostly by the college; for example, having a part-time faculty center that all part-time faculty can utilize

_____decentralized—handled mostly by the divisions/departments

12. District student data:

_____number of full-time credit students

_____number of part-time credit students

_____number of non-credit students

Respond to the following statements by circling one of the five responses:

13. The use of part-time faculty is an important issue in American community colleges.

| **Strongly Agree** | **Agree** | **Neutral** | **Disagree** | **Strongly Disagree** |

14. In general, this district effectively utilizes part-time faculty.

Strongly   **Agree**   **Neutral**   **Disagree**   **Strongly**
Agree   **Disagree**

15. In the years to come, the use of part-time faculty will increase in this district.

Strongly   **Agree**   **Neutral**   **Disagree**   **Strongly**
Agree   **Disagree**

Finally, we ask for your help in locating districts or colleges that have exceptional programs in effectively utilizing part-time/adjunct faculty. If your district (or another district or college with which you are familiar) has exceptional part-time/adjunct faculty programs or policies that you feel we should include in our study, please send information on the program(s) and/or give us the name of someone we might contact. Thank you for your assistance.

Exceptional part-time/adjunct faculty programs:

_____

_____

_____

Contact:

_____

_____

_____

If you have questions or concerns regarding this study, please contact:

John E. Roueche and Suanne D. Roueche
Project Directors
or
Mark D. Milliron
Senior Research Associate

Community College Leadership Program
Department of Educational Administration
College of Education
University of Texas at Austin
SZB 348
Austin, TX 78712-1293
(512) 471-7545
FAX (512) 471-9426

A p p e n d i x   B

State-of-the-Art Survey Respondents

COMMUNITY COLLEGE DISTRICTS OR SYSTEMS

Alamo Community College District, Texas
Coast Community College District, California
Community College of Allegheny County, Pennsylvania
Contra Costa Community College District, California
Cuyahoga Community College District, Ohio
Dallas County Community College District, Texas
Eastern Iowa Community College District, Iowa
El Paso County Community College District, Texas
Foothill-DeAnza Community College District, California
Houston Community College System, Texas
Iowa Valley Community College Distirct, Iowa
Kern Community College District, California
Los Angeles Community College District, California
Los Rios Community College District, California
Maricopa County Community College District, Arizona
Milwaukee Area Technical College, Wisconsin
Peralta Community College District, California
Saddleback Community College District, California
St. Louis Community College, Missouri
San Jacinto College District, Texas
Seattle Community College District, Washington
State Center Community College District, California
Tarrant County Junior College, Texas
Yosemite Community College District, California

LARGE-SIZED COLLEGES, NON-DISTRICT RELATED

Allan Hancock College, California
Antelope Valley College, California

Austin Community College, Texas
Belleville Area College, Illinois
Central Piedmont Community College, North Carolina
Cerritos College, California
County College of Morris, New Jersey
Cuesta College, California
Elgin Community College, Illinois
Erie Community College, New York
Essex Community College, Maryland
Front Range Community College, Colorado
Greenville Technical College, South Carolina
Indian River Community College, Florida
Johnson County Community College, Kansas
Joliet Junior College, Illinois
Kirkwood Community College, Iowa
Lakeland Community College, Ohio
Macomb Community College, Michigan
Metropolitan Community College, Nebraska
Nassau Community College, New York
Normandale Community College, Minnesota
Ocean County College, New Jersey
Oklahoma City Community College, Oklahoma
Pasadena City College, California
Portland Community College, Oregon
St. Petersburg Junior College, Florida
Santa Fe Community College, Florida
Suffolk County Community College, New York
Tidewater Community College, Virginia
Utah Valley Community College, Utah

AVERAGE-SIZED COLLEGES, NON-DISTRICT RELATED

Alexandria Technical College, Minnesota
Arapahoe Community College, Colorado
Bainbridge College, Georgia
Cecil Community College, Maryland
Central Virginia Community College, Virginia
Centralia College, Washington
Coastal Carolina Community College, North Carolina
Colby Community College, Kansas
College of Southern Idaho, Idaho
Connors State College, Oklahoma
Delgado Community College, Louisiana
Garland County Community College, Arkansas
Jackson State Community College, Tennessee

Jefferson State Community College, Alabama
Lake Tahoe Community College, California
Lees College, Kentucky
McHenry County College, Illinois
Middle Georgia College, Georgia
Miles Community College, Montana
Muskegon Community College, Michigan
Muskingum Area Technical College, Ohio
Northeast Community College, Nebraska
Passaic County Community College, New Jersey
Patrick Henry Community College, Virginia
Phillips Junior College, Mississippi
Pueblo Community College, Colorado
Rockland Community College, New York
San Juan College, New Mexico
Sauk Valley Community College, Illinois
Texarkana College, Texas
Treasure Valley Community College, Oregon
Wilkes Community College, North Carolina
Wilson Technical Community College, North Carolina

A p p e n d i x   C

Part-Time Faculty Study Interviewees

ARIZONA

Maricopa Community College District
Paul A. Elsner, Chancellor
Interviewee: Carol Scarafiotti, Dean of Instruction
                  Rio Salado Community College
                  640 N. 1st. Avenue
                  Phoenix, AZ 85003
                  602/223-4235

CALIFORNIA

College of the Canyons
Dianne G. Van Hook, Superintendent/President
Interviewee: Joseph Gerda, Mathematics Instructor and
                  Interim Assistant Dean of Instruction
                  26455 North Rockwell Canyon Road
                  Valencia, CA 91355
                  805/259-7800

Cuesta College
Grace N. Mitchell, Superintendent/President
Interviewee: Susan Cotler, Vice President of Educational Services
                  P.O. Box 8106
                  San Luis Obispo, CA 93403-8106
                  805/546-3100

De Anza College
Martha J. Kanter, President
Interviewee: Sandy Acebo, Vice President of Instruction
                  21250 Stevens Creek
                  Cupertino, CA 95014
                  408/864-5678

Modesto Junior College
Stanley Hodges, Jr., President
Interviewee: Ron Manzoni, Vice President of Instruction
435 College Avenue
Modesto, CA 95350
209/575-6058

Santa Barbara City College
Peter R. MacDougall, Superintendent/President
Interviewee: John Romo, Vice President for Academic Affairs
721 Cliff Drive
Santa Barbara, CA 93109-2394
805/966-5730

Vista Community College
Barbara Beno, President
Interviewee: Barbara Beno, President
2020 Milvia Street
Berkeley, CA 94704
510/841-8431

COLORADO

Community College of Aurora
Larry Carter, President
Interviewee: Cynthia Barnes, Dean of Educational Development
16000 E. Centretech Parkway
Aurora, CO 80011-9036
303/360-4700

FLORIDA

Santa Fe Community College
Lawrence W. Tyree, President
Interviewee: Barbara Sloan, English Chair
3000 NW 83rd Street
Gainesville, FL 32606
904/395-5168

St. Petersburg Junior College
Carl M. Kuttler, Jr., President
Interviewee: Emily Baker, Instructor-in-Charge Applied Ethics
St. Petersburg/Gibbs Campus
P.O. Box 13489
St. Petersburg, FL 33733
813/341-3600

Interviewee: Connie Howard, Curriculum Services Coordinator
                 Educational and Student Services
                 District Office
                 P.O. Box 13489
                 St. Petersburg, FL 33733
                 813/341-3600

Interviewee: Edward J. Long, Associate Vice President
                 Educational and Student Services
                 District Office
                 P.O. Box 13489
                 St. Petersburg, FL 33733
                 813/341-3600

Interviewee: Esther Oliver, Provost
                 Allstate Center
                 P.O. Box 13489
                 St. Petersburg, FL 33733
                 813/341-4440

Interviewee: Charlie Roberts, Provost
                 St. Petersburg/Gibbs Campus
                 P.O. Box 13489
                 St. Petersburg, FL 33733
                 813/341-3600

Interviewee: Ernie Ross, Dean, Academic Services
                 Clearwater Campus
                 P.O. Box 13489
                 St. Petersburg, FL 33733
                 813/791-2400

Interviewee: Robert W. Sullins, Vice President
                 Educational and Student Services
                 District Office
                 P.O. Box 13489
                 St. Petersburg, FL 33733
                 813/341-3600

Interviewee: Yvonne Ulmer, Director of Staff Development
                 Human Resources
                 District Office
                 P.O. Box 13489
                 St. Petersburg, FL 33733
                 813/341-3600

Interviewee: Trudy Williams, Associate Center Administrator
                 Academic Services
                 Tarpon Center
                 P.O. Box 13489
                 St. Petersburg, FL 33733
                 813/791-5750

Valencia Community College
Paul C. Gianini, Jr., President
Interviewee: Edmund Gross
                  Vice President of Instructional Affairs and Provost
                  West Campus
                  P.O. Box 3028
                  Orlando, FL 32802
                  407/299-5000
Interviewee: William Tapp, Faculty Development Specialist
                  P.O. Box 3028
                  Orlando, FL 32802
                  407/299-5000

ILLINOIS

Triton College
George Jorndt, President
Interviewee: Michael Botterweck
                  Vice President of Academic Affairs and Student Services
                  2000 Fifth Avenue
                  River Grove, IL 60171
                  708/456-0300

IOWA

Kirkwood Community College
Norman Nielsen, President
Interviewee: David Jensen, Associate Vice President of Instruction
                  P.O. Box 2068
                  Cedar Rapids, IA 52406
                  319/398-5411

KANSAS

Cowley County Community College
Patrick McAtee, President
Interviewee: Bob Paxton, Vice President of Instruction
                  125 S. 2nd Street
                  Arkansas City, KS 67005-1147
                  316/442-0430

MARYLAND

Hagerstown Junior College
Norman P. Shea, President
Interviewee: Michael H. Parsons, Dean of Instruction
                    11400 Robinwood Drive
                    Hagerstown, MD 21742-6590
                    301/790-2800

MICHIGAN

Schoolcraft College
Richard W. McDowell, President
Interviewee: Conway Jeffress, Vice President for Instruction
                    18600 Haggerty Road
                    Livonia, MI 48152-2696
                    313/462-4400

NEBRASKA

Metropolitan Community College
J. Richard Gilliland, President
Interviewee: Jenny Fauchier, Social Science Instructor
                    P.O. Box 37777
                    Omaha, NE 68103-0777
                    402/449-8400

NEVADA

Truckee Meadows Community College
John Gwaltney, President
Interviewee: John Scally, Vice President for Academic Affairs
                    7000 Dandini Boulevard
                    Reno, NV 89512
                    702/673-7090

NEW JERSEY

County College of Morris
Edward Yaw, President
Interviewee: Cliff L. Wood, Vice President for Academic Affairs
                    214 Center Grove Road
                    Randolph, NJ 07869
                    201/328-5000

Ocean County College
Milton Shaw, President
Interviewee: John Weber, Dean of Instruction
       P.O. Box 2001
       Toms River, NJ 08753
       908/255-4000

NEW YORK

Nassau Community College
Sean A. Fanelli, President
Interviewee: Sean Fanelli, President
       Garden City, NY 11530
       516/572-7500

Westchester Community College
Joseph N. Hankin, President
Interviewee: John Flynn, Vice President and Dean of Academic Affairs
       75 Grasslands Road
       Valhalla, NY 10595-1698
       914/785-6712

NORTH CAROLINA

Central Piedmont Community College
P. Anthony Zeiss, President
Interviewee: Mitchell Hagler, Assistant to the Vice President for Instruction
       P.O. Box 35009
       Charlotte, NC 28235
       704/342-6633

OHIO

Cuyahoga Community College District
Jerry Sue Thornton, President
Interviewee: Richard France
       Assistant Dean of Evening and Weekend Programs
       11000 Pleasant Valley
       Cleveland, OH 44130
       216/987-5229

Lakeland Community College
Ralph R. Doty, President
Interviewee: Judith Doerr
                    Dean, Social Science and Public Service Technologies
                    7700 Clocktower Drive
                    Mentor, OH 44060-7594
                    216/953-7079

PENNSYLVANIA

Community College of Allegheny County—Allegheny
John M. Kingsmore, President
Interviewee: James Holmberg, Vice President, Dean of Academic Affairs
                    808 Ridge Avenue
                    Pittsburgh, PA 15212-6097
                    412/237-2525
Interviewee: Allysen Todd, Chairperson, English Department
                    808 Ridge Avenue
                    Pittsburgh, PA 15212-6097
                    412/237-2525

SOUTH CAROLINA

Greenville Technical College
Thomas E. Barton, Jr., President
Interviewee: Martha Hart Herbert, Associate Vice President for Education
                    P.O. Box 5616
                    Greenville, SC 29606-5616
                    803/250-8187

TEXAS

Richland College
Stephen K. Mittelstet, President
Interviewee: Jackie Claunch
                    Vice President of Academic and Student Development
                    12800 Abrams Road
                    Dallas, TX 75243-2199
                    214/238-6193
Tarrant County Junior College
C. A. Roberson, Jr., Chancellor
Interviewee: Jim Worden, Vice Chancellor for Educational Affairs
                    1500 Houston Drive
                    Forth Worth, TX 76102-6599
                    817/336-7851

WASHINGTON

Centralia College
Henry P. Kirk, President
Interviewee: Bill Taylor, Dean of Instruction
600 West Locust Street
Centralia, WA 98531
206/736-9391

BIBLIOGRAPHY

Abraham, Ansley. *College Remedial Studies: Institutional Practices in the SREB States.* Atlanta, Ga.: Southern Regional Education Board, 1992.

Abrami, P.C., D'Appollonia, S., and Cohen, P.A. "Validity of Student Ratings of Instruction: What We Know and What We Do Not." *Journal of Educational Psychology,* 1990, *82* (2), 219–231.

Addy, Cathryn. "Some Thoughts on Faculty Evaluation." *Innovation Abstracts,* 1981, *III* (31).

Albert, L.S., and Watson, R.J. "Mainstreaming Part-Time Faculty: Issue or Imperative?" In M.H. Parsons (Ed.), *Using Part-Time Faculty Effectively.* New Directions for Community Colleges No. 30. San Francisco: Jossey-Bass, 1980.

Aleamoni, L.M. "Typical Faculty Concerns About Student Evaluation of Teaching." In L.M. Aleamoni (Ed.), *Techniques for Evaluating and Improving Instruction.* New Directions for Teaching and Learning No. 31. San Francisco: Jossey-Bass, 1987.

American Association of Community Colleges. Annual Fall Survey. Washington, D.C.: American Association of Community Colleges, 1991.

American Association of Community Colleges. *1992 Statistical Yearbook of Community, Technical, and Junior Colleges.* Washington, D.C.: American Association of Community Colleges, 1992.

Armstrong, D. "Information on Part-Time/Full-Time Faculty." Report to Florida State Board of Community Colleges, September 30, 1993.

Astin, Alexander W. *Four Critical Years: Effects of College on Beliefs, Attitudes, and Knowledge.* San Francisco: Jossey-Bass, 1977.

Astin, Alexander W. *Achieving Educational Excellence.* San Francisco: Jossey-Bass, 1985.

Babbie, E.R. *The Practice of Social Research.* Belmont, Calif.: Wadsworth, 1989.

Banta, T.W. "Use of Outcomes Information at the University of Tennessee, Knoxville." In Peter T. Ewell (Ed.), *Assessing Educational Outcomes.* New Directions for Institutional Research No. 47. San Francisco: Jossey-Bass, 1985.

Barnes, Cynthia. "Part-Time Faculty, Full-Time Excellence: The Faculty Development Program: Community College of Aurora, Colorado." *Teaching for a Change,* Summer 1991, Publication No. 1.

Barnes, L.B., and Barnes, M.W. "Academic Discipline and Generalizability of Student Evaluations of Instruction." *Research in Higher Education,* 1993, *34* (2), 135–149.

Barshis, Donald E., and Guskey, Thomas R. "Providing Remedial Education." In George B. Vaughan (Ed.), *Issues for Community College Leaders in a New Era.* San Francisco: Jossey-Bass, 1983, 76–99.

Barzun, Jacques. *Teacher in America.* Garden City, NY: Doubleday, 1959.

Beal, P.E., and Noel, L. *What Works in Student Retention.* Iowa City, Iowa: American College Testing Program/National Center for Higher Education Management Systems, 1980. (ED 197 635)

Behrendt, R.L., and Parson, M.H. "Evaluation of Part-Time Faculty." In Albert B. Smith (Ed.), *Evaluating Faculty and Staff.* New Directions for Community Colleges No. 41. San Francisco: Jossey-Bass, 1983.

Bell, Terrel. Keynote Address, Leadership 2000 Conference, Chicago, July 1991.

Beman, R.R. "Observations of an Adjunct Faculty Member." In M.H. Parsons (Ed.), *Using Part-Time Faculty Effectively.* New Directions for Community Colleges No. 30. San Francisco: Jossey-Bass, 1980.

Bender, L., and Hammons, J. "Adjunct Faculty: Forgotten and Neglected." *Community and Junior College Journal,* 1972, *43* (2), 20–22.

Bethke, R. "From Part-Time to Full-Time: A New Visibility." Unpublished manuscript.

Bethke, R., and Nelson, V.J. *Collaborative Efforts to Improve Conditions for Adjunct Faculty.* Paper presented at the NISOD International Conference on Teaching Excellence, Austin, Texas, May 22–25, 1994.

Biles, George E., and Tuckman, Howard P. *Part-Time Faculty Personnel Management Policies.* New York: American Council on Education/Macmillan, 1986.

Bloor, Earl G. "The Instructional Skills Workshop: A Mechanism for Instructional and Organizational Renewal." *Innovation Abstracts,* 1987, *IX* (10).

Boggs, G.R. "An Evaluation of the Instructional Effectiveness of Part-Time Community College Developmental Writing Faculty." Unpublished doctoral dissertation. University of Texas at Austin, 1984.

Bogue, Jesse Parker. *The Community College.* New York: McGraw-Hill, 1950.

Boice, R. *The New Faculty Member.* San Francisco: Jossey-Bass, 1990.

Boice, R. "Mentoring a New Faculty: A Program for Implementation." *Journal of Staff, Program, and Organizational Development,* 1992, *8* (3), 143–160.

Bonham, B.S., and Claxton, C. "Summary of Preliminary Findings: Research Project on Developmental Education." Boone, N.C.: Appalachian State University, National Center for Developmental Education, 1992.

Bonham, G. "Part-Time Faculty: A Mixed Blessing." *Change,* 1982, *14* (3), 10–11.

Borich, G.D. *The Appraisal of Teaching: Concepts and Process.* Reading, Mass.: Addison-Wesley, 1977.

Borich, G.D., and Madden, S.K. *Evaluating Classroom Instruction: A Sourcebook of Instruments.* Reading, Mass.: Addison-Wesley, 1977.

Boyer, Ernest L. *The Undergraduate Experience in America.* New York: Harper and Row, 1987.

Boyer, Ernest L. "Curriculum, Culture, and Social Cohesion." *Celebrations,* October 1992, p. 4.

Bowen, H.R., and Schuster, J.H. *American Professors: A National Resource Imperiled.* New York: Oxford University Press, 1986.

Bowen, W.G., and Sosa, J.A. *Prospects for Faculty in the Arts and Sciences.* Princeton, N.J.: Princeton University Press, 1989.

Bridges, William. "The End of the Job." *Fortune,* Summer 1994, *130* (6), 61–74.

Brophy, J. "Teacher Effects: Research and Quality." *Journal of Classroom Interaction,* 1987, *22* (1), 14–23.

Bushnell, D.S., and Zagaris, I. *Strategies for Change: A Report from Project Focus.* Washington, D.C.: American Association of Community Colleges, 1972.

Cage, M.C. "States Questioning How Much Time Professors Spend Working with Undergraduate Students." *Chronicle of Higher Education,* August 7, 1991, p. A1.

Callahan, J.P. "Faculty Attitudes Towards Student Evaluation." *College Student Journal,* 1992, *26* (1), 98–102.

Carter, D.J., and Ottinger, C.A. "Community College Faculty: A Profile." *Research Briefs,* 1992, *3,* 14.

Cashin, W.E. "Student Ratings of Teaching: A Summary of the Research." IDEA Paper No. 20. Manhattan, Kansas: Center for Faculty Evaluation and Development, Kansas State University, 1988.

Centra, John A. *The Relationship Between Student and Alumni Ratings of Teachers.* Princeton, N.J.: Educational Testing Service, 1973.

Centra, John A. *Faculty Development Practices in U.S. Colleges and Universities.* Princeton, N.J.: Educational Testing Service, 1976.

Claxton, Charles S. *Community College Staff Development: Basic Issues in Planning.* Atlanta, Ga.: Southern Regional Education Board, 1976.

Cohen, A.M. (Ed.). *Toward a Professional Faculty.* New Directions in Community Colleges No. 1. San Francisco: Jossey-Bass, 1973.

Cohen, A.M., and Brawer, F.B. *The American Community College.* San Francisco: Jossey-Bass, 1982.

Cohen, A.M., and Brawer, F.B. *The American Community College.* 2nd ed. San Francisco: Jossey-Bass, 1989.

Cohen, Marlene. "Benefits on a Budget: Addressing Adjunct Needs." Paper presented at the annual meeting of the Speech Communication Association, Chicago, October 29–November 1, 1992. (ED 355 578)

Cohen, P. "Student Ratings of Instruction and Student Achievement: A Meta-Analysis of Multisection Validity Studies." *Review of Educational Research,* 1981, *51* (3), 281–309.

Collins, Mary Beth, and Stanley, Karen. "Bringing Worlds Together: Internationalizing the Curriculum Through Focused Interaction." *Innovation Abstracts,* 1991, *XIII* (1).

Commission on the Future of Community Colleges. *Building Communities: A Vision for a New Century.* Washington, D.C.: American Association of Community and Junior Colleges, 1988.

Cross, Carol. "PBS Launches Initiative to Complete AA Degrees." *Community College Week,* August 29, 1994, p. 22.

Cross, K. Patricia. *Accent on Learning.* San Francisco: Jossey-Bass, 1976.

Cross, K. Patricia. "Teaching for Learning." Paper presented at the annual meeting of the American Association of Higher Education, Chicago, March 2, 1987.

Cross, K. Patricia. "Teaching to Improve Learning." Paper presented at the annual meeting of South Carolina Association of Colleges and Universities, Columbia, South Carolina, January 27, 1989.

Cross, K. Patricia. "Leadership for Teaching and Learning." *Leadership Abstracts,* 1990, *3* (5).

Cross, K. Patricia, and Angelo, Thomas A. *Classroom Assessment Techniques: A Handbook for Faculty.* Ann Arbor, Mich.: National Center for Research to Improve Postsecondary Teaching and Learning, 1988.

De Jong, C., Hartman, M., and Fisher-Hoult, J. "Mentoring New Faculty." *Journal of Staff, Program, and Organization Development,* 1994, *12* (1), 41–49.

Decker, E.H. "Utilizing Part-Time Faculty for Community-Based Education." In M.H. Parsons (Ed.), *Using Part-Time Faculty Effectively.* New Directions for Community Colleges No. 30. San Francisco: Jossey-Bass, 1980.

Dent, P.L., and Nicholas, L. "A Study of Faculty and Student Opinions on Teaching Effectiveness Ratings." *Peabody Journal of Education,* 1980, *25,* 135–143.

Dervarics, Charles. "Part-Time Faculty Member Juggles Daily Roles, Schedules." *Community College Week,* July 5, 1993, p. 7.

Doyle, Kenneth. "Construction and Evaluation of Scales for Rating College Instructors." Unpublished doctoral dissertation. University of Minnesota, 1972. Available from *Dissertation Abstracts,* 33 (5-A), 2163.

Doyle, Kenneth. *Evaluating Teaching.* Lexington, Mass.: D.C. Heath, 1983.

Eble, Kenneth E. *The Recognition and Evaluation of Teaching.* Salt Lake City, Utah: Project to Improve College Teaching, 1970.

Eble, Kenneth E. *The Aims of College Teaching.* San Francisco: Jossey-Bass, 1983.

Eble, Kenneth E., and McKeachie, W. *Improving Undergraduate Education Through Faculty Development.* San Francisco: Jossey-Bass, 1985.

Eells, William C. *The Junior College.* Boston: Houghton Mifflin, 1931.

Elbow, Peter. "Will the Virtues of Portfolios Blind Us to Their Potential Dangers?" In L. Black, D.A. Daiker, J. Sommers, and G. Stygall (Eds.), *New Directions in Portfolio Assessment.* Portsmouth, NH: Boynton/Cook Publishers, 1994.

Eliason, N.C. "Part-Time Faculty: A National Perspective." In M.H. Parsons (Ed.), *Using Part-Time Faculty Effectively.* New Directions for Community Colleges No. 30. San Francisco: Jossey-Bass, 1980.

Erwin, J., and Andrews, H.A. "State of Part-Time Faculty Services at Community Colleges in a Nineteen-State Region." *Community College Journal of Research and Practice,* 1993, *17,* 555–562.

Ewell, Peter T. "Some Implications for Practice." In Peter T. Ewell (Ed.), *Assessing Educational Outcomes.* New Directions for Institutional Research No. 47. San Francisco: Jossey-Bass, 1985.

Ewell, Peter T. "Assessment and Public Accountability: Back to the Future." *Change,* November/December 1991, *23* (6), 12–17.

Feldman, D.C. "Reconceptualizing the Nature and Consequences of Part-Time Work." *Academy of Management Review,* 1990, *15,* 103–112.

Feldman, K.A. "Effective College Teaching from the Students' and Faculty's View: Matched or Mismatched Priorities?" *Research in Higher Education,* 1988, *28* (4), 291–344.

Feldman, K.A. "College Students' View of Male and Female College Teachers: Part I—Evidence from the Social Laboratory and Experiments." *Research in Higher Education,* 1992, 33 (3), 317–375.

Feldman, K.A. "College Students' View of Male and Female College Teachers: Part II—Evidence from Students' Evaluations of Their Classroom Teachers." *Research in Higher Education,* 1993, *34* (2), 151–191.

Fox, G.C. "Factors that Motivate Part-Time Faculty." *Community Services Catalyst,* Winter 1984, *14* (1), 17–21. (EJ 297 072)

Frey, P.W. "Validity of Student Instructional Ratings: Does Timing Matter?" *Journal of Higher Education,* 1976, *47* (3), 327–336.

Friedlander, J. "Instructional Practices of Part-Time Faculty." In M.H. Parsons (Ed.), *Using Part-Time Faculty Effectively.* New Directions for Community Colleges No. 30. San Francisco: Jossey-Bass, 1980.

Futrell, M.H. "Toward Excellence." *National Forum,* 1984, *44,* 11–24.

Gaff, J.G. *Toward Faculty Renewal: Advances in Faculty, Instructional and Organizational Development.* San Francisco: Jossey-Bass, 1975.

Gaff, J.G. *General Education Today.* San Francisco: Jossey-Bass, 1983.

Gage, N.L., and Berliner, D.C. *Educational Psychology.* Chicago: Rand McNally, 1975.

Gagné, R.M. *The Conditions of Learning.* 2nd ed. New York: Holt, Rinehart and Winston, 1970.

Galluzzo, G.R., and Craig, J.R. "Evaluation of Preservice Teacher Education Programs." In W.R. Houston (Ed.), *Handbook of Research on Teacher Education.* New York: MacMillan, 1990.

Gappa, J.M. *Part-Time Faculty: Higher Education at a Crossroads.* ASHE-ERIC Higher Education Research Report No. 3. Washington, D.C.: Association for the Study of Higher Education, 1984.

Gappa, J.M., and Leslie, D.W. *The Invisible Faculty: Improving the Status of Part-Timers in Higher Education.* San Francisco: Jossey-Bass, 1993.

Gehrke, N.J. "Toward a Definition of Mentoring." *Theory Into Practice,* 1988, *27* (3), 190–194.

Gianini, P., and Sarantos, S. "Academic Rhetoric Versus Business Reality." In J.E. Roueche, L.S. Taber, and S.D. Roueche (Eds.), *The Company We Keep: Collaboration in the American Community College.* Washington, D.C.: Community College Press, 1995.

Gleazer, Edmund J., Jr. *Values, Vision, and Vitality.* Washington, D.C.: American Association of Community and Junior Colleges, 1980.

Gold, Y. "Psychological Support for Mentors and Beginning Teachers: A Critical Dimension." In T.M. Bey and C.T. Holmes (Eds.), *Mentoring: Contemporary Principles and Issues.* Reston, Va.: Association of Teacher Educators, 1992.

Graves, Debbie. "Number of Adults Going to College Is Rising." *Austin American Statesman,* August 25, 1994, pp. A1, A10.

Greening, John. "Learning Biology Through Writing." *Innovation Abstracts,* 1987, *IX* (9).

Greenwood, R.D. "Making 'What's-His-Face' Feel at Home: Integrating Part-Time Faculty." In M.H. Parsons (Ed.), *Using Part-Time Faculty Effectively.* New Directions for Community Colleges No. 30. San Francisco: Jossey-Bass, 1980.

Guba, E.G. "The Failure of Educational Evaluation." *Educational Technology,* 1969, *9* (5), 29–38.

Guthrie-Morse, B. "The Utilization of Part-Time Faculty in Community Colleges." *Community College Frontiers,* 1979, *7* (3), 8–17.

Hall, R.M., and Sandler, B.R. *Academic Mentoring for Women Students and Faculty: A New Look at an Old Way to Get Ahead.* Washington, D.C.: Association of American Colleges, 1983.

Halstead, J.S. "A Model for Research on Ratings of Courses and Instructors." Proceedings of the 78th Annual Convention of the American Psychological Association, 1970, *5,* 625–626.

Hammons, J. "Adjunct Faculty: Another Look." *Community College Frontiers,* 1981, *9,* 46–53.

Hammons, J., and Watts, G. "Evaluating Part-Time Faculty Performance." *Journal of Staff, Program, and Organizational Development,* Spring 1983, *1* (1), 18–22.

Hanson, G.R., and Kerker, R.M. "Evaluating the Effectiveness of TASP." In J.M. Matthews, R.G. Swanson, and Richard M. Kerker (Eds.), *From Politics to Policy: A Case Study in Educational Reform.* New York: Praeger, 1991.

Hauff, E.M., and Berdie, D.R. "Community College Part-Time Faculty: Who Are They?" *NEA Higher Education Journal,* 1989, *5* (1), 73–82.

Hawkins, B. Denise. "Sharp Pro and Con Division on Merits of Part-Time Faculty." *Community College Week,* July 5, 1993.

Hawthorne, E.M. "Anticipating the New Generation of Community College Faculty Members." *Journal of College Science Teaching,* 1991, *20* (6), 365–368.

Head, F.A., Reiman, A.J., and Thies-Sprinthall, L. "The Reality of Mentoring: Complexity in Its Process and Function." In T.M. Bey and C.T. Holmes (Eds.), *Mentoring: Contemporary Principles and Issues.* Reston, Va.: Association of Teacher Educators, 1992.

Heinberg, S. "Procedures for the Supervision and Evaluation of New Part-Time Evening-Division Instructors in California Junior Colleges." Unpublished doctoral dissertation, University of Southern California, 1966.

Hildebrand, M., Wilson, R.C., and Dienst, E.R. *Evaluating University Teaching.* Berkeley, Calif.: University of California, Center for Research and Development in Higher Education, 1971.

Hoffman, J.R. "The Use and Abuse of Part-Time Instructors." *Community Services Catalyst,* Winter 1980, *10* (1), 12–18. (EJ 225 946)

Jackofsky, E.F., and Peters, L.H. "Part-Time Versus Full-Time Employment Status Differences: A Replication and Extension." *Journal of Occupational Behavior,* 1987, *8,* 1–9.

Jarvis, D.K. *Junior Faculty Development: A Handbook.* New York: Modern Language Association of America, 1991.

Jenrette, M. "Staffing for a New Century: An Opportunity for Institutional Renewal." *Leadership Abstracts,* 1990, 3 (2).

Kay, R.S. "Mentor Management: Emphasizing the Human in Managing Human Resources." In T.M. Bey and C.T. Holmes (Eds.), *Mentoring: Contemporary Principles and Issues.* Reston, Va.: Association of Teacher Educators, 1992.

Keim, M.C. "Two-Year College Faculty: A Research Update." *Community College Review,* 1989, *17* (3), 34–43.

Kelly, D.K. "Part-Time Faculty in the Community College: A Study of Their Qualifications, Frustrations, and Involvement." Paper presented at the annual forum of the Association for Institutional Research, San Francisco, California, May 26–29, 1991. (ED 336 035)

Kerlinger, F.N. *Foundations of Behavioral Research.* 3rd ed. Chicago: Holt, Rinehart and Winston, 1986.

Kinnick, M.K. "Increasing the Use of Student Outcomes Information." In Peter T. Ewell (Ed.), *Assessing Educational Outcomes.* New Directions for Institutional Research No. 47. San Francisco: Jossey-Bass, 1985.

Klapper, P. "The Professional Preparation of the College Teacher," *Journal of General Education,* April 1949, *3,* 228–244.

Klemp, G.O. "Three Factors of Success." In D.W. Vermilye (Ed.), *Current Issues in Higher Education.* San Francisco: Jossey-Bass, 1977.

Kogler Hill, S.E., Bahniuk, M.H., and Dobos, J. "The Impact of Mentoring and Collegial Support on Faculty Success: An Analysis of Support Behavior, Information Adequacy, and Communication Apprehension." *Communication Education,* 1989, *38,* 15–33.

Komarovsky, Mirra. *Women in College: Shaping New Feminine Identities.* New York: Basic Books, 1985.

Kramer, G., and Washburn, R. "The Perceived Orientation Needs of New Students." *Journal of College Student Personnel,* 1983, *24* (4), 311–319.

Kurfiss, J.G., and Boice, R. "Current and Desired Faculty Development Practices Amond POD Members." *To Improve the Academy,* 1990, *9,* 73–82.

Leatherman, C. "Survey Finds College Officials Preoccupied with Finances." *Chronicle of Higher Education,* 1993, 47, 16.

Leslie, D.W. *Employing Part-Time Faculty.* San Francisco: Jossey-Bass, 1978.

Leslie, D.W., Kellams, S.E., and Gunne, G.M. *Part-Time Faculty in American Higher Education.* New York: Praeger, 1982.

Lewis, L.S. *Scaling the Ivory Tower.* Baltimore: Johns Hopkins University Press, 1975.

Lindquist, J. *Designing Teaching Improvement Programs.* Battle Creek, Mich.: W.K. Kellogg Foundation, 1979.

Little, J.W. "The Mentor Phenomenon and the Social Organization of Teaching." In C. Cazden (Ed.), *Review of Research in Education.* Washington, D.C.: American Educational Research Association, 1990.

London, Howard. "In Between: The Community College Teacher." In Philip G. Altbach and Sheila Slaughter (Eds.), *The Academic Profession.* Annals of the American Academy of Political and Social Science, volume 448. Philadelphia: American Academy of Political and Social Science, 1980.

Lorenzo, Albert L., and Banach, William J. *Critical Issues Facing America's Community Colleges (1994–1995).* Warren, Mich.: Macomb Press, 1994.

Lowther, M.A., Stark, J.S., Genthon, M.L., and Bentley, R.J. "Comparing Introductory Course Planning Among Full-Time and Part-Time Faculty." *Research in Higher Education, 31* (6), 495–517.

Luna, Gaye, and Cullen, Deborah L. "Mentoring Women and Minorities: Applications to Higher Education." *Journal of Staff, Program, and Organizational Development,* Fall 1992, *10* (3), 133–140.

Magarell, J. "Part-Time Professors on the Increase." *Chronicle of Higher Education,* 1978, *15,* 1–6.

Mangan, Katherine S. "Many Colleges Fill Vacancies with Part-Time Professors, Citing Economy and Uncertainty About Enrollments." *Chronicle of Higher Education,* August 7, 1992, A9.

Marsh, H.W., and Dunkin, M. "Students' Evaluations of University Teaching: A Multidimensional Perspective." In Association for the Study of Higher Education, *Higher Education: Handbook on Theory and Research.* Volume 8. New York: Agathon, 1992.

Mauksch, H.O. "What Are the Obstacles to Improving Quality Teaching?" *Current Issues in Higher Education,* 1980, *1,* 49–57.

Maxwell, William E., and Kazlauskas, Edward J. "Which Faculty Development Methods Really Work in Community Colleges? A Review of the Research." *Community/Junior College Quarterly of Research and Practice,* October–December, 1992, *16* (4), 351–360.

McGrath, Dennis, and Spear, Martin B. *The Academic Crisis of the Community College.* New York: State University of New York Press, 1991.

McGuire, John. "Part-Time Faculty: Partners in Excellence," *Leadership Abstracts,* 1993, *6* (6).

McKeachie, Wilbert J. *Teaching Tips: A Guidebook for the Beginning College Teacher.* 7th ed. Lexington, Mass.: D.C. Heath, 1978.

McKeachie, Wilbert J. "Student Ratings of Faculty: A Reprise." *Academe,* October, 1979, *65,* 384–397.

McKeachie, W.J., Lin, Y.G., and Mann, W. "Student Ratings of Teacher Effectiveness: Validity Studies." *American Educational Research Journal,* 1971, *8,* 435–445.

McNeil, J.D., and Popham, W.J. "A Critique of Widely Used Criteria in Assessing Teacher Competency." In G.D. Borich (Ed.), *The Appraisal of Teaching Concepts and Process.* Reading, Mass.: Addison-Wesley, 1977.

Miami-Dade Community College. "A Guide to Assessing Performance Portfolios." Miami: Miami-Dade Community College, 1994.

Miller, M.T., and Nadler, D.P. "Orientation Program Considerations for New Community College Faculty." *Community College Journal of Research and Practice,* 1994, *18,* 441–448.

Miller, R.I. *Evaluating Faculty Performance.* San Francisco: Jossey-Bass, 1972.

Miller, R.I. *Developing Programs for Faculty Evaluation.* San Francisco: Jossey-Bass, 1974.

Miller, R.I. *Evaluating Faculty for Promotion and Tenure.* San Francisco: Jossey-Bass, 1987.

Minerbrook, S. "A Different Reality for Us." *U.S. News and World Report,* May 11, 1992, p. 36.

Morgan, Joan. "Accrediting Agencies Defer to Institutions on Part-Time Faculty Issues." *Community College Week,* July 5, 1993, p. 6.

Mortimer, K.P., Bagshaw, M., and Masland, A.T. *Flexibility in Academic Staffing: Effective Policies and Practices.* ASHE-ERIC Higher Education Report No. 1. Washington, D.C.: Association for the Study of Higher Education, 1985.

Nadler, D. (Ed.). *Orientation Director's Manual.* Statesboro, GA: National Orientation Directors Association, 1992.

National Center for Education Statistics. *Faculty in Higher Education Institutions, 1988.* Washington, D.C.: Department of Education, 1990.

National Center for Education Statistics. *College-Level Remedial Education in Fall of 1989.* Washington, D.C.: U.S. Department of Education, 1991.

National Center for Education Statistics. *Staff and Faculty in Higher Education Institutions.* Washington, D.C.: U.S. Department of Education, 1993.

National Center on Education and the Economy. *America's Choice: High Skills or Low Wages!* Rochester, NY: National Center on Education and the Economy, 1990.

National Commission on Excellence in Education. *A Nation at Risk: The Imperative for Educational Reform.* Washington, D.C.: U.S. Department of Education, April 1983.

National Institute of Education. *Involvement in Learning: Realizing the Potential of American Higher Education.* Washington, D.C.: U.S. Department of Education, 1984.

Newman, Frank. *Report on Higher Education.* Washington, D.C.: Department of Health, Education, and Welfare, 1971.

O'Banion, Terry. *Teachers for Tomorrow: Staff Development in the Community-Junior College.* Tucson: University of Arizona Press, 1972.

O'Banion, Terry. *Community College Staff Development Programs for the 80s.* Frederick, Md.: Associated Faculty Press, 1981.

O'Banion, Terry, and Associates. *Teaching and Learning in the Community College.* Washington, D.C.: Community College Press, 1994.

Odell, S.J. "Evaluating Mentoring Programs." In T.M. Bey and C.T. Holmes (Eds.), *Mentoring: Contemporary Principles and Issues.* Reston, Va.: Association of Teacher Educators, 1992.

Ortego, Sheila R. "Involving Administrators in the Teaching Process: A Team-Teaching Approach." *Innovation Abstracts,* 1991, XIII (23).

Ory, J.C. "Changes in Evaluating Teaching in Higher Education." *Theory Into Practice,* 1991, 33 (1), 30–36.

Paoni, Frank. "I Know It When I See It: Great Teaching." *Innovation Abstracts,* 1990, XII (23).

Palmer, J. *Community, Technical and Junior Colleges: A Summary of Selected National Data.* Washington, D.C.: American Association of Community and Junior Colleges, 1987. (ED 292 507)

Parsons, M.H. (Ed.) *Using Part-Time Faculty Effectively.* New Directions for Community Colleges No. 30. San Francisco: Jossey-Bass, 1980a.

Parsons, M.H. "Realizing Part-Time Faculty Potential." In M.H. Parsons (Ed.), *Using Part-Time Faculty Effectively.* New Directions for Community Colleges No. 30. San Francisco: Jossey-Bass, 1980b.

Parsons, M.H. "Future Directions: Eight Steps to Parity for Part-Time Faculty." In M.H. Parsons (Ed.), *Using Part-Time Faculty Effectively.* New Directions for Community Colleges No. 30. San Francisco: Jossey-Bass, 1980c.

Parsons, M.H. *Part-Time Occupational Faculty: A Contribution to Excellence.* Columbus, Ohio: Ohio State University, 1985.

Parsons, M.H. "Managing Part-Time Faculty: The Silent Majority." Paper presented at the second annual international conference for Community College Chairs and Deans, Phoenix, Arizona, 1993.

Pascarella, E.T., and Terenzini, P.T. "Patterns of Student-Faculty Informal Interaction Beyond the Classroom and Voluntary Freshman Attrition." *Journal of Higher Education,* 1977, *55,* 540–52.

Pascarella, E.T., and Terenzini, P.T. "Interaction Effects in Spady's and Tinto's Conceptual Model of College Dropout." *Sociology of Education,* 1979, *52,* 197–210.

Pascarella, E.T., and Terenzini, P.T. *How College Affects Students.* San Francisco: Jossey-Bass, 1991.

Pascarella, E.T., Terenzini, P.T., and Wolfle, L. "Orientation to College as Anticipatory Socialization: Indirect Effects of Freshman Year Persistence/Withdrawal Decisions." Paper presented at the annual meeting of the American Educational Research Association, Chicago, 1985.

Pascarella, E.T., and Wolfle, L.M. "Persistence in Higher Education: A Nine-Year Test of a Theoretical Model." Paper presented at the annual meeting of the American Educational Research Association, Chicago, 1985.

Pedersen, Robert. "Growing Dependence on Part-Time Faculty." *Community College Week,* July 5, 1993, p. 4.

Peters, T.J., and Waterman, R.H. *In Search of Excellence.* New York: Warner Books, 1982.

Phelan, A. *Boundary-Spanning Professionals: Value-Adding Roles for Part-Time Faculty.* Pratt Institute's Strategy to Enhance Its Curriculum. Paper presented at a conference sponsored by Empire State College on value-added learning, Saratoga Springs, N.Y., June 1986. (ED 279 233)

Philbrick, Kathilyn Durnford. "The Use of Humor and Effective Leadership Styles." Unpublished dissertation. University of Florida, 1989. Available from *Dissertation Abstracts,* 51–06A, 1861.

Pickett, V.R. "Focusing on the 'Right' Questions." In R.J. Brass (Ed.), *Community Colleges, the Future, and SPOD.* Stillwater, Okla.: New Forums Press, 1984.

Pintozzi, Frank. "Developmental Education: Past and Present." Paper developed for Task Force on the Future, School of Education, Kennesaw College, 1987.

Popham, W.J. *Educational Evaluation.* 2nd ed. Englewood Cliffs, N.J.: Prentice Hall, 1988.

Preus, Paul K., and Williams, Douglas F. *Personalized Faculty Development: Rationale, Application and Evaluation.* Bear Creek, Ala.: CESCO Press, 1979.

Ratcliff, James L. "Faculty Evaluation as a Measure of Organizational Productivity." *Innovation Abstracts,* 1984, *VI* (15).

Recktenwald, Rita, and Schmidt, Carrie. "Writing to Learn Math: A Dialogue." *Innovation Abstracts,* 1992, *XIV* (13).

Reiman, A.J. "An Intervention Study of Long-Term Mentor Training: Relationships Between Cognitive-Developmental Theory and Reflection." Unpublished doctoral dissertation, North Carolina State University, 1988.

Reiman, A.J., and Edelfelt, R. *School-Based Mentoring Programs: Untangling the Tensions Between Theory and Research.* (Research Report No. 90-7). Raleigh, N.C.: Department of Curriculum and Instruction, North Carolina State University, 1990.

Richardson, R.C. "The Associate Program: Teaching Improvement for Adjunct Faculty." *Community College Review,* 1992, *20* (1), 29–34.

Rogers, G.E., and Steinhoff, C.R. "Florida Community Colleges Meet the Challenge: Preparing Students for Minimum Competency Testing." *Community College Review,* Spring 1991, 33–38.

Ross, Harry A. "Policy Considerations for the Use of Part-Time Faculty in Public Community Colleges." Unpublished doctoral dissertation, West Virginia University, 1982.

Roueche, John E. *Salvage, Redirection, or Custody?* Washington, D.C.: American Association of Community Colleges, 1968.

Roueche, John E. "Staff Development: Nipping at the Heels of the Master." *Community and Junior College Journal,* 1982, *56* (6), 28–31.

Roueche, John E. "Insuring Excellence in Community College Teaching." *Leadership Abstracts,* 1990, *3* (10).

Roueche, John E., and Baker, George A. *Access and Excellence: The Open-Door College.* Washington, D.C.: Community College Press, 1987.

Roueche, John E., Baker, George A., and Rose, Robert. *Shared Vision: Transformational Leaders in American Community Colleges.* Washington, D.C.: Community College Press, 1989.

Roueche, John E., and Kirk, Wade. *Catching Up: Remedial Education.* San Francisco: Jossey-Bass, 1973.

Roueche, John E., and Mink, Oscar G. *Holistic Literacy in College Teaching.* New York: Harcourt Brace, 1980.

Roueche, John E., and Pitman, John C. *A Modest Proposal: Students Can Learn.* San Francisco: Jossey-Bass, 1973.

Roueche, John E., and Roueche, Suanne D. *Developmental Education: A Primer for Program Development and Evaluation.* Atlanta, Ga.: Southern Regional Education Board, 1977.

Roueche, John E., and Roueche, Suanne D. "Innovations in Teaching: The Past as Prologue." In Terry O'Banion (Ed.), *Innovation in the Community College.* New York: ACE/Macmillan, 1989.

Roueche, John E., and Roueche, Suanne D. *Between a Rock and a Hard Place: The At-Risk Student in the Open-Door College.* Washington, D.C.: Community College Press, 1993a.

Roueche, John E., and Roueche, Suanne D. "Has the Friendship Cooled and the Love Affair Ended? Responding to Realities of At-Risk Students." *College Board Review,* Spring 1993b, *167,* 12–17, 26.

Roueche, John E., and Snow, Jerry J. *Overcoming Learning Problems.* San Francisco: Jossey-Bass, 1977.

Roueche, Suanne D., and Comstock, Veronica N. *A Report on Theory and Method for the Study of Literacy Development in Community Colleges.* Technical Report NIE-

400-78-0600. Austin: Program in Community College Education, University of Texas, 1981.

Rubin, A., and Babbie, E. *Research Methods for Social Work.* 2nd ed. Pacific Grove, Calif.: Brooks/Cole, 1993.

Scheibmeir, Alan J. "An Investigation of Part-Time Faculty Staff Development in Public Community Junior Colleges in the United States." Unpublished doctoral dissertation, University of Texas at Austin, 1980.

Schein, E.H. *Organizational Culture and Leadership: A Dynamic View.* San Francisco: Jossey-Bass, 1985.

Schein, E.H. "Organizational Culture." *American Psychologist,* 1990, *45,* 109–119.

Schein, E.H. *Organizational Culture and Leadership.* 2nd ed. San Francisco: Jossey-Bass, 1992.

Schuster, J.H., and Bowen, H.R. "The Faculty at Risk." *Change,* September 1985, 13–21.

Schuster, J.H., Wheeler, D.W., and associates. *Enhancing Faculty Careers: Strategies for Development and Renewal.* San Francisco: Jossey-Bass, 1990.

Seidman, Earl. *In the Words of the Faculty.* San Francisco: Jossey-Bass, 1985.

Sillman, D. "Sources and Information: Using Part-Time Faculty Effectively." In M.H. Parsons (Ed.), *Using Part-Time Faculty Effectively.* New Directions for Community Colleges No. 30. San Francisco: Jossey-Bass, 1980.

Singleton, R., Jr., Straits, B.C., Straits, M.M., and McAllister, R.J. *Approaches to Social Research.* New York: Oxford University Press, 1988.

Smith, Page. *Killing the Spirit: Higher Education in America.* New York: Viking, 1990.

Smith, R.A., and Cranton, P.A. "Students' Perceptions of Teaching Skills and Overall Effectiveness Across Instructional Settings." *Research in Higher Education,* 1992, *33* (6), 747–764.

Smith, Richard R. "Can Participatory Programs Realize Part-Time Faculty Potential?" In M.H. Parsons (Ed.), *Using Part-Time Faculty Effectively.* New Directions for Community Colleges No. 30. San Francisco: Jossey-Bass, 1980.

Smith, Starita. "Worley Beats Incumbent Murray in Place 8 Race for ACC Board." *Austin American Statesman,* May 8, 1994, B5.

Spinetta, K.I. "Part-Time Faculty Instructors in the California Community Colleges: A Need to Revise Current Policies." *Community College Review,* 1990, *18,* 43–49.

Study Group on the Conditions of Excellence in American Higher Education. *Involvement in Learning: Realizing the Potential of American Higher Education.* Washington, D.C.: National Institute of Education, 1984.

Tabb, C.E. "Community College Teacher Attitudes Regarding Academically At-Risk Community College Students." Unpublished doctoral dissertation, Ohio State University, 1991. Available from *Dissertation Abstracts, 52,* 3810A.

Terenzini, Patrick T., and Pascarella, Ernest T. "Toward the Validation of Tinto's Model of College Student Attrition: A Review of Recent Studies." *Research in Higher Education,* 1980, *12,* 271–282.

Texas Higher Education Coordinating Board. *Study on the Use of Part-Time Faculty in Texas.* Austin: Texas Higher Education Coordinating Board, January 1990.

Texas Higher Education Coordinating Board. *Guidelines on the Use of Part-Time Faculty.* Austin: Texas Higher Education Coordinating Board, July 1991.

Texas Higher Education Coordinating Board. "Proposed Performance-Based Funding Process for Texas General Academic Institutions." Unpublished document. Austin: Coordinating Board, Texas College and University System, April 1992.

Thies-Sprinthall, L. *Becoming a Teacher Educator: A Curriculum Guide.* Raleigh, N.C.: Department of Curriculum and Instruction, North Carolina State University, 1990.

Tinto, Vincent. *Leaving College: Rethinking the Causes and Cures of Student Attrition.* Chicago: University of Chicago Press, 1987.

Toy, Terrence J. "Increasing Faculty Involvement in Retention Efforts." In Lee Noel, Randi Levitz, Diana Saluri, and Associates (Eds.), *Increasing Student Retention.* San Francisco: Jossey-Bass, 1985, 383–401.

Trice, H.M., and Beyer, J.M. *The Cultures of Work Organizations.* Englewood Cliffs, N.J.: Prentice Hall, 1993.

Tucker, Allan. *Chairing the Academic Department.* Phoenix, Ariz.: American Council on Education/Oryx, 1993.

Tuckman, Howard P. "Who Is Part-Time in Academe?" *AAUP Bulletin,* December 1978, *64,* 305–315.

Tuckman, Howard P. "Part-Time Faculty: Some Suggestions of Policy." *Change,* January–February 1981, *13,* 8–10.

Tuckman, Howard P., and Caldwell, Jaime. "The Reward Structure for Part-Timers in Academe." *Journal of Higher Education,* November 1979, *50,* 745–760.

Tuckman, Howard P., and Tuckman, Barbara. "Sex Discrimination Among Part-Timers at Two-Year Institutions," *Academe,* Spring 1980, *6,* 20–25.

Tuckman, Howard P., and Tuckman, Barbara. "Who Are the Part-Timers and What Are Colleges Doing for Them?" *Part-Time Faculty in Colleges and Universities.* 1981 Current Issues in Higher Education No. 4. Selected papers presented at the annual national conferene of the American Association for Higher Education, Washington, D.C., March 1981. Washington, D.C.: American Association of Higher Education, 1981.

Tuckman, Howard P., and Vogler, William D. "The Part in Part-Time Wages." *AAUP Bulletin,* May 1978, 70–77.

Twale, D.J. "Social and Academic Development in Freshman Orientation: A Time Frame." *NASPA Journal,* 1989, *27,* 160–167.

U.S. Department of Education. *Digest of Education Statistics.* Washington, D.C.: U.S. Department of Education, 1993.

Valek, Millicent. "Faculty Mentors: New Roles, New Relationships." *Innovation Abstracts,* 1987, *IX* (14).

Vaughan, George B. "Faculty and Administrative Renewal." In D. Angel and M. DeVault (Eds.), *Conceptualizing 2000: Proactive Planning.* Washington, D.C.: Community College Press, 1991.

Vaughan, George B., and Associates. *Issues for Community College Leaders in a New Era.* San Francisco: Jossey-Bass, 1983.

Vogler, D.E. "Administering Part-Time Instruction." *Community Services Catalyst,* Winter 1980, *10* (1), 19–22. (EJ 225 947)

Weber, John. "Thoughts and Actions on Students Retention." *Innovation Abstracts,* 1985, *VII* (30).

Weiss, H.C. "The Stakeholder Approach to Evaluation: Origins and Promise." In A.S. Bryk (Ed.), *Stakeholder-Based Education.* New Directions for Program Evaluation No. 17. San Francisco: Jossey-Bass, 1983.

Whaley, C.R., and Wolfe, D.M. "Creating Incentives for Cooperating Teachers." *Journal of Teacher Education,* 1984, *35* (4), 46–48.

Wherry, R.J. "Control of Bias in Ratings." Department of the Army, Adjutant General's Office, Personnel Research and Procedures Division, Personnel Research Branch, 1952. (PRS Reports 914, 915, 919, 920, 921)

Williams, J.M. *A Study of Professional Development Practices of Part-Time Instructors at Selected League for Innovation Community Colleges.* Laguna Hills, Calif.: League for Innovation in the Community College, 1985. (ED 269 093)

Wilson, R.C., Gaff, J.G., et al. *College Professors and Their Impact on Students.* New York: Wiley, 1975.

Wilson, R.C., Wood, L., and Gaff, J.G. "Social-Psychological Accessibility and Faculty-Student Interaction Beyond the Classroom." *Sociology of Education,* Winter 1974, *47,* 74–92.

Wlodkowski, R.J. *Enhancing Adult Motivation to Learn.* San Francisco: Jossey-Bass, 1985.

Wolfe, D.M. "Designing Training and Selecting Incentives for Mentor Programs." In T.M. Bey and C.T. Holmes (Eds.), *Mentoring: Contemporary Principles and Issues.* Reston, Va.: Association of Teacher Educators, 1992.

Wolfle, D. *America's Resources of Specialized Talent.* Report of the Commission on Human Resources and Advanced Training. New York: Harper and Row, 1954.

Working Party on Effective State Action to Improve Undergraduate Education. *Transforming the State Role in Undergraduate Education: Time for a Different View.* Denver, Colo.: Education Commission of the States, 1986.

Wranosky, Vernon L., and Mitchell, Kenneth E. "Science and Art: A Cross Discipline Approach." *Innovation Abstracts,* 1987, *IX* (4).

Yarrington, Roger. (Ed.). *New Staff for New Students.* Washington, D.C.: American Association of Community and Junior Colleges, 1973.

Zey, M. *The Mentor Connection.* Homewood, Ill.: Dow Jones-Irwin, 1984.

INDEX

About the Authors

John E. Roueche is professor and director of the Community College Leadership Program at The University of Texas at Austin, where he holds the Sid W. Richardson Regents Chair in Community College Leadership. He has served as director of the program since 1971. He is the author of thirty-three books and more than 150 articles and monographs on the topics of educational leadership and teaching effectiveness. He is the recipient of numerous national awards for his research, teaching, service, and overall leadership, including the 1986 National Distinguished Leadership Award from the American Association of Community Colleges, the 1988 B. Lamar Johnson Leadership in Innovation Award from the League for Innovation in the Community College, and the Distinguished Research Publication Award from the National Association of Developmental Education. He received the 1994 Distinguished Faculty Award at The University of Texas at Austin.

Suanne D. Roueche is the director of the National Institute for Staff and Organizational Development (NISOD); editor of *Innovation Abstracts,* NISOD's weekly teaching tips publication; editor of *Linkages,* NISOD's quarterly newsletter; and lecturer in the Department of Educational Administration, College of Education, The University of Texas at Austin. Author of more than twelve books and more than thirty-five articles and book chapters, she was presented with the 1988 Distinguished Research and Writing Award by the National Council for Staff, Program, and Organizational Development. Suanne and John Roueche received the 1994 Distinguished Senior Scholar Award from AACC's Council of Colleges and Universities for *Between a Rock and a Hard Place: The At-Risk Student in the Open-Door College.* She is the recipient of numerous state and national awards and recognition for her leadership and service, including the "Great Seal of Florida" and The University of Texas at Austin's College of Education Distinguished Service Award. She has been named an Arkansas Traveler, a Kentucky Colonel, and a Yellow Rose of Texas.

Mark D. Milliron is a Ph.D. candidate in the Community College Leadership Program at The University of Texas at Austin, where he was a 1993–1994 Kellogg Research Fellow. He is a graduate of Arizona State University, where he received the 1992 Teaching Excellence Award from the International Communication

Association while completing his M.A. in organizational communication. He has taught at The University of Texas at Austin and at Rio Salado Community College, Arizona. A researcher and writer, Milliron is a contributing author to *Innovation Abstracts* and an instructional module designer for the National Community College Chair Academy's Leadership Institute.